# KISS LORI FOR ME

EDITOR
Elayne Wells Harmer, www.theelementsofediting.com.

PAGE LAYOUT AND FORMATTING
Ivica Jandrijević, www.writingnights.org

BOOK DESIGN
Ivica Jandrijević

Articles from the Marion (Ind.) *Chronicle-Tribune* are reprinted with permission.

ISBN 978-1-7365629-1-8

Books are available in quantity for promotional or premium use. For information, email lorireaves@me.com.

Patagonia Press, Salt Lake City, Utah. First edition, 2022.
Printed in the United States of America.

# KISS LORI FOR ME

## A Vietnam Corpsman's Sacrifice, His Widow's Undying Love, and Their Daughter's Quest to Find the Truth

## DR. LORI GOSS-REAVES

I dedicate this book to my mother, Marty Goss Cannon, whose steadfast love for my father never died. She poured all the love she had for him into me. Her strength and determination to go on after my father was killed in Vietnam set an example of deep courage. The stories she chose to share with me charted a course for my life that led to a quest for the truth and a search to "know" this man who loved us deeply. My mother's goal was for my father to not be forgotten. It is my honor to share their beautiful love story and pass the torch to my father's grandchildren and great-grandchildren. May their lives be a reflection of the legacy left for them by their Grandpa Larry and Granny Marty, my heroes.

*Kiss Lori For Me* is a touching and riveting story that draws the reader in and keeps them involved with main characters we care about. We follow along as Lori searches for answers as to what really happened to the dad she lost, a Navy Corpsman killed in Vietnam. Over the course of decades seeking the truth, she becomes part of a whole new family.

### PAUL "DOC BUZZ" BAVIELLO
First Battalion, Fifth Marines
Vietnam 1969–1970
Author of *Corpsman Up*


An inspirational book for all veterans. Partner on a journey with a devoted daughter and experience sacrifice, emotions, tearful moments, intrigue, and an unfailing family love. After capturing the truth, Lori let the healing begin with a trip to the land where her father sacrificed his life.

### COL. WAYNE ELLIS, U.S. ARMY (RET.)
Second Battalion, 505th Infantry Regiment, Third Brigade, 82nd Airborne
Vietnam 1968–1969


*Kiss Lori For Me* is a sublime and beautifully written story, already a classic in my eyes. Lori not only "found" her father in her search but also blessed his memory and the memory of countless of his comrades, giving understanding to many who have lived on without hope. I am one of them, and I thank you, Lori.

### JAMES A. RUFFER, MD
42nd Officer Candidate Class (OCC), USMC
USN medical doctor, USAF flight surgeon
Vietnam 1969–1970
Author of upcoming book *At What Cost*

Raw. Riveting. Inspirational. My life is forever changed because of Lori writing and my reading this book. I thank the author for the courage to begin this journey, the tenacity to persevere, and the vulnerability to share so much of herself and to write and put it out there for the rest of us to experience. I thank her husband and family who stood by her as she walked this journey.

### WILLIAM DAVID MOORE, MD
Fellow of the American Congress of Obstetricians
and Gynecologists (FACOG)

Hurt people hurt people; healed people heal people. Lori's painful yet rewarding journey from hurt to healing is inspiring and challenging, not only for those who lost a loved one in war, but for anyone willing to reflect on their own journey. Your own life could be transformed as you travel with Lori through her healing journey.

### JACK BRADY, PhD
Associate professor (Ret.), Criminal Justice, Indiana Wesleyan University

*Kiss Lori For Me* is a must-read. As a Gold Star Daughter who knows too well the way war can destroy families, I feel that this book inspires hope. The most profound part of Lori's story for me is the wisdom of her young mother who became a widow at age twenty-three. Marty Goss preserved and built her husband's memory for their daughter and continues to do so today. Their love is truly a blue-heart love story. Lori's father can be very proud that his daughter became a doctor just like he aspired to be. This is because of the strength of the woman he married, and the essence of the man Lori found on her journey.

### SHARI BENNETT
Daughter of Capt. Robert D. Bennett, U.S. Air Force,
Air Commando pilot, 4400th Combat Crew Training Squadron, DET 2A
Distinguished Flying Cross, Purple Heart
USAF service: 1952–1962; Vietnam 1962 (KIA)

# Table of Contents

## PART 1: UNDYING LOVE

# PART 2: THE SEARCH

# PART 3: FINDING PEACE

# Acknowledgments

This book has come to fruition only because of the encouragement and belief of others.

To **Mrs. Hubbard**, my sixth-grade teacher: You asked me about this book before I even started writing. When I shared my concerns about finding the time, you said, "Then the time is not right yet. God knows and will give you the words when it's time, and it will be the best." Your words brought tears to my eyes and peace to my heart. Thank you!

To **Dr. Jerry** and **Mary Behrens**: When I lacked clarity on how to begin, you adamantly encouraged me to write this book—the one I have known I needed to write since I was a child. Thank you for calling me brave and for believing in me.

To **Stan Burkart**, my father's most loyal friend: Thank you for carrying my dad in your heart all these years. You would have given your life for his in a heartbeat—I know of no greater love than that. Somehow my dad knew that you—of all of the people my dad could have befriended in boot camp and Corps school—were the best. I am very thankful you choose to be a part of our lives.

To **Ray** and **Ginny Felle**: Thank you for loving me unconditionally and sharing your numerous files with me. Your willingness to connect me to Doc Marty Russell allowed me to learn about my dad's final hours. Thank you for giving me live footage of my dad five days before his death. Your visits to our home created memories I will cherish forever. Thank you.

To **Steve** and **Aggie Girten**, my other Kentucky family: Thank you for embracing my children and being so generous with your love. Your excitement about this book encouraged me. Your kindness and expressions of love continue to touch my heart.

To **John** and **Cass Holladay**: Thank you for taking me under your wing in 2007. We share a love for redheads and laughter. Your supportive emails made me laugh and guided my path when I joined the world of academia.

To the late **John Edwards**: Thank you for leading me up the trail on Valentine's Ridge and for telling me everything you remember about the battle on Valentine's Ridge. Thank you for calling me regularly and making me laugh. You are a legend in my mind.

To **Camron Carter**: I am very thankful you survived the battle on Valentine's Ridge. My dad would be so happy to know the kind of man whose life he helped save. You have lived each day in gratitude and served God well. Thank you for contacting me and inviting me into your life.

To **Gary Mayo:** Thank you for telling me about my dad's childhood in Home Corner, Indiana, and for displaying a memorial at your home for your hometown heroes Larry Jo Goss and Donald Smith. Your relentless attempts to connect me to people from my dad's youth is a blessing to me.

To **Marty Russell, Don Carter, Dan Wszolek, James Nat Lloyd, Richard Foster, Doc Lindell,** and **Arthur Sayward:** You were near my father when he was killed. Your willingness to come alongside me and share your memories gave me pieces to the puzzle I desperately needed. Thank you! I am glad you made it home.

To **Janice Conklin:** Thank you for sharing Eddie's written accounts with me and generously donating to the Larry Jo Goss Peace Home.

To **Jim Lockwood** and **Larry Bearden:** Thank you for sharing your memories, reading through countless documents, and supporting me during challenging times in the search.

To **Doc Landry:** Thank you for praying for me and teaching me about being a Navy Corpsman in Vietnam.

To Second Platoon's **Sonny Wells, Ray Holmes,** and **Jon Ahlschwede Jr:** Thank you for sharing your buried memories with me. I am very glad you made it home.

To the **Marines and corpsmen who spent the night on Valentine's Ridge and fought the next day:** Your story deserves to be told. Please know how much I respect you and thank God that you made it home.

To the **countless Vietnam Veterans** who encouraged me as I wrote this book: Thank you for serving our country and for honoring my dad. He would have enjoyed growing old with you.

To **Elayne Wells Harmer** and **Cody Lawrence Reaves,** for giving hours of your time to edit this book. Your belief that this story needed to be told gave me the energy to keep going. Your encouragement carried me to the finish line.

To my research assistants, **Hannah, Megan, Abbey,** and **Kyla,** thank you for working alongside me as we sought a publisher for this book. Your enthusiasm for learning and suggested edits made this book better. Thank you for believing in this project and being my objective eyes as we poured through fifty-year-old documents. I also want to thank the IWU Scholarship Council for providing funds for this research.

To my mom, **Marty,** and my **Aunt Mona:** The interviews you allowed me to have with you shaped the beginning chapters of this book. Your memories helped me form the story of my dad—a story that must be told because of who he was!

To my husband, **Eric**, and my children, **Chris**, **Cody**, **Colton**, **Courtnee Jo**, **and Casey**: Thank you for sharing me with this work. You never complained as I spent countless hours on this labor of love. You are my heart and my life, and I thank God daily for each of you. As I grew to know my dad better through writing this book, I saw pieces of him in all of you. They say you marry someone like your dad—Eric, he would be so proud of you!

To our daughters-in-law, **Kylie** and **Becky,** and our grandchildren, **Madelyn Ann**, **Olivia Grace**, **Jordan Lawrence**, **James Matthew**, and **Emilia Claire**: Your Grandpa Larry would have dearly loved you!

# Foreword

This is a unique story about the Vietnam War written by Lori, the daughter of Larry and Martha Goss. Her book, though sad and gut wrenching, adds much to the literature on the Vietnam War.

I first met HM2 Larry Goss, her father, when he checked in with me in December 1967 in a bunker at the Rockpile, a Marine position near the DMZ. He was with me for several days and during that time he told me, "If I make it through, I want to become a doctor."

Larry was then made the senior Corpsman of Kilo Company. Six weeks later, he was killed on Valentine's Day 1968, while ministering to wounded Marines in a terrible battle on a ridge west of Ca Lu, forever after known as Valentine's Ridge.

Larry and nine Marines who died that day were not recovered until three weeks later. Their skeletal, decomposed remains were brought down into the Ca Lu perimeter by their brother Marines and Corpsmen where they were laid out on the ground. Major John Oliver, the Battalion XO, Richard Black, the Battalion Chaplain, and I put on surgical gloves and identified each one by their dog tags and other personal effects they had in their pockets.

Larry Goss, had a personal picture of his wife and infant daughter Lori in his left breast pocket. When I saw that, I said, "Oh God, Larry."

I'll never forget repeatedly swallowing my own vomit. When our task was done we put them in body bags and they left via helicopter. We just didn't talk about it afterwards; each man held those horrific sad remembrances inside and the war went on. Their bodies had not been mutilated by the NVA soldiers.

Long after the war, when I corresponded with and eventually met Lori Goss and her husband, Eric Reaves, I learned that Larry Goss and his young wife Martha had both kept daily journals and written loving letters to each other. The preserved letters fueled the need for Lori to tell us about this man whose life was snuffed out but was never forgotten by those who knew and loved him.

Lori is a very strong woman with an equally strong Christian faith, which stands out to all who know her.

Eric, her kind and understanding husband, and their children, as well as Lori's mother Martha, have supported her throughout. To them much credit is due.

Lori's research spans over twenty years of time and includes trips to our home in Wyoming, eyewitness accounts by survivors of the battle on Valentine's Ridge, and information on the relief effort by India Company of 3/9. Lori also attended Marine reunions and found the input and support of multiple 3/9 Marines and Corpsmen.

After countless telephone and internet exchanges, a myriad of hours going over all of the information Lori collected, and two trips to Valentine's Ridge in Vietnam we now have the final product.

Larry can be very proud of his little daughter; I know we all are as well.

**JERRY BEHRENS, MD**
Casper, Wyoming
Battalion Surgeon, Third Battalion
Ninth Marine Regiment, Third Marine Division
Vietnam 1967–1968

# Preface

For as long as I can remember, I have known that I would one day write a book about my dad. There were many other things I wanted to accomplish first, but I believed the right time would come one day.

Being the daughter of a Navy corpsman who was killed in action in Vietnam created for me a challenge to stay in the present while remaining connected to the past. I knew it was important for my children to know the legacy of their grandfather, but I didn't want them to be negatively affected by his loss the way I had been. For this reason, it took me fifty-four years to complete this book. Over time, pieces of the puzzle were revealed, though all did not fit. As I searched for the truth about how my father was killed, I found some stories that were true and some that proved to be fiction. Through this journey, I learned the importance of forgiveness and the power of love.

When a child grows up without a parent, the stories passed down create an image of the person they long for. These stories craft the child's identity and understanding of love. My journey was filled with roadblocks and blessings. During the moments when I was tempted to discontinue the quest, someone came along beside me and believed. It was their belief in me that propelled me forward. This book is written with the fatherless in mind.

Deep inside us all is a longing to know the love of our mom and our dad. When circumstances take them away from us, a void is created that time alone cannot heal. But as I sought to "find" my father, I found so much more. It is my hope that you find a part of yourself in the pages that follow and that, in doing so, you love deeper and savor longer the people you have the opportunity to love—because love never dies.

# Introduction

Dear Student:

We are sponsoring a trip to Washington, D.C., on Veterans Day, Thursday, November 11, 1982.

Our group will visit the White House, Lincoln and Jefferson Memorials, Arlington Cemetery (special service for Veterans Day), the Capitol Building, and the Smithsonian Institute. You will be surprised about the amount of time for sightseeing especially since most federal employees are not working on Veterans Day.

Payment schedule is as follows:

$20.00 Non-refundable seat reservation by October 1, 1982

$105.00 Balance due by October 25, 1982

Sign up in the office now if you can go with us.

I was a fifteen-year-old sophomore in high school when I brought this flyer home from school. My high school principal was organizing a one-day field trip to Washington, D.C., by plane. I was excited. I had been out of Indiana just twice, both times by car—once to visit relatives in Kentucky and once for a family vacation to Tennessee.

My mom, Marty, was fearful of flying but knew I needed to go. The trip cost $125, a huge expense for her, and she paid not just for me but also for my step-brother Joey. Knowing how important the trip was to me, she said she would find a way. The itinerary showed plans to visit several prominent sites in our nation's capital but made no mention of the Vietnam Veterans Memorial. As I discovered years later, the memorial was under construction during the planning of this school trip. And as it turned out, our November 11 trip coincided with the Memorial's five-day dedication ceremony, presided over by Pres. Ronald Reagan, which ran November 10–14.

My mom made a phone call to Larry Stoner, the high school principal organizing the trip. He knew only a little about my loss but understood the love of a father; he had a daughter of his own. Mr. Stoner assured my mom that he would include a stop at the Vietnam Veterans Memorial Wall. I would be able to find my father's name on the Wall—a man I loved but did not know.

About 1,300 miles away, in Casper, Wyoming, Dr. Jerry Behrens was planning a similar trip to Washington, D.C., with a group of Vietnam Veterans. Jerry had served as the battalion surgeon for the Third Battalion, Ninth Marines from August 1967 to August 1968. The battalion was comprised of four line companies—Kilo, Mike, India, and Lima—along with the Headquarters Company. Jerry lost ten corpsmen during his tour. Their names were etched on his heart the moment they took their last breath, and now they would be among the 57,939[*] names etched on the black granite

---

[*] According to a 2019 audit by the Vietnam Veterans Memorial Fund, 58,390 names are on the Wall, but due to corrections, duplicates, or individuals who lived or are of unknown status, the Wall represents 58,276 individuals.

wall. One of his corpsmen—and one of those names—was my father, Larry Jo Goss.

Jerry knew Doc Goss had a wife and little girl at home. Larry had spoken of them fondly. Jerry had a wife and little girl at home, too. After returning home from Vietnam, Jerry became an orthopedic surgical resident at the University of Wisconsin, then started his practice in Casper, Wyoming.

Jerry thought about his experiences in Vietnam virtually every day. Jerry focused on how lucky he was to be alive, not the "what ifs," and lived his life with purpose. Every January 13, Jerry marked the anniversary of the attack on the convoy that could have taken his life, and thought of 2nd Lt. Michael George, Headquarters Company, who was killed that day. Just seconds before the attack, standing right in the spot where the enemy had ambushed them several months before, Mike had said, "Jerry, why don't you come over and sit by me?" That move, from the right side of the truck to the left, took Jerry away from the worst of the enemy's fire. To honor that Marine who had saved his life, Jerry named his own son Michael. Jerry would never forget the act of sacrifice and bravery of his friend—qualities, I would come to learn, that my father shared.

Throughout my childhood in Indiana, my mom and I wondered about the men who served with my dad in Vietnam. She had a container in the basement filled with military papers, each containing a piece of the puzzle. Among the papers were Western Union telegrams reporting that my dad went missing in action on February 14, 1968. Additional telegrams stated that a search was underway to find him. Another told her that hostile forces might have taken him. For three long weeks, my mom held onto the hope that my dad was still alive. But in early March, a final telegram shattered her dreams and her heart: they had found my dad's body and changed his status from MIA to killed in action KIA.

Though this telegram gave us an answer, it raised even more questions. How did he die? Was he really dead? Who else died in the battle? Was anyone with him when he took his last breath? Who found his body? What were his injuries? Why were his dog tags not returned? Why was he left on the ridge for twenty-one days? As I grew older, I wondered about the men who knew the answers—the men who had been there the day my father died. I knew I needed to find them one day. And I promised myself that I would, no matter how long it took.

I began actively searching for the answers when I was eighteen. I looked through my dad's scrapbook, turning over each page in my hand and thinking how many of the photos he once held. One of those papers was dated December 24, 1967—the day my dad reported for duty in Vietnam. And at the bottom was a signature: Jerry Behrens.

Nearly fifteen years after Jerry signed that paper, on Veterans Day, November 11, 1982, he and I were both at the Wall. But it would take more than a decade for us to connect. Though we did not meet that day, my short time at the Wall served as the catalyst for my search. Thousands of veterans—maybe tens of thousands—had showed up that day at the Wall. And as I looked at each one, the same question entered my mind: Did he know my dad? Over the coming years, I would get to ask many veterans that question. And in my search to find answers, to find my father, I found his legacy of love.

# PART I
## *Undying Love*

With my parents at Grandma Bradford's house in Marion, Indiana, Nov. 25, 1967.

# CHAPTER ONE

# My Mom's Gift to Me

I was only six months old when my father, PO2 (Petty Officer Second Class) Larry Jo Goss, a hospital corpsman, was killed in action in Vietnam on February 14, 1968, during the Tet Offensive. I have no memories of the four months we spent together, and yet I cannot remember a time he was not a part of my life. Every year on my birthday, my mother gave me gifts. Some were ordinary gifts that little girls usually receive: baby dolls, books, dress-up clothes, and teddy bears. But the gifts I remember best were those that had belonged to my dad.

We had a barrel in the basement filled with his letters, but I didn't know about all his things she had saved. One year she gave me my dad's briefcase, filled with the ink pen and stationery he used to write letters home from the Vietnam War. Sometimes her special gift was a collection of my dad's things, like audio tapes on reel to reel, his stethoscope and medical kit, and a stack of letters labeled "boot camp," "Field Medical School," and "Vietnam." Once she even gave me a bottle of his aftershave that was a quarter full. Knowing that his hands once held the bottle made me want to hold it too. I would close my eyes while I twisted off the cap. Doing something I knew he had done while touching something he had touched made me feel close to him. I loved knowing what my dad smelled like. With my eyes still closed, I imagined him standing in front of a mirror, getting ready for his day, while his twenty-one-year-old handsome face looked back at him. I tried to age him but couldn't. The photographs my mom gave me over the years were the only thing I had to form an image of him in my mind.

Sometimes these images turned into moving pictures of my dad putting on his aftershave before work and then kissing Mom and me goodbye with his briefcase in hand. I inhaled the scent from the open bottle and pretended this fantasy was real.

My mom made it her life's mission to make sure I knew everything I could about my loving father. Through moves, frequent turbulence, and countless trials, she held on to every item he ever touched, preserving his character, his voice, and his wit. Over time, as she shared bits and pieces of his life, I came to know my dad.

A grief-stricken widow at the age of twenty-three, my mother faced a choice: bury my dad's memories along with his body, or pass them on to his only child. She chose the latter. Every morning she woke up and made the decision to focus on what was in front of her: their baby girl. With no military assistance program to help her cope and no instruction manual to show her the way, my mom pushed forward. She was a pioneer, charting a difficult course in a time when Vietnam was an unpopular and controversial topic.

I remember learning in school about the "Vietnam conflict" and feeling great sadness. My dad had given his life in Vietnam, leaving a hole in my heart I did not know how to fill. There were no support groups for children like me in our town, and no social workers in our schools. And though there were approximately twenty thousand children across the country whose fathers were killed during that war, I did not personally know any other child who had suffered the same loss I did. In fact, I thought I was one of few.

In school, I tried to understand the politics and details of the Vietnam War but found both confusing. No matter what the history books said, I knew in my child's mind that my dad had fought in a *war*, not a "conflict." My mom told me that Dad believed it was his duty, after receiving his draft notice, to do his part so that communism would never take root in the United States. His four great-uncles, Tom, Oscar, Fred, and Bill Hutchison, had served in World War II and all made it home alive. My dad assured her he would, too.

In our home, the Vietnam War was never taboo. The shame many soldiers felt when they returned home to an ungrateful country was never associated with my dad or his service. My mom made it clear that my dad served because of his deep love for the two of us and his country. He wanted my mom and me to always be safe. Our future was his main priority.

Even though I heard my mom's words, I still could not understand *why*. Why did our country go to war with North Vietnam? Why did my dad have to go? Couldn't he have left the country after being drafted? Some people told me my dad was a hero, but I didn't want a hero—I just wanted my dad! In my mind, he'd had options. I dreamed of the three of us living together in Canada. And even though Mom had received the call telling her that he was KIA, my young mind created the fantasy that he was possibly still alive. And I held to that dream for twenty-seven years.

As I entered college, I had the privilege of speaking about my father's service in high school history classes. This experience exposed me to Vietnam Veterans for the first time. As they shared their stories, I learned about the horrendous conditions they faced in Vietnam. These brave men served during a time of intense division in our country—a country they loved and were willing to die for. I also learned that the "conflict" truly was a war. The brotherhood they felt for each other taught me about loyalty, honor, and love. They were so young in Vietnam—most in their late teens or early twenties—and forced to make monumental decisions in the midst of grave danger. Those who did not make it back home paid the greatest sacrifice, and their families would never be the same.

While searching for all I had lost, many people told me that everything happens for a reason—that my dad was not supposed to come back. No one, however, could tell me why. But I needed to make sense of the tragedy. I needed to know why.

*To everything—turn, turn, turn*
*There is a season—turn, turn, turn*
*And a time to every purpose under heaven*
*A time to be born, a time to die*

**THE BYRDS**

I distinctly remember singing these words in junior high choir and wondering if they were true. Later, I found myself reading similar words in my Bible in Ecclesiastes 3:1–2, "There is a time for everything, and a season for every activity under the heavens: a time to be born and a time to die." Did my dad die because it was his time? What was the purpose of my growing up without a dad? If he had survived the battle on February 14, 1968, would he have made it home? No one had the answers to these questions.

* * * * *

My grandma Mary—whom we affectionately called "Mamaw"—had introduced me to God before. Mamaw was my mom's mother and the only "father figure" I had ever known. Whenever I spent a Saturday night at her house, we would walk across the street to her church the next morning. Mamaw had faced many hard times, but her faith was strong. She read her Bible every day and trusted God to meet her needs, and she was not afraid to die. I would often hear her say, "When it's my time to go, it's my time to go." She was not concerned about her earthly body, as she believed her spirit would be with God the moment she passed away. Was Mamaw right? Did we really die when it was "our time"?

At school, when kids would talk about their dads, I would tell them about my grandma. She worked a job usually reserved only for men: lifting picture tubes at a factory called RCA. She had big muscles and labored tirelessly in her yard tending to her roses. Though she lived in a very modest house, she had the most beautiful yard in town. My grandma was my protector, and showed through her actions how much she loved me.

In first grade, a boy made fun of me because I did not have a dad. My teacher took a special interest in me that year and asked the office secretary to call my mom. She was at the doctor, so Mamaw walked almost a mile to the school to pick me up. As we walked back to my grandma's house, she said, "Lori Jo, don't you ever let anyone tell you that you don't have a dad. You have a wonderful dad who lives in heaven. He is looking over you right now."

I wanted to believe he could see me. I wanted to believe he was lying in the clouds looking down and smiling as we walked back to Mamaw's house, but I didn't feel his presence. Maybe that's because I had no working memory of him.

But even though I don't remember it, I feel fortunate to have spent four months (minus his month at Field Medical School) with my dad. I imagine that time must have been as precious to him as the memories of my own babies are to me. On my thirty-sixth birthday, my mother gave me a photo of my dad cradling me in his arms and gazing into my eyes. It is my favorite picture of the two of us. I wish I knew what he was thinking as he looked at me. Did he wonder if he would return home from Vietnam? Did he fear that he would die in country, leaving me to grow up without a dad, just like he did? Did he have hopes of who I might one day become, and wonder if he would get to watch my life unfold? My dad knew that providing for a family took hard work, but he was ready for the challenge. He was determined to give me what he never had: financial stability, safety, and a father's love.

My favorite photo of my dad and me, taken by my mom
at Aunt Marge's house (October 1967).

# CHAPTER TWO

# Larry's Story

My dad's story began in 1946, in an impoverished neighborhood in Marion, Indiana, called "Home Corner." He was the third child of parents who could not seem to live with (or without) each other. Their relationship was toxic, and like most children who face such harrowing circumstances, my dad suffered greatly as a result.

His parents, Harry and Marie, married at the age of sixteen. Their first child, Eddie Lee, was born one month premature and died seven days later. Marie never forgave Harry for their baby's death, which she claimed occurred because they had a physical altercation and she was left outside in the snow. The two remained together, however, and later had a daughter, Mona Sue. Marie vowed she would never bear Harry another son, but in October 1945, Marie became pregnant with my dad. She and Harry had recently divorced, and he was about to marry a woman named Willie, who was also pregnant with Harry's child. Just six weeks after my dad's birth, Harry had another son: my dad's half-brother, Harry Richard.

Perhaps unsurprisingly, Harry did not claim my dad as his son. Marie said it didn't matter—Larry was hers. Decades later, when I spoke with Marie at a nursing home not long before she died, I still could not understand why she said, "it didn't matter." It certainly mattered to my dad. But our discussion made clear that Marie saw things from only her perspective. She simply could not put her son's needs above her own. And so my dad lived his life without a father. He felt the loss I know so well. This was only the beginning of our similarities, and it was the first pattern I resolved to break.

It's human nature to look back and wonder why a person did something that caused so much pain. The common mantra is that you should never judge another until you've walked a mile in their shoes. And I think that's true, though I've always liked Harper Lee's phrasing better: "You never really understand a person until you consider things from his point of view—until you climb into his skin and walk around in it."[*]

I tried to see things from Marie's perspective, but I could not come to grips with how she blithely ignored how much my dad needed a father—someone who, even if not present, would call him his own. And how could Harry? To this day, I'm not sure I know. But I knew that day, as I sat with Marie, that my dad was resilient. He decided to learn from his parents' mistakes and live life differently. His resolve continued with me, and my children are better off because of it. Dad knew the struggles of generational poverty and believed an education was his ticket out.

But how did my dad reach that conclusion? As part of my search for that answer, I interviewed my dad's older sister, Mona. She shared details with me about her and my dad's difficult years growing up without their dad or any reliable man in the father role. Although Harry would occasionally visit his two children, he never acknowledged my dad as his son, as that would have upset Willie, to whom he remained married for the rest of his life. Still, my father called Harry "Daddy," and I can only imagine how it must have hurt my dad not to be called "son" in return.

---

[*] Harper Lee, *To Kill a Mockingbird* (Philadelphia: J. B. Lippincott & Co., 1960).

Though my dad had no father and an often-absent mother, Mona told me about the stable influences on their lives. My dad's grandma on his mother's side, Grandma Bradford, loved him dearly. Her daughter—my dad's Aunt Marge—loved him too. He was their "Larry Jo." For the first two years of his life they, along with a friend they called "Aunt Lucy," provided the majority of his care, as Marie worked out of town and would often disappear for weeks at a time.

Until my dad turned four, Grandma Bradford and Aunt Marge lived with Marie. They moved out, however, when Aunt Marge married Russell and Grandma married a man nicknamed "Pop." After they left, Marie allowed a lady they called "Grandma Macky" to move in to take care of her two kids. Though Grandma Macky was there, my dad and Mona were often neglected and left alone. When my dad was only ten, Aunt Marge penned this letter to Harry.

Dear Harry,

I am writing to ask that you please do something to help Larry Jo and Mona Sue. No children should have to live the way they do. Mona Sue is sad all of the time. Larry Jo needs his dad. Marie's home is like a house of ill repute. [. . .]* You are the only person who can get them out of that situation. Will you please help your children?

Sincerely,

Marge

I don't know if Harry ever received this letter, but I assume he did. One thing I know for sure is that he never acted on Aunt Marge's urgent and heartfelt request.† I know Harry could have made my dad and Mona's life better, but he chose his other family instead.

---

* Ellipses within brackets indicate that I've removed portions of a letter or an account.

† After Harry and Willie both passed away, their daughter Bonnie Kay found the letter and gave it to me.

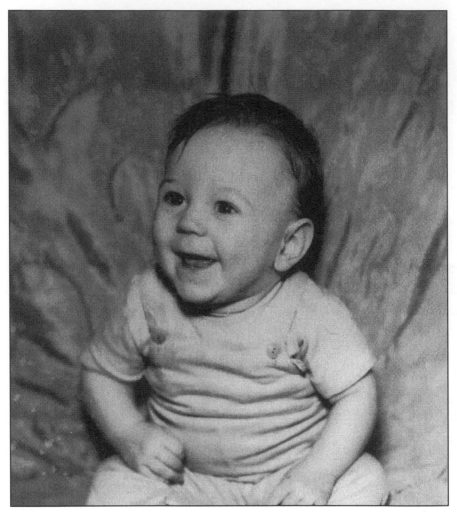

My sweet dad at about six months (1947).

Larry Jo and Mona Sue in Marion, Indiana (1949).

Aunt Mona did not minimize the hardships this caused, but she also emphasized the fun she and my dad had together. He liked to "push her buttons," she recalled with a laugh, but always in a loving way. When she would get mad at him, he would laugh and flash his infectious grin. He was a jokester through and through. Stories of his mischievousness and orneriness make me smile and remind me of my own daughter and four sons. Mona also shared that my dad knew as a little boy that he wanted to grow up and become a doctor one day. School was hard for her but very easy for him.

Of all the memories Mona shared, she said that their most favorite times together were spent at Big Barbee Lake. Grandma Bradford rented a fishing cottage there each summer, as did my dad's Uncle Bill. Mona tearfully shared how playing in the water quenched his spirit and allowed him time to enjoy being a boy, since home was filled with stress, work, and responsibility.

As I collected stories and tried to create a mosaic of my father, his elementary classmates were invaluable. Each vignette they passed along—no matter how brief—gave me another window into my dad's personality and interests. One told me that, at the age of six, my dad had two paper routes. One friend helped him fold the newspapers and told me how far my dad could throw. Another friend, Dennis Holcom, shared that my dad kept a baseball mitt under his desk so they could play catch before and after school. That same friend also told me of the depths of my dad's poverty, describing how he often wore the same clothes to school two or three days in a row.

One of Dad's friends, Gary Mayo, said that he looked up to my dad because he was different from the rough boys in the neighborhood, who were not-so-affectionately known as the "Home Corner hoodlums." Gary said most of the boys were mean, but my dad was always kind. He fondly recalled games of hide-and-seek in the woods across from my father's house, and said my dad would beat him in a footrace every time. He also mentioned my dad's deep love for sports and the pickup games of basketball they would play after school. Gary said, "Larry was very athletic and could outrun a deer. He had great sportsmanship but the grin he gave you when he shot a basket over you was priceless."

Gary's memories allowed me to envision my dad as a little boy and the place called Home Corner that shaped him. Gary said the neighborhood was a very tough place to grow up. He described his apprehension as he walked up to the entrance of Evans Elementary School for the first time. He carried that feeling the whole first day of school until my dad asked him if he wanted to play basketball. Right away, Gary said, he could tell that Larry was different. And the years spent with my dad confirmed that: Gary never heard my dad cuss and never saw him get mad.

But like all little boys (and girls), my dad did get mad. Aunt Mona said he did not get mad often, but "you didn't want to be around him when he did." She recalled a time when some older boys were picking on her and my dad came to her defense. He knocked one of the big boys off his bicycle and made it clear that you did not mess with his big sis. He was always there for her, and she was there for him, too. Mona helped him deliver his newspapers around the VA Hospital, even when it was rainy and cold. Each Saturday they collected their money, and after turning in what they owed to the newspaper company, their mother expected the rest.

When my dad was nine, Marie had another son. In the next five years, she went on to have three more children, all by different men. With no husband to support them, she expected my dad to be the man of the family. After school, he and Mona babysat their four younger siblings, and Marie often expected Mona to skip school to care for them. Mona finally found a way to escape the stress: She married at seventeen, became pregnant, and moved away.

* * * * *

A few years later, when my Aunt Mona and her husband, Chet, moved back to Marion, she told my dad he could move in with her if things got too bad at home. The summer before his senior year of high school,

Marie moved out to the county (and into a new school district), and expected my dad to babysit his siblings while she worked. He wanted to finish his senior year at Marion High School, though, so he took Mona up on her offer. He moved in with her and Chet, and their daughter, Debbie. My dad was wonderful with his little niece—a clear indication of the kind of father he would be one day.

That summer, heading into his senior year, he took a full-time job at General Tire, a factory near Mona's house. No longer would he have to argue with his mom when she demanded his paychecks to support her young kids. Marie was terrible at managing money, unlike my dad. He bought a '58 Thunderbird, saved for college, and set his eyes on Ball State University in Muncie, Indiana. He was determined not to let anything stop him from reaching his goals.

He continued working at the factory in the evenings while going to Marion High during the day. He loved being a Marion Giant, and no one cheered louder at basketball games in the Marion Coliseum. He was outgoing and friendly and enjoyed attending school dances after the games. His first cousin Donna told me that one night after a dance they attended together, my dad was late getting her home. Her father, Russell, did not hesitate to ground her for a whole month. My dad felt responsible, so he spent every Friday night for the next month at Donna's home, dancing with her.

My dad graduated from Marion High School in 1964. With his devoted grandma and sister by his side, he beat the odds and reached this momentous milestone. As he walked across the stage to receive his diploma, he had a characteristically big smile on his face. On that day, just like in the many stories I collected from his childhood, his sunny disposition shined through. I believe God created him that way; his cheerfulness was a gift that carried him through his turbulent childhood, and it would carry him through the hard days in the jungles of Vietnam. But at that time, my dad had no plans to go to war. He had big dreams and his high school diploma—now all he needed was enough money to pursue a college degree.

Dad walks across the stage at his graduation from Marion High School on June 4, 1964.

After the ceremony, Dad holds his diploma in the school parking lot.

Celebration party at Grandma house.

Nevertheless, like countless newly minted high school graduates, my dad signed up for the draft on July 31, 1964, not long after he walked across the stage and turned eighteen. His draft card showed that he had hazel eyes, brown hair, measured 5'10", and weighed 140 pounds. Physical characteristics noted were two scars under his left eye—a detail I had never heard about until I saw his draft card.

Though my dad had to register for the draft, he never wavered in his desire to go to medical school. He was determined to create a life free from the daily struggles that come with poverty, and to earn a college degree. Fortunately, he had the work ethic to make both happen. Unfortunately, he did not have the money. Without a single college graduate (let alone a doctor) in his family and without the resources to pursue his dream, he doggedly created a plan that would get him there—he just needed to work at the factory a little longer, where his intelligence and diligence had recently earned him the supervisor position.

And his plan worked. In the summer of 1965, just one year after graduating from Marion High, he applied to Ball State University and was accepted. He received a student number, 37388, and paid ten dollars to hold his place for the spring quarter of 1966, beginning in January. I can only imagine his elation!

**BALL STATE UNIVERSITY**

OFFICE OF
ADMISSIONS

MUNCIE, INDIANA

be RDR                                    no ca

STUDENT

Notice of OFFICIAL UNDERGRADUATE ADMISSION for:

NAME Goss, Larry Jo

STUDENT NUMBER  37388

ADDRESS 528 W. Wiley
Marion, Indiana

INDIANA RES. ☒  NON RES. ☐

TO THE spring          QUARTER, 19 66    ISSUED ON          July 20, 1965
directed          TERM, 19

FINAL ADMISSION AS A freshman     STUDENT

CURRENT ADMISSION STATUS

☐ DISTINCTION  ☒ WARNING  ☐ REGULAR

☐ PROBATION  ☐ TO BE DETERMINED

☐ OTHER

– SEE OTHER SIDE –

Memo to Student:

The attached $10.00 receipt must be presented together with your Notice of
Admission Card at the Cashiers' Window on the day you are scheduled to register in order for you to secure a Permit to Register Fee Card for the
Quarter indicated.  This fee is non-refundable and loss of this receipt will
require another $10.00 payment.

BE SURE TO BRING BOTH CARDS WITH YOU ON THE DAY YOU REGISTER.

R. L. Klinedinst, Burser
Ball State University

NAME: Goss, Larry Jo

FOR:

PAYER SHOULD COMPLETE ABOVE LINES

**BALL STATE TEACHERS COLLEGE**

MUNCIE, INDIANA

**OFFICIAL RECEIPT**

APPROVED BY STATE BOARD OF ACCOUNTS FOR
BALL STATE TEACHERS COLLEGE, 1958

CASH_____CHECK NO._____MONEY ORDER_____

THIS INSTRUMENT NOT A RECEIPT UNTIL VALIDATED

VALIDATION

**FORM B-34**

IN APPLYING FOR OR INQUIRING ABOUT REFUND ADDRESS THE:
**OFFICE OF THE BUSINESS MANAGER AND TREASURER**

But less than four months before he was set to arrive on campus, my dad's plans crashed and burned. He received an envelope in the mail that contained a draft notice from the selective service system. The letter ordered him to report for induction into the United States Armed Forces.

---

SELECTIVE SERVICE SYSTEM

**ORDER TO REPORT FOR INDUCTION**

Approval Not Required.

The President of the United States,

To

Larry Joe Goss
713 Lancelot Drive
Marion, Ind. 46952

Indiana Local Board No. **138**
Selective Service System
The Glass Block
113-25 West 3rd Street
Marion, Indiana · 46952

(LOCAL BOARD STAMP)

December 16, 1965
(Date of mailing)

| SELECTIVE SERVICE NO. | | | |
|---|---|---|---|
| 12 | 138 | 46 | 136 |

GREETING:

You are hereby ordered for induction into the Armed Forces of the United States, and to report

at ____Local Board Office, 418 Glass Block, Marion, Ind._____
(Place of reporting).

on ____Jan. 20, 1966____ at ____5:45 a.m._____
(Date)                              (Hour)

for forwarding to an Armed Forces Induction Station.

_____
(Member or clerk of Local Board)

**IMPORTANT NOTICE**
(Read Each Paragraph Carefully)

IF YOU HAVE HAD PREVIOUS MILITARY SERVICE, OR ARE NOW A MEMBER OF THE NATIONAL GUARD OR A RESERVE COMPONENT OF THE ARMED FORCES, BRING EVIDENCE WITH YOU. IF YOU WEAR GLASSES, BRING THEM. IF MARRIED, BRING PROOF OF YOUR MARRIAGE. IF YOU HAVE ANY PHYSICAL OR MENTAL CONDITION WHICH, IN YOUR OPINION, MAY DISQUALIFY YOU FOR SERVICE IN THE ARMED FORCES, BRING A PHYSICIAN'S CERTIFICATE DESCRIBING THAT CONDITION, IF NOT ALREADY FURNISHED TO YOUR LOCAL BOARD.

Valid documents are required to substantiate dependency claims in order to receive basic allowance for quarters. Be sure to take the following with you when reporting to the induction station. The documents will be returned to you. (a) FOR LAWFUL WIFE OR LEGITIMATE CHILD UNDER 21 YEARS OF AGE—original, certified copy or photostat of a certified copy of marriage certificate, child's birth certificate, or a public or church record of marriage issued over the signature and seal of the custodian of the church or public records; (b) FOR LEGALLY ADOPTED CHILD—certified court order of adoption; (c) FOR CHILD OF DIVORCED SERVICE MEMBER (Child in custody of person other than claimant)—(1) Certified or photostatic copies of receipts from custodian of child evidencing serviceman's contributions for support, and (2) Divorce decree, court support order or separation order; (d) FOR DEPENDENT PARENT—affidavits establishing that dependency.

Bring your Social Security Account Number Card. If you do not have one, apply at nearest Social Security Administration Office. If you have life insurance, bring a record of the insurance company's address and your policy number. Bring enough clean clothes for 3 days. Bring enough money to last 1 month for personal purchases.

This Local Board will furnish transportation, and meals and lodging when necessary, from the place of reporting to the induction station where you will be examined. If found qualified, you will be inducted into the Armed Forces. If found not qualified, return transportation and meals and lodging when necessary, will be furnished to the place of reporting.

You may be found not qualified for induction. Keep this in mind in arranging your affairs, to prevent any undue hardship if you are not inducted. If employed, inform your employer of this possibility. Your employer can then be prepared to continue your employment if you are not inducted. To protect your right to return to your job if you are not inducted, you must report for work as soon as possible after the completion of your induction examination. You may jeopardize your reemployment rights if you do not report for work at the beginning of your next regularly scheduled working period after you have returned to your place of employment.

Willful failure to report at the place and hour of the day named in this Order subjects the violator to fine and imprisonment. Bring this Order with you when you report.

If you are so far from your own local board that reporting in compliance with this Order will be a serious hardship, go immediately to any local board and make written request for transfer of your delivery for induction, taking this Order

He was stunned—there had to be a mistake. He had his notice of official undergraduate admission to Ball State University and money for his tuition in the bank. My dad contacted the university and was told they had never received his $35 admissions deposit. How could that be? Before the deadline, his mom told him she was going to Muncie. Since Ball State was in Muncie, she would deliver his admissions deposit for him. He gave her the deposit in cash.

But Marie never went to the university. She never delivered his deposit. Instead, she spent his hard-earned money on alcohol.

My dad's heart broke. He felt angry, sad, and betrayed. He had experienced many disappointments, but nothing like this. A third blow came when my dad went to his bank and found the money he saved for college was gone. His mother's name was placed on it when he opened the account as a youth. His sister Mona said their mother's name was on everything of hers until she got married. The same was true for my dad, but he never thought his mom would do this to him. Mona remembers that time vividly. My dad still lived with her, but he would not tell her what was wrong. One day he finally told her: "Mom wiped out my savings account. It's all gone." Not only had Marie partied with his deposit, she had spent all the money he saved for Ball State.

My dad wrote a desperate letter to a local politician and to the draft board, asking for the error to be corrected. He received an official letter back denying the request; they would not grant him a college deferment.

SELECTIVE SERVICE SYSTEM

Indiana Local Board No. 138
Selective Service System
The Glass Block
113-25 West 3rd Street
Marion, Indiana - 46952
(LOCAL BOARD STAMP)

IN REPLY, REFER TO:

December 30, 1965

Mr. Larry J. Goss
713 Lancelot Drive
Marion, Ind. 46952

Dear Mr. Goss:

We regret to inform you that your request for a postponement has been denied. Therefore you are still ordered to report for induction on January 20, 1966 unless you wish to enlist before that date.

Sincerely,

Mac E. Love

When Plan B failed, my dad—used to solving his problems alone—developed Plan C. Instead of reporting to the Army, he would talk to a Navy recruiter to see what his options were. Harry had served in World War II as a sailor; maybe that would be an option for him too.

When my dad talked to a recruiter and made clear his desire to have a career in medicine, the recruiter suggested he become a hospital corpsman, an enlisted medical specialist in the U.S. Navy. The recruiter explained that when my dad returned home from Vietnam, he could pursue his dream of earning his M.D. and his education would be free. But the recruiter neglected to tell my dad that not all corpsmen serve on Navy ships. The Marines could take Navy corpsmen to serve with them on the front lines.

My dad's enlistment in the Navy gave him a ninety-day delay, pushing back the date—January 20, 1966—that his original orders required him to report for basic training. Across town, a beautiful girl named Marty prepared to celebrate her twentieth birthday on January 20. Though they had never met, their paths would cross during his extra days at home. And once they did, the two would be inseparable.

## CHAPTER THREE

# His Blue Kentucky Girl

My mom, Martha Gipson, was beautiful both inside and out. Raised in Paducah, Kentucky, she was the beloved belle of the town—sweet, kind, and easy to love. She was the oldest of seven living children born to Earl and Mary. Martha's quick wit, sense of humor, infectious laugh, and cheerful disposition got her through many challenging times. Her father had, to put it plainly, a poor work ethic, which caused the family to live in extreme poverty throughout her growing years.

Growing up, Marty (as her friends called her) spent most of her time nurturing her siblings while her mama worked tirelessly, taking on every odd job she could find. When Marty was twelve, her family packed up and moved with only what they could carry, hoping for a better life in Gas City, Indiana. Mary's brothers worked at a factory in Indiana and assured Earl he could find work. Although he was hired, Earl often chose to stay in bed rather than go to his job. This forced the family to move often when the rent became due.

My mom was well liked by her teachers. During her senior year, a teacher submitted her name to the Twin City Bank in Gas City and she was offered a job. With no means of transportation, she walked to work from her parent's rental home in Jonesboro (a neighboring town) when she could not find a ride. She was only eighteen, but wise and mature. She obtained a loan from the bank to purchase a car for three hundred dollars. However, she had no license to drive it. She left the car at home, hoping that her dad would use it to go to work. One day, after working an eight-hour shift and then walking home, she found the car in the driveway and her dad in bed. She mustered up the courage to confront him. As he lay in bed, she asked him to get up and go to work because her siblings needed food. He got out of bed, picked her up by the neck, and threw her onto the front yard. He placed her belongings there as well and told her to never return.

Marty slept at a girlfriend's house that evening and went to work the next morning. When her boss heard she was homeless, he took over and quickly found her a home. She had a place to stay by the end of the night: a bedroom at the home of Mrs. Nelson, a sweet elderly lady who lived alone and was willing to take a chance on Marty.

My mom didn't make much at the bank, but she had enough to get by. Anything extra she shared with her mama and younger siblings. She was generous, kind, and well liked by her supervisors, and it wasn't long until she received a promotion from bookkeeper to bank teller. Her tall, slender frame caught the eye of a bank examiner, and they began dating. Marty was quite a catch.

My mom continued to live with Mrs. Nelson for three years. During that time, she joined a bank-sponsored bowling league at Crown Lanes. Every Wednesday evening, she and her friends would meet up to try and knock down some pins. They didn't knock down many, but they had fun.

Though Marty did not know it, Larry had just started working at the bowling alley. His aunt and uncle, Fred and Fran Hutchison, were the owners. Their son Ronnie (Larry's cousin) had not been getting good grades. Since Larry had left his full-time job at the factory to enjoy some down time before his commitment to the Navy began, he offered to do Ronnie's job for three weeks so his cousin could focus on school. Aunt Fran was delighted.

My competitive dad bowling a 278 at Crown Lanes in Gas City, Indiana (1965).

\* \* \* \* \*

On March 23, 1966—just thirty-four days before he was scheduled to leave for boot camp—Larry saw Marty for the first time. For him, it was love at first sight. Marty's beautiful, thin lips and sapphire blue eyes captivated him as he approached her group to take their drink orders. Larry tried to give her a signal by flashing his dashing smile.

As soon as he walked away, Marty's friend Dorothy Winters said, "Did you see the way he looked at you? He likes you." Marty thought nothing of it until he returned a little later. As Larry gently handed her a Coke, he said, "I'm going into the service so I don't have a lot of time, but if you want to improve your bowling game, I can give you private lessons."

Marty called the bank examiner as soon as she got home and broke up with him. She didn't mean to break his heart, but there was something about the young man at the bowling alley she could not resist. Larry had no idea that Marty was eighteen months older, but it wouldn't have made a bit of difference if he had. Their age difference was something they would joke about often. From that night on, Marty and Larry saw each other every day until he left for boot camp on April 26, 1966.

During the long weeks of separation that followed, my parents wrote each other many letters. Marty kept all her communication very positive; boot camp was hard, and she didn't want to add to Larry's burdens. When "Pop" passed away in July, Marty didn't give him the news, since the funeral would be two days before boot camp ended.

Larry graduated from boot camp training on his twentieth birthday, July 7, 1966. His adoring Marty and sister Mona were there, beaming with pride as he graduated at the top of his class. Officer Green, a tough old drill sergeant, had taken a liking to Larry and given him a leadership position. Though the men were all enlisted Navy, they were affectionately called "Green's Marines" because of the sergeant's no-guff reputation.

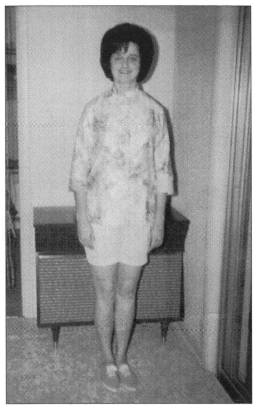

*Left:* My beautiful mom's senior picture in the high school yearbook (1963).

*Right:* Mom sent this picture to Dad when he was in boot camp (June 1966).

During boot camp, Larry befriended a fellow sailor, Stan Burkart, from Battle Ground, Indiana. Officer Green was especially hard on Stan and Larry helped him whenever he could. Their friendship grew stronger in corpsman school since they had much in common, including a love of sports and a desire to study hard. Years later, Stan found me. He said that my dad's kindness always stayed with him. Stan's stories added pieces to the puzzle and gave me vital insight into my dad's few years as a young adult.

Dad brought a handkerchief home from boot camp inscribed with a cartoon of Officer Green and his nickname. Years later, when I married a cartoonist, I would think about that handkerchief and wonder if my dad loved cartoons. I know that my dad would have loved being a father-in-law to my talented husband.

Stan Burkart and Dad at boot camp (shown in circles).

Basic Training leaders including my dad (fourth from right), selected as master-at-arms. A master-at-arms is a Navy rating responsible for discipline and law enforcement. He also made Third Class at Great Lakes in April 1967.

# CHAPTER FOUR

# Summer Love

L arry knew he had about a week and a half with Marty before he left for the Naval Hospital Corps School, and he couldn't waste any time. Marty was in love, too, and anxious to make those few days special for him. When he returned home, she had a birthday surprise for him: her brand-new driver's license, which he had encouraged her to get before he left so she could care for his beloved '58 Thunderbird. Larry wasn't used to people making a big deal about him on his birthday, so he was thoroughly touched. In fact, that birthday was the only surprise party he ever had.

On a break between boot camp and corps school, my parents relaxed at Mona's house (July 1966).

Dad loved his Thunderbird and motorcycle, but he loved my mom even more.

Larry proposed to Marty on July 13, 1966—fifty years to the day on which I'm writing this line. Getting married at the age of twenty was a big deal, and he wanted her to have the perfect engagement ring. He had enough cash to pay for the ring in full, and they went together the following day to make the bank withdrawal and select a ring. My parents were now officially engaged!

On July 21, Larry left for training at the Naval Hospital Corps School in Great Lakes, Illinois. He found rides home every weekend because he and Marty had memories to make. Sometimes they would meet at his grandma's lake cottage on Big Barbee. Larry loved the water and Marty did not, but she would go anywhere with him. They danced and played cards and laughed a lot. While Marty planned their wedding, Larry found an apartment for them in Chicago.

The happy couple after getting engaged (July 14, 1966).

Mom's engagement picture, July 1966.

My parents picked their wedding date to coincide with a weekend break from corps school: October 8, 1966. Their whirlwind courtship had been a time of true bliss, and looking through their pictures from those months, I see a couple deeply in love. They were so young and thought they had a lifetime of happiness ahead of them.

One of the ways my dad showed his overflowing love for my mom was through poetry. This is the first of many that he sent her, written on a card attached to a bouquet of flowers:

> *Twelve little roses,*
> *Each to say*
> *Why I am happy*
> *You came my way.*

However, one obstacle surfaced: Because Larry was only twenty, he needed a parent's signature to get married. But since the night he found out that his mom had spent his admission deposit on alcohol and evaporated his savings, he had barely spoken to her. Thanks to her, he was now in the military instead of college. Even worse, his mother had expressed no remorse and had never apologized.

And it got even worse. Marie knew Larry would likely be deployed to Vietnam, and if he were single, she would be his next of kin. The life insurance payout the government offered was $10,000. So, when Larry asked for his mother's signature to get married, she refused. Marie's rejection left my dad with only one option: he had to ask his biological father, Harry, to sign. Though Harry had never claimed my dad as his son, his name was on Larry's birth certificate. His signature would suffice.

My mom recalled how nervous my dad was when he picked up the phone to call Harry. Although my dad had a relationship with Harry's brother, John, and his wife, Ginny, he hadn't talked to Harry in years, so he had no idea how his father would respond when he answered the phone. It took great courage to make that call.

When Harry answered, Larry got right to the point.

"I've met a beautiful girl named Marty, and I hope you can meet her one day," he said. "I love her very much and want to make her my wife, but Mom won't give us permission to marry. If I could pick someone to be my father, I would want it to be you. Would you be willing to sign the document so we can get married?"

Harry was more than happy to give his legal approval and blessing. And from that day forward, he gave my father something he had never given him before: his love and support.

Not only were my parents able to be married, but now that Harry had acknowledged Larry as his son, my dad could get to know his four half-siblings: Harry Richard, Connie, Jack, and Bonnie. The youngest of the bunch, Bonnie Kay, was only six years old, and she and my dad developed a special closeness right away. In

September, for the first time, Marty met Harry's wife, Willie, at the Grant County Courthouse. Harry's signature on their application for a marriage license meant that nothing could stop them now. In one short month, Marty would become Mrs. Larry Goss.

Their growing affection, expressed beautifully through their letters—prior to, on, and after their wedding—tell of their abiding love. Larry was at corps school when he received this note from his fiancée:

Wednesday Night
September 14, 1966
11:23 p.m.

Dear Sweetheart,

How are you tonight? Probably in bed and asleep by now, dreaming about me (I hope).

It is really turning cold tonight and it's raining too. I just got home from bowling. I did terribly. I didn't feel very well to start with, every game got worse. I'm so glad I'm home and in a good warm bed. One thing missing, you here beside me.

Every time I'm in the bowling alley I think you should be there. Every time I look at the counter, I want to see you there. I remember how you always smiled at me when I was bowling, you always looked so happy.

I wish tomorrow was Friday. I can hardly wait to see you.

Ronnie can't get Saturday night off, he said he tried really hard but Dick wouldn't let him.

I can't believe this will be our last long weekend together. Friday and Saturday night were terribly short, but now only one night.

I hope you have a good trip home Friday night. I'll be ready and leave right after work.

I got a letter from you today. I was so happy to hear from you. I read it several times. I hope I get one tomorrow.

Larry, I love you. I can't stand the thought of being away from you. I'll be waiting for you Friday night with open arms.

All of my love always,
Marty

On October 8, 1966, their wedding day finally arrived. I can only imagine how elated and loved my dad felt that day—in a month's time, he was accepted as Harry's son and marrying the woman of his dreams. In a little church in Jonesboro, Indiana, Larry and Marty were wed. Marie did not attend the wedding, but her mother, Ruth Bradford, and Marty's mother, Mary Gipson, did. My parents promised to love each other until "death do we part," but my mother knew that death would never extinguish her love for Larry. As she held a bouquet of blue and white carnations, her face glowed with joy. They had never been happier, and their future was as radiant as her smile.

On their wedding day, Larry wrote the following words for Marty on a notepad. Years later, I realized that my love of poetry came from him.

*A Wife's Love is like a rose*
*Hung on your chest.*
*It reveals beauty and charm at its best*
*My wife's love is the world you see*
*For it means so very much to me*
*I'm so glad that God above,*
*Gave to me such a wife's Love*
*Your Husband*

Mary Geneva Gipson, Marty, Larry, and Ruth Christine Bradford.

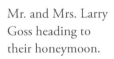

Mr. and Mrs. Larry Goss heading to their honeymoon.

Larry could not get enough time off from the Naval Hospital for a real honeymoon, so they had just the weekend. But they were finally man and wife! The joy that filled their hearts all weekend would be enough to get them through. Marty booked a honeymoon suite at a Holiday Inn out of town, but Larry thought it was too expensive, so he had her change it to a regular room. Sunday afternoon, as he drove back to Chicago, thoughts of his bride flooded his mind.

His first day back at the Great Lakes Naval Hospital, Larry wrote Marty two letters. He wrote her three more letters that week and then drove home on Friday to move her back to Chicago with him.*

Dearest Darling,

Well dear, it's been 40 hours since we were happily joined together. We had a very beautiful wedding. I couldn't have asked for a more wonderful or beautiful girl to spend the rest of my life with. I thought the Holiday Inn was really nice and being there alone with you made it even better. I know everything will work out beautiful for us. We were brought together and joined together as man and wife and the rest of our life will be wonderful as we'll both be making each other happy.

I just got back from the personnel office and all I need is that copy of our marriage license and they'll start the barrel-a-rolling up here. I hope it gets through and you start receiving your checks. We need everything that they'll give us. I hope we'll be able to spend the whole 3 1/2 years together. I don't want us to be apart any more than we have to. I love you very much and I want you to be happy. I'll try my whole life through to make you very, very happy. I truly will. [. . .]

---

* I've inserted bracketed ellipses ("[. . .]") in my dad's letters whenever he wrote intimate expressions to my mom. I'm including them just to show how many of them he wrote.

I feel so good knowing that you're my wife and the mother of our children. I couldn't have asked for a better wife. I know you'll make me the happiest man in the world.

Well dear, I'm going to sign off so you can get this early. I love you very much.

With All My Love
Larry

OCTOBER 10, 1966
1800 [6:00 P.M.]

Dearest wife,

Hi sweetheart, how's my dearest darling tonight? I love you very much. I received two wonderful letters from you today "a hurry right home and we'll be married quicker than you think"! See already! How's that?

I'm glad you like my relations; they think you are about it and so do I. My grandmother has really fallen in love with you. The girl I married would have to be approved more than ever by my grandmother. You passed 100%.

Well this week will go pretty slow, but in four long days you'll be in my arms once again. Today all we did was watch television and I went to the personnel office and started your allotment $92.50. Not bad for saying I do! I also had to fill out a thing to get your "ID" card. I wasn't sure about everything, but I said you were 5'5" 130 lbs., hazel/blue eyes. How did I do? I was going to put down your description as: The most wonderful girl with the most fascinating smile and the most radiating personality." The most likeable girl in this whole wide world.

"I Know A Smile I Love"

I Know A Smile I Love to See,
A voice I Love to hear,
I know a hand I Love to hold,
A presence I hold near.
I know a heart—a loving heart
That's thoughtful, fine and true,
I know them all, and Love them all
For they belong to you.

Well dear I guess I'll close for now. I love you very much. Hope you have a very pleasant week. See you soon!

With All My Love
Forever & Always
Mr. Larry Goss
Your Loving husband

P.S. Well Mrs. Goss it's been two days we are like old married people now. But we love like we are red hot out of the frying pan. [. . .]

# CHAPTER FIVE

# A Growing Family

Though my mom and dad never got to raise me together, they did get to experience a taste of what it would have been like when Mom's five-year-old sister, Rhonda, came to stay with them for a month in their Chicago apartment. My dad was the father Rhonda never had, and her love for him continues to this day. In contrast to my lenient mom, my dad was a disciplinarian. Rhonda loved sleeping in their bed, right in between them, "like a baby bear," and my dad wasn't happy about it. After all, they'd only been married for two months! Dad allowed "baby bear" to remain in the middle and forty-six years later, my Aunt Rhonda told this story at his footstone dedication ceremony. His love and kindness affected her immensely.

*Left:* My parents await my arrival (May 1967).

*Right:* Mom at eight months pregnant (June 1967).

I was born July 25, 1967, at the Naval Hospital in Great Lakes, Illinois, exactly nine months and seventeen days after my parents' wedding day. My mom said they weren't trying to conceive, but weren't trying to prevent it, either. I choose to believe that God knew I was supposed to be here on this Earth for my mom's sake. My dad had turned twenty-one just two weeks before I was born. Although he was young, he was mature beyond his years. And with the war in Vietnam looming on the horizon, he still focused on the here and now: his wife, his baby girl, and his work in the medical field.

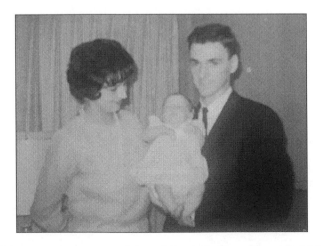

With my parents at a cousin's wedding in Indiana (Aug. 20, 1967).

At that time, my dad was classified as an HM3/USN: Hospital Corpsman 3rd Class, U.S. Navy. He was assigned to a duty station at a hospital in Chicago, where he learned about podiatry and pharmaceuticals. He liked both areas so much, he considered specializing in one of them when he went to medical school. A dedicated student, Dad was promoted up to a HM2 quicker than most corpsmen. He was a tireless worker.

When I was little, my mom would tell me stories of how she timed him while he held his breath underwater in the bathroom tub, and the countless times she held his feet while he did nightly sit-ups. She explained that completing these physical fitness challenges helped him move up the Navy career ladder—and that meant more pay and more security for us, his family.

On many Fridays, when my dad had finished his day at the hospital, he would load up our little red VW Bug and head to Marion so my grandmas could enjoy me too. And one time, Aunt Marge and her family brought Grandma Bradford up to Chicago to visit. They both loved babies and enjoyed me tremendously.

*Left:* Dad in his Ball State T-shirt with me,
Grandma Bradford, and Mom in Chicago (August 1967).

*Right:* Dad with Aunt Marge and cousins Michael
and Phillip in Chicago (August 1967).

In September, Mom and Dad's one-year anniversary was approaching, and life was the best it had ever been for them. On Thursday,

September 14, my dad came home from work and kissed my mom hello, the way he did every day. Then he sat her down to tell her the most devastating news: he had received his orders for Vietnam.

They both knew this was inevitable but hoped the war would end before this day came. But they did not anticipate that instead of serving the wounded on a Navy vessel, my dad would be on the front lines of the battlefield, serving with the Marines. The Army had medics and the Navy had corpsmen. The Marines, however, had no medical personnel. That meant that some Navy corpsmen were assigned to the Marines. My dad's orders informed him that this was his assignment. He would not find out which unit or what location, though, until he got to Vietnam.

As my mom struggled to catch her breath, my dad reassured her that he would make it home. He was scared, just as she was, but he hid it the best he could. He was good at calming her fears and telling her everything was going to be OK. This time he was not sure it would be, but he had to remain positive for her.

In very short order, they had to make a decision about Field Medical School. My dad had two choices: He could go to California, where he would train at Camp Pendleton for four weeks and then be home for a month, or he could go straight from training to Vietnam. He chose the first, which meant he'd have thirty days of leave after school was done. They would make every moment count. This also meant he had to quickly find us a place to live.

Because my dad wanted to ensure that we were well cared for while he was gone, he decided to move us back closer to the family before he left. He asked his Aunt Marge and Uncle Russ if they would rent him the room above their garage, and they said yes. He knew we would be safe and supported there.

Our little car would not hold all of our belongings so my dad called Harry to ask if he would help us move home. He obliged and did his best to make up for the years he had lost with his son. So, when I was only two months old, we moved back to Indiana.

After getting us settled, my dad headed west. He had never seen the ocean or the mountains before. The beauty of California captivated him, but his heart remained with his family in Indiana. He wrote letters to my mom every day at Camp Pendleton and wanted desperately to be with us.

*Left:* Dad holds me outside our Chicago apartment (Sept. 30, 1967). Harry and Willie Goss arrived that day to help my parents pack up and move back to Indiana.

*Right:* Dad got to see his father enjoying time with his granddaughter (Sept. 30, 1967).

With my happy parents on their first anniversary, Oct. 8, 1967, in Indianapolis.

* * * * *

Though my dad could not be with us physically, he did everything he could to stay close to us. At a young age, I heard the saying, "The greatest gift a father can give his children is to love their mother." Because of his letters and audio tapes, I always knew how deeply my dad loved my mom.

I don't remember the first time she showed me one of his letters, but I am beyond thankful that she held them so close all these years. For fifty-two years she kept his last letter in her purse, along with her last letter to him. She had asked to be buried with all his letters, but recently told me she felt that was selfish; copies of each letter would suffice. Though I'm touched by her thoughtfulness, I can't imagine her ever being without them.

Up to this point, my parents' letters are a joyful read, brimming with happiness and anticipation. But as the war and my dad's death creep closer, reading them becomes difficult. So many people search for a profound and abiding love like theirs—a flame that still burns just as bright as when they saw each other for the last time over half a century ago. But so few people find it. So to find it and have it ripped away? Perhaps that's why, even with the passing of time, my mom's love and longing for my dad has not wavered. It has only grown.

## CHAPTER SIX

# Letters from Camp Pendleton

My mom kept a daily calendar from 1965–1967. Entries showed their first date, the day they got engaged, and numerous details of the two years they had together. It was one of many treasures my mom saved that made this book possible. At the top of September 1967, she wrote, "11th month in our apartment. 8th visit home." It was important to her and my dad that they stayed connected to family and that their loved ones were able to bond with me too.

One entry showed its significance by the circle mom placed around it. September 14 said "Larry got orders."

Mom's calendar, September 1967.

On October 11, 1967, three days after their one-year wedding anniversary, my dad left for California. One year was not enough. He had hoped for so much more, but the war was picking up in Vietnam. He did not want to go. The letters that follow contain the majority of my dad's words. Though I considered sharing only bits and pieces here, I decided it was important to share most of every letter because they show my dad's personality. They also give us a window into the last few months of his life.

LETTER 1
OCTOBER 11, 1967
10:30 A.M.

Dear Marty,

I am on my flight to Los Angeles now. We have already been served breakfast. I am doing fine. <u>I miss you very much. I love you.</u> It only took us only 35 minutes to get to St. Louis and after a 45

56

minute wait we were on our way to California. It is now 10:45 and we are going over the Rockies. Pike's Peak has snow on top of it and it is real pretty.

11:30 A.M. We are now going over the Grand Canyon. It is some sight. Have arrived everything is fine.

I love you.
Larry
Kiss Marty & Lori

This postcard makes me think of all the things my father experienced for the first time in his last sixteen months of life. Becoming a husband and a dad, seeing the mountains, swimming in the ocean. My daughter, Courtnee Jo, made a similar journey to California, but for college. On one of her flights home, she took a picture of the Rockies and Grand Canyon. My dad would have loved to talk with his only granddaughter about this experience they both shared, forty-nine years apart. My youngest son, Casey Jordan, also attends college in California now. My dad would have loved visiting there to watch him act, sing, and dance—three things my dad also loved to do.

Dad's second letter beautifully expressed his longing for my mom and his deep desire for her to feel happy and deeply loved.

LETTER 2
OCTOBER 12, 1967

Dear Darling,

I miss you very much. I look at your pictures, but I need to hold you. How is my darling little daughter? I hope she is being good for her mother. I will only be gone until November 14th, so that won't be too long. I will try to write you every night because I know how much these letters mean to you and I want you to always be happy and feel wanted, because you are. I wanted to hold you again the first time I looked out the plane window and saw you waving. I really miss your beautiful smile and the way you make me feel wanted and needed. I love you very much.

We are here, but school doesn't start until tomorrow and only lasts for 4 weeks, so I'll be starting home about the 15 of Nov. As far as I know now, I got my 30 days of leave. I also need one set of whites, so please send them as soon as possible. I have to have them for my second week. You don't need to send them air mail, that's just wasting money. Where we stay is pretty nice, we are right on the ocean and the breeze is real refreshing.

The barracks are fairly nice, but a little dusty because of the Marine tanks that run around here. We have to walk a mile and a half to chow everyday three times and when we go to classes or anything else it's March March March! We get our Marine clothes tomorrow and then our Navy clothes will set around and collect dust. But the reason I need my whites is because we have a big inspection, and this is to make sure you have the number of Navy clothes you were supposed to.

Tell everybody Hi and that I am doing fine. I love you very very much. Kiss my daughter for me.

Larry
I love you very much
xxxxxxx x 1 million for each hour of each day I'm gone.

This letter taught me many things about my dad. The line about money made me smile—the first time I read it, I finally figured out where my frugality came from. Nature versus nurture? I vote for nature on this one!

Dad (right) and a fellow corpsman at Camp Pendleton's Field
Medical School. He was there Oct. 11–Nov. 14, 1967.

LETTER 3
OCTOBER 13, 1967

Dearest Darling,

Well dear, how are my girl's feeling today? I hope fine. I miss
you very much, but we will only be apart for five weeks, so I think
I'll make it. How's my car coming along? I don't think you'll have
any trouble with it. You were driving it pretty well, when you were
with me. <u>Be Careful.</u> Ha! Ha! Ha!*

Well here at Camp Pendleton things are going along smoothly.
We received all our clothes today. They are really nice. I like them
better than the Navy's. We also received all our combat gear. Boy,
there is a lot of it. We were also issued a M14 rifle and it is really
a fine weapon.

---

* Dad was joking with my mom about a little accident she'd had while he was in corps
school, which busted out the front headlight in his car. I loved his gentle teasing "Ha!
Ha! Ha!" and could almost see his smile as he wrote the words.

Well enough of that. How are you doing? I hope Lori isn't giving you any trouble. She is so sweet; she's probably hardly noticed. How is she getting along with her bells?* She seemed to really like them. Tell everybody I am doing fine and that I will see them soon.

Well dear I'll sign off for now. I love you very much I can't wait until I'm home for those 30 days. WE will live the next 13 months in those 30 days.

Love you always,
Your Husband Larry

Dad (far right) looking sharp in his new uniform.

---

* The bells were a toy that hung above my baby bed. Dad picked them out for me. Mom said he thought I would enjoy playing with them and he was right.

Learning to shoot an M14 rifle.

LETTER 4
OCTOBER 14, 1967

Dearest Darling,

Well how are my girls doing today? I miss you both very much. I hope everything at home is coming along o.k. I know that everybody is treating you fine, because everybody likes you very much. I miss you very much and wish I were home every night, like in Great Lakes. It was really something to appreciate, coming home to a beautiful wife every night. I really miss you always having a pleasant smile greeting me at the door. I hope to call you every Sunday and hear your sweet voice. We won't be able to talk long but I'll remember every single second. It will keep me going until I can hold you tight once again.

Tell everybody back home I'm doing fine. We have started into training now and it is pretty interesting. "Boy" I'm going to be a Marine! It isn't easy but it's not as bad as people think. For us anyway. We are treated with respect, because we are petty officers.

And what they are teaching us is for our own good, because we'll need it all where we are going.

If you wanted to go to Kansas<sup>*</sup> in November, I am sorry I didn't discuss it with you but we really don't have the money and they don't have the space. I'm only going to stay for two days and then I'm coming home to you my darling. We will talk more later. I want to be with you, because you and Lori are my whole life now.

Well today after training I went swimming in the ocean. It was really nice. Those big waves just about pick you up and take you away with them. The water tastes just like saltwater you'd make at home. The <u>sandy beach</u> is something to see. It goes <u>on</u> and <u>on</u> for miles and those <u>waves</u> coming in are just <u>breathtaking</u>. I'm going to ask for Hawaii for my duty station after Vietnam and you and Lori can come with <u>me</u> and live by the <u>sea</u>.

Well honey I have to go. Miss you very much. See you in my dreams. I love you very much.

Always and Forever Yours.

Your Husband,
Larry
kiss x 1 million

My deep love of the ocean made sense to me when I read this letter. I wonder if God looked down on my dad at the ocean, knowing he was experiencing this for the first and last time. I am sure heaven is much better than a beach in California, but I'm glad my young dad who had never traveled the world got to experience the beauty of the mountains and coast before he left his earthly home.

---

<sup>*</sup> My dad planned to go to Kansas on his way home to visit his half-brother Jimmy who had contracted polio. He was concerned about Jimmy receiving proper care and attention. This visit would also allow him to say goodbye to his mother and half-siblings, Billy, Tina, and Bobbie Kay.

LETTER 5
OCTOBER 15, 1967

Dearest Darling,

How are my two wonderful girls today? I love you both very much. I hope that Lori is feeling better now, she'll have to get used to not seeing her daddy for some time. How's my big girl doing? She sounded pretty good on the phone today. I really needed to hear your sweet voice. When I get in Vietnam, I'll probably listen to those tapes every spare minute just to hear your sweet voice. You don't know how it really makes me feel. I love you very much.

Well, today I went down to the beach and walked around. I took a few picture of the ocean with my buddy's polaroid. The ocean is really something to see. It's never the same. We watched some people fish today. I also saw a stingray. The sea gulls are all around out here. They are something as they fly down and grab fish out of the water. Pelicans also.

Well I guess I'll go. I love you very much; Tell everybody Hi for me. I'm doing fine.

Your husband
Larry
KISS

My dad knew I needed him. His consideration for my mom and me came through in every note he wrote.

LETTER 6
OCTOBER 16, 1967

Dearest Darling,

How are my two very sweet girls today? I love you both very very much. I miss you more than you could ever guess. I sure will be glad when this school is over and I can be back in your arms. And to kiss your sweet lips again is what I really need. Send me some more pictures of you and Lori. I need them to build my <u>morale</u>.

We really worked out today marching, running and other exercises. I am really tired. I'll really be in great shape when I get home, <u>You</u> better be ready.

Well, things here are coming along fine. It really isn't that bad. But you are tired at the end of the day. It just makes me sleep better. The breeze off the ocean is really nice, keeps things cool at night.

Tell Grandma this training out here is making a man out of her boy. But I'm still a boy at heart in love with a very wonderful girl. Whose love keeps me going, because it gives me something to live for and to raise my little girl up into a little woman is my dream.

Well I guess I'll go. I have to hit the sack. I love you very very much.

Your husband always,
Larry
KISS        KISS        KISS

Tears formed in my eyes as I read my dad's desire to raise me up into a little woman. My mom and I were his focus. He was so devoted to us—and would have continued to be for our entire lives.

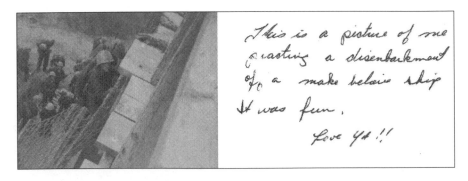

Training at Camp Pendleton. On the back, Dad wrote, "This is a picture of me practicing a disembarkment of a make-believe ship. It was fun. Love ya!!"

64

Field training at Camp Pendleton.

LETTER 7
OCTOBER 17, 1967

Dearest Darling,

I love you very much. How are you and my little daughter? I hope she's getting along better. I hope her shot doesn't hurt too much. I really hate to hear her cry. It really gets to me. How is our big room coming along?* It is really a nice place. How is the weather there? Probably getting fairly cold. Here things are hot and dusty. The dust is the only thing I hate out here, everything else is just beautiful. The View of the Ocean from our Barracks is really nice. At night the sky just above the ocean turns a dusty red, it is really pretty. We'll come out here on our vacations, o.k.?

---

* The big room was the area above Aunt Marge and Uncle Russ's garage my dad had rented for us. He wanted us safe and knew their support would be good for my mom while he was gone. This converted apartment is the place we shared together during my dad's last thirty days at home.

How is everybody at home? I hope fine. How are Danny and Donna doing?* They really don't have long together. We were really lucky to be together for a year. And we'll have many more.

I love you so very much. I believe "Absence Makes the <u>Heart</u> Grow Fonder."

Well, I guess I'll go see you soon. Love you very much.
your husband
Larry

LETTER 8
OCTOBER 18, 1967

My Dearest Darling,

I received your most wanted letters today. They are what I have been waiting for and needing. I thought your letters were very sweet. I hope Lori starts feeling better. Just hold her and make her feel loved and she will be alright. I really miss her very much also. I hope these next 26 days fly by. I want to hold you in my arms and never let go. I hope I will be able to someday.

Does your brother still have his tape recorder? If he does, start sending me tapes and I'll buy a tape recorder here. I want to hear your voice. I will feel a whole lot better if I do. It will make me feel more like you are here with me and also I can hear Lori talk maybe. It is going to be rough without you and Lori, because I love you very much and we really haven't been apart since we were married. I hoped it would have never happened, being apart.

How's everything there? I hope you start going out and visiting people. I know moving Lori is probably pretty hard, because with both of us it was a job and she is growing more every day. In your

---

* My dad's cousin Donna married Danny in August 1967, shortly after Danny's draft notice arrived in the mail.

letter you said she was 26" long. "Boy" she is really growing, just think what she'll be when I get home.

If you get Ray's tape recorder, don't forget to turn it all the way up. . .so it will be loud enough when I hear it. I hope you get it quick. I want to hear your voice every spare minute.

Well things here at Camp Pendleton are coming along just fine, except the training is getting tougher. We run with field packs and a cartridge belt, which has canteens numbering 2 and 2 clips for our M14 riffles. They are a nice weapon. We run about 2 ½ miles at the end of the day. What an ending. Next Wednesday we go on a 3-day overnight outing. We march at top speed and double time for 6 miles to the spot. With no rest, it's a force march. "Boy" are they getting us ready. Well I guess I'll sign off. I love you very much. See you soon.

With love always.
Your husband,
Larry

My dad was so honest about his needs and so expressive about his love. Mom was his stronghold. Her love and support sustained him through the long days of training he had to endure. He was barely twenty-one, yet he knew what his young daughter needed: to be held and to feel loved.

LETTER 9
OCTOBER 19, 1967

Dearest Darling,

I received 3 more letters from you today, totaling 6 now. The pictures were really good. I'm going to put two in my locker alongside of yours. I hope everything at home is coming along o.k. I really miss you more and more each day. I hope I can take the whole 25 days left. I love you very very much. I hope I can show you how much one of these days.

Things here are just the same as always. Classes all day and physical training at days end. "Boy" it really keeps you busy. The clothes we wear are real nice and comfortable too but the boots are just a little tight on the top of my right foot. I hope it stretches a little.

The pictures that you sent turned out real good. The ones of Lori are real cute. I like the ones where she is sitting against the pillow smiling just a little and the one where she's playing with her bells. I like the others also and that picture of you and I is the only one we got of just us, I think. I like it.

I hope the tape recorder of Ray's works. I want to hear your voice every day, not just once a week. I love you very much. [. . .] See you very soon.

Your Husband,
Larry
PS. Kiss my daughter for me. <u>I love you.</u>

My dad was filled with hope. I write that word a lot too, and now I understand why.

Playing with the bells dad bought me (October 1967).

LETTER 10
OCTOBER 20, 1967

Dearest Darling,

Just received your seventh letter today. I'm glad you're sending them each day. How are you and little Lori? You said she's laughing out loud now, I really bet that's something. I hope you can send it to me on those tapes. I would really like that. But if Ray's tape recorder doesn't work, I don't want you buying one.

How are you doing personally? I hope you aren't too sad. I never want you to be sad, because I love you very much and you mean a great deal to me. Without you I don't know what I'd do. You make me feel like I'm a whole man. Having a wonderful wife and a darling daughter. I love you both very much.

How are things there with you? Has Joe* found a job yet? Is he going to live at home and help your mom? Please keep me informed. You are doing a good job on everything else. Just like being there myself.

Here another day is over and I'm closer to the time I'll be home in your arms. I hope it flies by. We work six days a week here so I won't have but one day to sit and think for a long time about being away from you. If I thought too long I might go AWOL and come home to see you. I really miss you dear.

Your Husband,
Larry
KISS & HUG

My dad was a family man, concerned about the well-being of others. He did not want his wife to ever feel sad. He loved laughter and had great hope for their future. Like other service members, he

---

* Joe, Ray, and David are my mom's younger brothers.

longed to be home with his family. I know he would've made our happiness his top priority. Because I knew that, I have done my best to bring joy to my mom's life and enjoy mine to the fullest. I owe him that and so much more.

LETTER 11
UNDATED

Dearest Darling,

I'm glad Lori was awake when I called, and I hope you get the tape so I can hear her every day. I bet she has really grown. She'll probably look twice as big when I get home. I'm glad she was given a complete physical. Well, how are you feeling? I hope that you get out more now that you're used to me being gone. I don't want you sitting around worrying all day. I love you very much and I want to get you anything you want. You haven't had much in the last year, so go out and buy yourself something. I want you to be happy. I'll try and bring Lori back a musical toy like we saw in Indianapolis.

Well my day was very enjoyable today. I talked to my very sweet wife and then I went down to the beach and got a little sun. After that I played pool for a while and now I'm here writing my most dearest. I hope she had a most enjoyable day too. I get to go to the rifle range tomorrow and shoot my M 14 rifle and the 45 pistol. I hope it is enjoyable but like everything it will be messed up.

Tell everybody at home that I am doing fine. Hope to see them all soon. Wish I could be home lying beside you. [. . .]

Love
Your Husband, Larry

My prudent father wanted my mom and me to have nice things. He bought me a blue merry-go-round musical toy for Christmas that year. He and my mom picked it out together. I still have it, tucked away securely in my safe; for years, I kept it in my bedroom. It's a gift I'll always treasure as a reminder of my dad's love.

I took this photo around Christmas 2017 in my home in Marion, Indiana, fifty years after my parents gave me this blue merry-go-round.

LETTER 12
UNDATED

Dearest Darling,

How are you today? I hope fine. Well, I bet you are wondering why my letters are slowing down. Well, we are going out on overnight stays and they are keeping us busy all the way up to midnight, so the writing is hard to squeeze in. We go on a 3-day overnight hike tomorrow morning. I hope things are a little easier, so I can write you a few lines. We will be back Saturday so I will still call on Sunday. I hope you aren't mad.

Well now, how is everyone at home? Hope you are feeling well and slimmer. "Oh Boy, now you are mad!" I'd love you if you were 450 pounds. You're still my sweet lovable Marty. And you are all mine.

How's my darling daughter? I hope her leg is better by now. I'm sure it is. Now to answer some of your questions. I haven't bought any shoes, because I don't need them. I haven't bought any pants for the same reason. When I get back from Vietnam I'll buy them then. I haven't called Jack and Linda, because I really haven't had time. They really have jammed about 8 weeks into 4 weeks. Sunday I'm tired so I just rest.

Well I guess I'll close for now. I love you very much and I wish you happiness and riches. I'll give them to you someday very soon. Tell everybody hi from me. See you all soon.

Love forever,
Your husband Larry

My mom is very inquisitive, and my dad answers her many questions in these letters. They were able to send audio tapes to each other. He really wanted to hear her voice and the sounds of his almost three-month-old baby girl.

LETTER 13
WEDNESDAY, OCTOBER 25, 1967

Dearest Darling,

Well it is now 12:30 we have been out in the field about 4 hours and it isn't peaches. We are in small tents. 2 men per tent and it is crowded. I hope you are doing fine. I love you very much. I hope that we won't have things separating us all our lives. Well I have to go again. Will talk more later. Love You Very Much.

Thursday 6:00 p.m.

You can see how busy we have been. I haven't had a spare minute. We go on a six-mile force march in a half an hour. Well I hope you are doing better than me. We have no lights after dark, no wash basins, we use our helmets. We eat out in the wind. The dust is so bad you can't keep clean.

I hope you and Lori are doing fine. I love you very much. I miss you very much. I'm glad to hear you're getting more used to the VW and that you are going places more. I want you to get back to your old way and old friends. You have really done without, for the last year. You are my ideal wife. I love you very much. Write more later when I get time.

Love You. A Kiss for You and Darling Lori

Saturday 2:00

Well, we are finally back, and I am really dirty. I'll probably have to stand under the shower for about two hours to get all the dirt and dust off. Last night we had to fight off the enemy from our fox holes and we had to sleep in them all night long and it was dirty and not too much room for anything. The morning we got up and marched back. All we did was march up hills that I think were really mountains all the time we were out and watching for the enemy who were always ambushing us. The enemy were Marines. We both used blanks, but they could hurt you if you got close. I sure am tired. I'm going to get cleaned up and relax. See you soon.

Your Husband Always,

Larry

P.S. Take care of my little girl. I love you both very much.

P.S. [. . .]

I could not envision what my dad was describing until many years later, when one of my dad's fellow corpsmen, Ray Felle, showed me a picture of the tents. In 2014, on my daughter's college visit to California, Ray sent a message encouraging me to visit Camp Pendleton. I didn't realize it was close, but I enjoyed seeing the place where my dad trained. All I could think of as I stood there was, *I wish Dad could see us*. I wanted him to know how much his grandchildren, son-in-law, and daughter sought to know him, and that we loved him fiercely.

I understood my dad's expressions of love for my mom but was surprised to read how much he thought about me. I was only three months old, yet he wanted to make sure I was well cared for. Even thousands of miles across the country, he was a great dad.

LETTER 14
UNDATED

Dearest Darling,

I love you very much. I really enjoyed our talk today. I thought Sunday would never get here. I love hearing your sweet voice, that's why I want to get a tape recorder, so I can hear your voice anytime I want. I really miss you. I thought Lori sounded real cute today. It sounds like she is really getting grown up. She seems real happy too. I know you are giving her the best of care and I don't worry. You're a fine wife and mother and I love you very much.

I'm glad to hear that everybody is treating you real nice. I know they all like you very much. Nobody could dislike you, you're too sweet. "Watch for rain."

Things here will be fairly easy this week, because we are in the classrooms all week. We'll stay in our barracks, where it is fairly clean and there is plenty of hot water. We start our medical part this week and next. Our first two weeks were all military. I didn't really like it too well, but we had to know it before going over.

How is grandmother doing? I hope she isn't working too hard. I bet Donna and Danny are getting pretty shaky now with only two weeks to go. I hope he gets somewhere close. Being apart is

74

really rough. The service is for single men. Well I guess I'll go for now. See you soon. Love you very much.

Miss you terribly.
Your Husband,
Larry

Donna, me, Mom, Grandma Bradford, Aunt Marge,
and Aunt Mona in Marion (October 1967).

LETTER 15
UNDATED

Dearest Darling,

How is my very wonderful wife on this pleasant evening? I miss you very much. We only have two more weeks and then I'll be home in your wonderful arms. I also get my 30-day leave. I don't have to be back out here until Dec 16 at 1800. I leave at 2200 for Vietnam. I'm glad I decided to take my leave afterwards. Those

75

30 wonderful days with you will be the most wonderful days of my life. Hurry 14 days and fly by.

How is my sweet little daughter? I miss her so very much too. I hope she is feeling better. She sounded better Sunday. I really got a kick out of hearing her laugh. I'm glad Aunt Marge is there to help you with her. We are real lucky to have got to live with them. I love you very much and miss you terribly. Tell everybody I'm feeling fine and wish I was home.

Love you. Your husband Larry
P.S. I bought a tape recorder today.
I Love You Very Much.
KISS

LETTER 16
UNDATED

Hello Darling,

How are you this evening? By now you are probably asleep. I wish I was there beside you, hugging you tight. I'd give almost anything to have you out here with me. I can't stand being away from you. How is my darling daughter doing? I hope she is over being sick. How is your cold coming along? You are probably over it by now. I went to my first show this evening and saw James Bond in "You Only Live Twice." It was really a fine flick. Not too much sex, but it was real good. I hope we can do something every weekend when I'm home like a show or dancing.

Well it's now down to 14 days and a wake up and I'll be heading home to your sweet lips. Oh, how I want you so. I love you very much with all my heart and soul. Well there isn't much to write about things here. Just classroom work until next Wednesday. It is really boring. I can hardly keep awake. Well tell everybody at home that I'm doing fine and I wouldn't mind hearing from them.

Your loving husband, Larry

P.S. I love you very much. Kiss for you from me

LETTER 17
UNDATED

Hello Darling,

I received two wonderful letters from you today. I can't find as much to write about as you. I feel real bad too. I love you as much as anybody could. I don't know what I'll do for a year without you. I'll probably go nuts.

I sure wish I could have been home for that Halloween party. I bet it was really a blast. What would we have gone as? Adam and Eve. Not bad huh! [...]

I'm glad to hear that Lori is feeling better and her sleeping with you is a fine idea. It probably makes her feel more secure. I hope I'll be able to have my old spot back when I come home. I don't like the cold floor.

Have you written my mother and told her anything yet? I'm going to write her fairly soon and tell her when I'll be out. Will you also send me her phone number and address?

Well I guess I'll close for now.

Love you with all my heart.
Love forever,
Larry

When I had young children, I often wanted to call my dad for his advice. I was happy he shared his views on co-sleeping in this letter to my mom, because my husband and I allowed our children to sleep with us when we were too exhausted to put them back in their beds. It's nice knowing that Dad would have approved! His sense of humor was one of his greatest traits.

Another piece of his personality came through in his next letter: his desire to provide for my mom and me. Mom had bought me medicine and was down to her last dollar. My dad was concerned:

LETTER 18
UNDATED

Dearest Darling,

How is my most charming? I love you very much. I received three most wonderful letters from you today. They were real long too. I like them. I only wish I could have as much to write about. I also want to thank you for the <u>Doublemint</u>. I really enjoy it especially when I know you sent it. [. . .]

I'm glad to hear Lori is doing better. I can't hardly imagine you being down to $1. I know you paid a lot, but down to $1 is kind of low. I hope you don't have to buy too much more medicine, it really mounts up. I also see what you have to pay out a month $106, doesn't leave much.

I'll try to send you money home while I'm overseas. I don't want you to want for anything. I'm glad to hear that Uncle Fred and Aunt Fran won first place at the Halloween contest. I bet they were really a sight. I think I'll send you a hundred dollars tomorrow and let you keep it. I hope we use most of it on my 30 days having the time of our lives. We live day by day now. I also got my orders changed to the 3rd Marines now. I don't know why, but I'm now on the DMZ. They must be planning something. Maybe the war will be over soon. I sure hope so. I love you very much, sleep tight.

Your Husband Forever & Always
Larry

My dad was preparing to go to war, yet his mind was on taking care of us. The DMZ was the worst place my dad could be! Why were his orders changed? God knew that in the 3rd Marine Division, my dad would meet Dr. Behrens and some other wonderful men. God also knew that in this division my dad's company would also be ordered to "go get a mortar" on a hill where my dad would take his last breath.

LETTER 19
UNDATED

Dearest Darling,

How are my dear sweet wife and lovely daughter? We are almost down to our last full week. I'll be home before you know it. I really miss you both very much. I hope everything at home is all-right. I know you are doing a fine job with <u>Lori.</u> I wish I was home with you, so I could help you with her. I bet she is really getting to be something. 14 pounds is a lot to be carrying around. And with her being sick, it's probably twice as bad. I'm glad that she is talking more, I bet you really get a kick out of that. Things here are getting pretty boring. Siting in class all day makes you tired and sleepy. A lot of the material is the same as we had in corps school. I am learning new things though. We go on another outing next Wednesday, so things will look up a little.

Then we get a long weekend, Friday afternoon, Sat. and Sun. I will probably go to Disneyland. I hear it is really beautiful. Then on Tuesday I leave here on my way home to you. I wish it was tomorrow. I miss you so. I can't wait to hold you in my arms and squeeze you tight. Then, well!

Hope to see you real soon. I love you with all my heart.

Your Husband,
Larry
Kiss from me to you

Reading this stack of letters, I felt profound admiration for my mother. She had shared some very personal letters, many of which had intimate notes intended only for her. He was passionate about her and very romantic. I'm sure it may have been a bit awkward for her to share these personal parts with me, but I am so grateful that did. Seeing his powerful love for her helped me understand the importance of romantic, physical love that God himself designed. Those parts of his letters allowed me to see my father's heart, and that was one of the greatest gifts she ever gave me. My dad never got to go to Disneyland. I assume he decided not to go because of money. I went for him in 1989. Doing things he wanted to do helped me feel like I was living for both of us.

LETTER 20
UNDATED

Dear Marty (My Darling Sweetheart),

I love you very much. I enjoyed our sweet talk today and I got it on my tape recorder and I'm going to listen to it every chance I get. I love hearing your very sweet voice. I really miss it and you very much.

I'm glad you didn't want to go out to Kansas with Uncle Tom.[*] I don't want you going on long trips, it's too dangerous. I want you home with me in our little room. I don't think you would be too happy out there anyway. There isn't enough room in the trailer for us all. They can see Lori when they're home next time.

Are you going to move in with Donna when I go over to V.N? If you are, we'll move our stuff over before I go. And if Uncle Russ wants we'll leave our bedroom suite upstairs so he can have a

---

[*] My dad was referring to the discussion about my mom riding to Kansas with my dad's Great-Uncle Tom. This would have allowed her and me to be with him for two more days. Years later, on December 19, 1987, my wedding day, Uncle Tom walked me down the aisle.

guest room for company. If you want to live there I don't care. Aunt Marge and Uncle Russ are the nicest people I could ever leave you with. Think about it from all points.

Well I guess I'll go for now. I'm going to listen to the tape before I go to bed. I'll dream all night about us. Only 8 days more. Goodnight. I love you.

Your Husband
Forever & Always,
Larry
P.S Kiss Lori for me. I'll make up for mine when I get home.

I couldn't help but think about my adult children when I read this letter. They are protective of their families and passionate. My kids certainly have their grandfather's genes!

LETTER 21
UNDATED

Dearest Darling,

I received three wonderful letters from you today the pictures of Lori were really beautiful. I'm not mad about you getting some pictures made. It's when you start getting color 8"x10" or take pictures of useless things that I would get disturbed about.* Giving everybody a small picture is really nice. They don't cost much, and they still have a picture.

I'm glad to hear that Lori is feeling better. I bet she was really in pain. I hope she doesn't have any more trouble. If she does, we'll have to put her to work to pay for her doctor bills. I'm not mad that you're taking her to Doctor Bailey. For these small things it

---

* My mom told me that the first argument she and my dad had was over the expensive color film she wanted for my christening—he thought the black-and-white film was good enough.

wouldn't pay to take her over to Bunker Hill.* We'll take her there for shots and her blood test. These things get fairly expensive. I hope she doesn't get sick too much, because this can really chew your allotment up fast.

I didn't get my whites in time for inspection, but he just said get some. It took them 2 whole weeks to get here. That's pretty slow.

I'm glad I decided to come straight home from here. I should get into Indianapolis at 11 o'clock at night. I'll be able to see Danny off and maybe Uncle Tom if he stays down there a little longer.

I haven't had a flat tire except once on all of my cars. The guy didn't charge you very much, why? How did he fix it? Did he take the tire off or fix it right on the car itself?

I don't know about Mona driving that long distance and the way she drives, something had to give. So is she staying with Aunt Jenny or not?

I sure am glad that you and Donna are seeing a lot of each other and tell Danny he's her second father. [. . .]

And by the way are you exercising any? You'd better be.

Your Loving Husband
Larry
P.S. I love you very much, <u>kisses</u> coming to you every minute don't start ducking now!!!
See you in <u>Seven days</u>

During his short, thirty-day absence, my dad picked his cousin Danny to be his surrogate for me. Danny had received his draft notice and my dad thought he would be leaving for boot camp, though he never did. Later, in an audio tape from his bunker in Vietnam,

---

* Bunker Hill was an Air Force Base thirty-two miles from where we lived. My medical care would have been free but my dad supported mom's decision to take me to a doctor in town. My funny, frugal, full-of-love dad was always thinking of others.

my dad said, "Tell Danny that if anything happens to me over here, he's gonna have to be a father to Lori."

LETTER 22
UNDATED

Dearest Darling,

How are you on a fine day like today? It's getting fairly cool out here now maybe in the 70s. I'll probably freeze when I get home, with the temp. down in the 30s, but I'll have you to keep me warm won't I?

How is my darling daughter doing? I hope she will be more talkative Sunday when I call. I only got a couple of sounds out of her on tape. You sound real good on the tape. I listen to it often. It is really something to hear you talk to me. I love you very much and will cherish every moment I'm with you and every minute I can hear your lovely voice when I'm not.

We'll go out in the field tomorrow so you won't get any letters from me anymore, because when I get back it will be too late for you to get them before I'm home. I'll think of you every night and call you again Sunday. I'll be home at 11:00 Tuesday night. If you want you can call Dad and ask him if he wants to go with you, so you won't have to worry about getting lost. I hope that Donna and Danny are up too. I want to tell him goodbye and good luck. I love you very much. [. . .]

Your Husband,
Larry
P.S. See you in my dreams.

I realized from reading his letters how important we were to his morale. Without FaceTime and texting, my dad had to rely on Mom's letters, tapes, and phone calls to get him through. The calls were very limited, but he could replay the tapes and feel us near him, 2,200 miles away. Soon it would be 8,384 miles away in Vietnam. My dad also wrote about his father in this letter, and even called him "Dad."

That night when my dad got home to the Indianapolis airport, a big happy group of people were there to greet him—including his dad.

Dad at the Indianapolis airport with Mom, Grandma Bradford, and his dad, Harry Goss (Nov. 14, 1967).

My parents made the most of every moment during the next thirty days. My mom's calendar lists it all: our first and only professional family photo, family dinners with extended family, and sacred times with just the three of us.

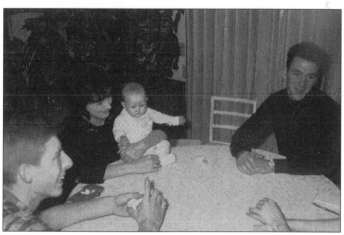

*Above:* Professional family photo taken in Marion on Nov. 21, 1967.
*Below:* Cousin Ronnie Hutchison, Mom, me, and Dad at Aunt Fran's house.

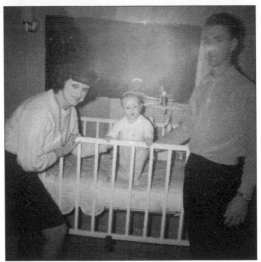

*Above:* At Grandma Bradford's for my first Thanksgiving (Nov. 23, 1967).

*Below:* Thanksgiving night in our little apartment above Aunt Marge's garage.

# CHAPTER SEVEN

## Vietnam

For the next thirty days, my parents savored every moment the three of us had together. One December night while they were lying in bed, Elvis Presley's song "Blue Christmas" played on the radio. My mom sobbed uncontrollably. My dad held her and remained strong, but inside he felt the sadness too.

Mom did not want to talk about the possibility of Dad not surviving his tour in Vietnam, but he needed to prepare her for the worst in case it happened. In her mind, he was coming home.

We celebrated our first and last Christmas together on December 13, 1967, and my precious daddy left the next day. He was killed exactly two months later. In that short time, he wrote my mom twenty-seven letters and sent her five complete audio tapes. She wrote him every day but one and sent him audio tapes too. These treasures allow me to hear their voices and savor their love.

Our last night together as a family, Dec. 13, 1967.
The next day, my dad left for Vietnam.

My mom has kept dad's letters close to her heart—literally and figuratively—for the past fifty-two years. She allowed me to borrow them, with the condition that I always kept them in her safe, tucked inside of my own safe for extra protection. She also gave me permission to share them here along with their journal entries.

Prior to my dad's departure for Vietnam, he and my mom purchased two diaries, one for each of them. They vowed to both write each day about their day's events so when they were together again, they could read out loud to the other the things they experienced when they were apart. On the top of each page, Mom and Dad wrote a number that told how many days it would be until Dad came home. Inside the cover of Dad's diary, Mom wrote:

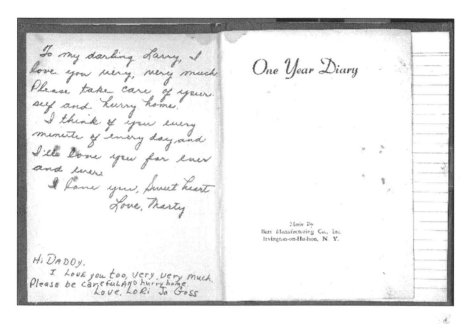

The inside cover of the diary Dad took to Vietnam.

My mom did not see my dad's entries until after his death, when his belongings arrived in a box. She took me to his grave and opened the package there. Her excruciating pain is unbearable to think about for very long.

I've included all of his letters and journal entries here. Both discuss the particulars of war, but they also talk about the mundane aspects of daily life. I again chose to include the majority of his words because they teach us so much about his character, his values, and his love.

LETTER 1, ON THE PLANE
DEC. 18, 1967

Hello Darling,

I miss you very much. I'm thinking of you every minute. I can hardly hold myself from coming home to you and telling them to hang it in their ear. I hope things over there keep me busy. It really tears me up knowing that you and I are apart. I hope these months go fast; I miss you so much. How is my lovely little daughter coming along? I hope she starts talking soon so I can hear her on the tapes. I want to hear you too so don't let her take all the tape. I've only got about 9 more hours to wait on the plane so maybe after that I won't think so much. I hope you can keep busy too. I know you worry more than me. Lori will keep you busy and she'll be there to cheer you up when you feel low. I love you both very, very much. Write more later.

Your Husband
Larry Jo Goss

LETTER 2, JAPAN
UNDATED

Just arrived in Japan. It's real pretty. I still have 4 hours to go before getting to Okinawa. I miss you very much. I am going to hurry home. Kiss Lori for me. I love you with all my heart.

Love,
Larry
Merry Christmas Darling
Love You Always

LETTER 3, OKINAWA
UNDATED

Hello Darling,

Well dear, I'm here in Okinawa. We are all checked in and have received our shots. I had to get a Gama Globulin and that's all. 5 cc in the rear. Wow! The living quarters are adequate. The food is o.k. too. I'd still like home cooked myself.

I Love You very much and I miss you more than I thought. I'd give anything to hold you tight once again. You've really got me hooked, but I like it. How is my charming little daughter? I miss her too. I hope she starts talking soon. If you get a chance pick up my bowling ball from Gas City.

It took us 17 hours to get here and we lost a day also. It is now twenty to five in the afternoon. Where you are it is twenty to seven in the morning on the 19th, here it is the 20th. The temp here is about 65 degrees. It's real comfortable. It was 16 degrees in Alaska and 34 degrees in Japan.

[same page, new note] Good Morning Darling,

How is Princess (you) doing? I love her very much. I haven't got a flight out to Vietnam yet. Probably today or tomorrow. We went in town last night. Two Sergeants and myself and they really have some beautiful things. I wanted to buy you everything. I won't get paid until I get to Nam, so I'll send money from there. I'll probably send some every month.

I love you very, very much.
Kiss Lori for me.

Just got the word we are leaving at 6:30 in the morning 22 Dec 67 will arrive in Vietnam at 11:30. I will write more then. I love you very, very much. Will be thinking of you every minute. Please take care of yourself and Lori. [. . .]

See you soon.


Your Loving Husband
Larry


LETTER 4, DONG HA, VIETNAM
DEC. 29, 1967


Hello My Darling,

I miss you very much. I love you more than you'll ever know. I have yours and Lori's pictures in front of me now. I hope to see you in person very soon. I mean in a year or on my R & R if in Hawaii. How have you been? I hope fine. I want you to write and tell me if anything is wrong. I'm going to send you money, so you won't have to worry about ends not meeting. I love you.

How are the people back home? Please keep me informed. I know you will. The pictures I sent home to you, send them to me in your letters, I'll send them back, because they would get destroyed here. [. . .]

I'm sleeping in the bunker now with sandbags all around to protect us from mortars. It really isn't bad, a little cramped though. I washed my clothes in a stream today real modern Huh! Chow is getting worse, but it keeps you going. I don't need anything so don't go and start sending things. I'll tell you if I need something o.k. We have a PX here. A truck comes out once a week with everything. I've got $52 on me now, so I don't need any green stuff. I got $43 for travel pay when I got here, and I won $6 playing cards in Dong Ha. I'll send you my pay in checks every month and you can put them in the bank. Save about $300 in 4 ½% and put the rest in 5 ½ % o.k.?

If everything works out o.k., we'll be rolling in dough! Too good to be true isn't it? I move on to Ca Lu in about five days so I don't know what it will be like there. We make sweeps all over the place. But I'll get your mail. Things are o.k.! Tell everybody I said Hi and that I won't be able to write much, and that you'll keep them informed o.k. You're no. 1. I love you very very very much.

Love,
Larry

P.S. I'm in Kilo Company now, so my address is:
Larry Jo Goss HM2 B50 42 75
Kilo Company 3rd BN 9th Marines 3rd Marine Division
F.P.O San Francisco California and zip code 96602, I think?
But you have it on my tape box
Love Always

My mom wrote the following address down on a card to make sure her letters and care packages made it to him every time. Writing it down made her cry.

> Larry Jo Goss
> 3rd Battalion 9th Marines 3rd Marine Division
> The Rockpile near the town of Dong Ha

I noticed in each letter that my dad wrote endearing words on the inside flap of the envelope. Perhaps he wanted to use every inch of space to tell her how much he loved and missed her, or maybe he just wanted her to know even before unfolding the letter. When I read his December 29th letter for the first time, my heart ached when I read "I love you more than you'll ever know." Those words were prophetic, because his death would take away our ability to experience and "know" the fullness of his love.

LETTER 5
DEC. 30, 1967

Dearest Darling,

Miss you very much. I love you more & more. Wish I could make your picture talk. I would give anything to hear your voice again. I hope your tape gets here soon. I will play it every night before I retire if I do and dream sweet lovely things, <u>you just you.</u> How is my charming little daughter today? I bet she is getting more exciting every day. Learning new things and picking up things other people do. What did she get for Christmas? Is she playing with her dolls yet? How is she doing with her walker? How did you like the clothes mom sent for Lori? I thought they were real cute. [. . .]

Today we started on a new bunker house for the new Corpsmen we have been getting lately. It is quite a job. First, we dug into the ground about 3 feet, then we stacked 4 feet of sandbags around the outside. We then fixed up a wooden floor and insides out of ammo boxes. Crude but it's home. There really isn't much happening now because of the monsoon season. Just a few snipers and maybe an ambush once a week. Things will pick up about March and April. I hope not. I love you very much. Hope to see you soon. Kiss Lori for me.

Love,
Larry

LETTER 6, THE ROCKPILE
JAN. 1, 1968

Dearest Darling,

I love you very much. Today is Jan. 1, 1968. Happy New Year! It won't be much of a year for you and me, but we will have many more to celebrate. This will be a good year for you and my darling daughter. She will learn so much in this one year that you will be kept busy just writing and telling me about them. I hope you can get her first words down on paper and send them to me. I hope she keeps you so busy that your year goes by like a flash. For me, well, I will be thinking of you every minute wanting to hold you and hear your sweet voice once again, but my year will go fast too, I hope. I just keep thinking of how it will be when I get home to you. I know you will have stored up much love for me and me for you also. We will probably explode on first touch. I hope we don't lose anything while being apart. Things like this happens, but I have faith in both of us. We will always love each other and that's all that matters.

How is Donna coming along? Is she getting any fatter? I bet old Dan is getting anxious for it to start kicking. How is grandmother? Did she stop working like she said? I sure hope so. If she needs any help, we'll try to help her.

Well, you are probably wondering what we are doing here. Well, things are quiet, because of the holiday truces. The VC have broken it once, which was last night, when they mortared Ca Lu and wounded a few men, none killed. The truce lasts until tomorrow morning at 6 o'clock. The VC are moving in supplies during this truce. I don't see why they let them, but I guess a day's peace is worth many of hell. Not really! But I just work here. 150 trucks we spotted along one road just after the Christmas truce. Planes destroyed 36 and damaged 16 that's still a lot of ammo and mortars left to hit us soon. Old Charlie is very well trained. He hits when he is at an advantage. In other words, he picks the spot where he can do the most damage and gets away with the least killed. The only thing that keeps him from really getting us is the helicopters. They really tear Charlie up. Well I will be here in the Rockpile one more week and then will move on to Ca Lu. I will be senior corpsman of K Company.

Well, I guess I'll close for now. Will write more later. Tell everybody I said hello. I love you very much. Hope you are fine in health. [. . .]

Love you always
Your Husband who thinks the world of you.
Larry "G"

JOURNAL
JAN. 1, 1968
357 [DAYS LEFT IN TOUR]

Happy New Year Darling,

Well today is a new year. I don't feel anything. This year is going to be one I will remember. I hope I can tell my grandchildren about it too. Today we took it easy and just sat around and enjoyed the truce. No fighting here today. Very quiet, the guns are sleeping for the first time since I've been here. It feels good not to have your eardrums popping every five minutes. Well, we got to listen to the Bob Hope Christmas Show from Saigon. He was real funny. The girls were something just hearing them talk sexy.

Don't get much over here. Well I guess I'll retire and dream about my beautiful wife and daughter.

Good night.

LETTER 7, THE ROCKPILE
JAN. 2, 1968

Hello Darling,

I want you to go ahead and buy yourself that color TV for your birthday (small RCA) ok! I'll send you the money in February. You'll get it about the 10th of the month. Also, when you send me a tape you can use the same box I send you, but put it in an envelope and tape it and write on the envelope. Then I can use the same box over and over again. So easy huh! I love you very much. Kiss Lori for me.

Larry
P.S. Here's a couple for you.
Goodnight

JOURNAL
JAN. 2, 1968
356 [DAYS LEFT]

Well, today was just like any other. Work Work Work! The weather was chilly, but pleasant. No enemy activity. The twin 40 had some practice tonight, blowing up some hills outside our perimeter. Quite a show to watch. I wish I had a movie camera. Well, I'm going to Camp Carroll tomorrow to buy some film for my camera, film is hard to get out here. I also taped a tape to my darling wife today. I love her very much. It is really something just thinking you are talking to her. I feel really good afterwards. Well that's all for today. I hope it doesn't get too cold.
Goodnight.
God bless my wife and daughter and family.

JOURNAL
JAN. 3, 1968
355

Today has been a cool and nasty day. I about froze on the run to Camp Carroll. That's what we did today. I went in the early convoy to Carroll to buy some film, which I didn't get. I finally bought some tapes and peanuts. As for the time being, I'm writing by candlelight and sitting on an old suitcase like box. Real modern.

Well I sent my darling wife a tape today and I sure hope I get a letter soon. I can't wait to hear her sweet words. I miss her very much. Knowing there's no way you can see her is hard to take. My tour has hardly started. I hope the next 11 months fly by. It is very lonely out here where all you hear is 105 & twin 40 guns going off pounding the hills around us. But I'm glad they are.
Goodnight Martha
Goodnight Lori
I love you both very much

JOURNAL
JAN. 4, 1968
354

Today was a very fine day. Moderately warm and no rain. We finished our bunker and moved in. Plenty of room. Very warm and home-like. I wrote Martha & Grandma today and played cards. A real full day. These kinds of days fly by. The only kind to have. Well, that's all for today. God bless Martha- Lori & and all my family and families everywhere. Good night.
I love Marty & Lori

LETTER 8
JAN. 4, 1968

Dearest Darling,
I Love You Very Much. How are you and Lori? I miss you both very much. I think of you constantly. I try to visualize what you're doing all the time. I hold you at night knowing that we are in bed together. Only if it could really be. I love you Darling.
Well we finished our bunker today and we are in it now. It is real roomy. It took a lot of work. It doesn't help quieting the big

guns. They are so loud. They shake everything, when they go off. But I'm glad they're there.

I know you probably have listened to my tapes by now. If you want to keep them it's ok. All you have to do is buy the 3 for $1.00 and then use the same box I send. It will save us money that way we won't have to buy those plastic mailers. Also send me about 4 pen light batteries 1.5 volts and two rolls of 126 slide film. That's all I need. Send airmail, use as small of box as you can find. Do not insure. OK! I'll write you if I need anything else. I've only got one more picture to take and then I'll send the film home. I also got two rolls of Kodacolor for prints. A buddy gave them to me. Real nice of him huh. I'll send them also when I finish them.

Well I guess that's all for now. I love you very much "Sleep warm."

Love,
Larry

P.S I'm sending newspaper pictures that show how things are over here. Keep them. Goodnight Darling
Kiss Lori for me

[He drew a picture of lips indicating two kisses before the words, "FOR YOU."]

JOURNAL
JAN. 5, 1968
353

Today was a very delightful day. Hot and sunny. A real good day to get a tan if you have the balls to lay out. But today I kept busy as a housewife on wash day. I washed my clothes. But then I had to construct a clothesline and then carry water, then heat the water on a gook stove. Wash by hand and then hang it up and watch it so it would still be there when dry. I'm hinting something.

Chow was exceptionally good tonight. Fish macaroni & cheese and peaches Wow! I had two helpings. They must have felt sorry for us. Played a little cards and now ready for bed. 10:30. I'm thinking of home. Marty & Lori. Very lonesome.

Goodnight

God bless Marty & Lori

Watch over them please

JOURNAL

JAN. 6, 1968

352

Today was another hot day. I finished my roll of slide film today and sent it home for processing. Haven't received a letter yet from home. Should be soon. I've got to hear some good old home news by that charming little wife. Today we cleaned up the BAS Ward for Pt. and did a little more sandbag filling. Fun and relieves tension. The Marines of Mike Company spotted some "gooks" digging in some bunker right outside our perimeter. Today there should be a little fire soon from blazers in the sky. Thank God for them. Well it is nice and cool tonight, wonderful sleeping weather so I say Goodnight.

Going to Dream of Martha

LETTER 9, THE ROCKPILE

JAN. 6, 1968

Dear Darling,

I miss you very much. I hope to be receiving a letter soon. I really miss hearing from you. I love you very much. How is my daughter feeling? I hope she didn't get sick like the last time I was away. She'll be going over for her 6-month checkup soon, time really flies. When you're over there you can pick up film to send me again. Two rolls. I'm sending home 1 roll of slides today. You can send them back when you're done looking at them. I'll send you the prints too, maybe you'll get free film, take them to Hook's 17 cents a piece.

Nothing has happened here. I will be leaving for Ca Lu on Tuesday. No more good living. Have to keep low all the time there. The last picture on the slides is me in all the gear I wear when out with the "grunts."* Kinda hot! Heavy and bulky too!

Only 14 days until your birthday. Are you going to buy that color TV? It's alright with me. I think RCA's is either $299 or $329. After that we'll have to save up for our Hawaiian Honeymoon. Won't it be nice, just you and me. Who will watch our darling Lori for 8 days? I really hate to leave her with anybody, but this should be our time alone. Write me and tell me what you think. You can bring her at no extra cost and she will be a year old by then. It's up to you. I would like to see her. Well, tell everybody Hi and that all's well.

"I'll love you always."

Love,
Larry

Kiss Lori for me
Couple for you too. <u>Great aren't they!</u> Real thing soon.

---

* I think my dad would have been delighted that I used this picture of him for the cover of this book that narrates his life and love.

JOURNAL
JAN. 7, 1968
351

Today was another fine day. First of all, I worked on my flak jacket putting the "Road Runner" on it and then making a beautiful naked girl to remind me of Martha. It's not too bad. We also played some football today and got beat. I skinned my arm up, but it saved 7 points. I also went to church. It was a wonderful feeling. I don't know why but it was. Then we played cards and knowing I lost 5 dollars "Boy" that isn't like me. Now I'm ready for bed and I think I'll sleep well. So, God bless Marty & Lori and Goodnight.
Love Martha with All My Heart

JOURNAL
JAN. 8, 1968
350

Today was a nasty rainy day. I had classes all day on the Vietnamese people and customs. I enjoyed it. The people have been in war since they were born. From about 600 B.C. all together. The people are like our own American Indians. They live a rough life and don't complain. Everything is done by hand. Well I'm going to retire early and get some sleep.
God bless Marty & Lori
Goodnight.

JOURNAL
JAN. 9, 1968, CA LU COMBAT BASE
349

Well, this was the worst day yet. First of all, it was raining cats and dogs and the mud was out of this world. The mud on the roads was up to your knees.* When you walked it was splashed all over you. Immediate camouflage. The mud on your boots is outlandish. Your feet are always wet. Our biggest problems. I left the Rockpile on a convoy to Ca Lu where I am now. "The mud hole of Vietnam."

We started out on a 6 bed truck then switched to a tank and then another tank. Then because the tank couldn't make it up a hill, we had to carry it up and put it on another truck. On into Ca Lu and getting there I still had to carry my gear about a mile through mud and slop at my new home.

Goodnight

God bless Marty & Lori

Dad's picture of the convoy from the Rockpile to Ca Lu.

---

* In 2018, my husband Eric and I traveled with Dr. Jerry Behrens and his wife, Mary, to Vietnam. We walked down Route 9, the very road my dad traveled and wrote about this day.

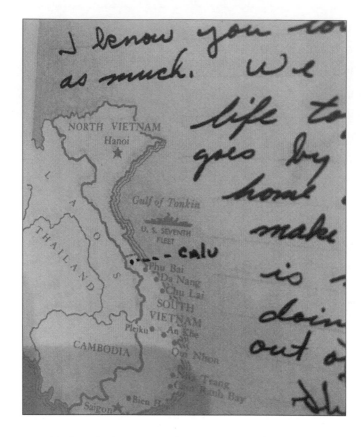

Dad marked Ca Lu on the map in one of his letters.

LETTER 10
JAN. 9, 1968

Dear Darling,

I miss you very much. How is my daughter? I miss her too. Well, today has really been a nasty day, with all the rain and mud. But this is a normal day in the Monsoon Season. I had classes on the Vietnamese people and their customs, and it was very interesting. They have never been without war. The French were here before us and before that they had great war troubles throughout the country. They do most of their work by hand. They seem to like it. They haven't changed a bit in 2000 years.

I will leave for Ca Lu tomorrow and that's where I'll stay for a while. I hope. I haven't received a letter from you yet. I'm getting very lonesome. I've got to hear your voice or read a letter soon or I'll go batty. I really miss you. "Boy" the people back in the world sure do have it made. Running water, lights, heat, and most of all the people they love. I hope the days start getting a little faster. But maybe when I receive your first letter, I'll feel a little better. I love you very much.

How are all the people doing with the temperature? Low in the 20s is pretty cold isn't it? We get the temperatures about every day. Have you driven in the snow yet? Well tell everybody Hi! I have to go.

Love,
Larry

JOURNAL
JAN. 10, 1968, CA LU COMBAT BASE
348

Well, today I went out and met all my new Corpsmen. A journey of about 2 ½ hours through mud and slop up and down hills. I really love this. Help! The food is getting worse everyplace I go. I hope we don't move to any worse place than this. It could only be hell. There's no showers here just the good old stream. Good old cold running water. Same with clothes down in the old stream. Well I've said enough. So, Goodnight. Hurry my mail please.
God bless Marty & Lori
I love them very much
Won $4.50 cards

LETTER 11

JAN. 10, 1968, CA LU COMBAT BASE

Dear Darling,

How are you? I miss you very much. I am now at Ca Lu. It is really a mud hole. I started out yesterday from the Rockpile and it was raining. It had been for two days. The roads were nothing but <u>slop</u>. I don't see how the trucks make it. We had to switch to a tank just outside of Ca Lu because it was too muddy for trucks. The tanks took us for a short distance, but couldn't make it up a hill, so we had to carry everything to the top, falling on our ass's all the way. We were mud from head to toe. The truck took us on in and then I had to carry my gear about another mile by hand to our outpost. We didn't have any trouble on the convoy. We had two tanks in front and two in the rear for protection. After getting here I looked the place over and didn't like what I saw. Mud as far as you could see and 3 feet deep. You're muddy all the time and your feet are never dry. But I can take it for a year knowing you're home waiting for me. I love you very much. How is everybody at home? Do the boys* keep you busy? I hope you are getting along ok. I hope you aren't having any money problems. I'll send my check home 1st of Feb. How is Grandma doing with her business? Probably slow with the weather you're having. Here just 24-hour rain. I hope she gets back on her feet and takes it easy. You can pay her the last $50 out of the money I send and pay for whatever you have bought. Tell Uncle Russ he could have made it all the way over here, but he would have wanted to go back as quick as possible. I hope to go home soon. The days will go faster.

---

* The boys my dad refers to are Aunt Marge and Uncle Russ's sons, Phillip and Michael Cummings. They were twelve and seven when my dad went to Vietnam.

Well, I'll sign off for now. Kiss Lori for me and love her a lot. I love you both very much. Will be waiting on your letters.

Love,
Larry
P.S. Sleep Warm, I'll be dreaming of you.

JOURNAL
JAN. 11, 1968
347

Today the sun was shining a little, the mud is not semi slop, but we manage to carry on. The Corpsmen were all doing their jobs to satisfaction. No complaints. I walked my regular 2 hours up and down. I'm keeping in shape. I also played housewife and did my laundry. In a crude way but it's fairly clean. We played cards and were up to about 12 midnight. Won about $2.00. Had a fine time but could have used the sleep. Caught two rats and that was our excitement.
Goodnight
God Bless Marty & Lori
Keep their Hearts full of Love

JOURNAL
JAN. 12, 1968
346

Today was the best day yet here at Ca Lu. It was hot and the sun dried up a lot of the mud. I made a trip to OP Texas today and the Corpsmen were putting in metal piss tubes and I had them put a screen on the one holer. I also took three pictures of the terrain from Texas of the lower valley. I also took it of our post. Then I went down to the bridge where we take baths and wash clothes.

I took a short bath. Water cold!!! I then went for chow. After chow I built a new washstand and put in a soaker pit for our used wash to drain. I kept fairly busy I'd say.

Goodnight

God bless Martha & Lori

I love them very much

They're My Whole World

*Top:* Sitting on a weapon, January 1968.

*Bottom:* Dad (center) takes a mud bath.

LETTER 12

JAN. 12, 1968

Dearest Darling,

I received 3 letters and two Christmas Cards today. They really make a guy feel better.

I have listened to a little of the tape but I haven't got by myself yet to listen to it all the way through. I have read one of your letters and the two cards. They were really nice. Thank you. The picture of Lori is really good. I got it in front of me now. She is really cute. I also got two letters from Indianapolis. One from Dad and another from Bonnie Kay. They were telling me how they were down to see you January 1. Also, of the toys Lori got. They said she had plenty. They also said she is saying Mommy and maybe Dad. I hope you are giving her plenty of Love. You are probably giving her more than I can even expect. I know you love her very much. I also know you got an ice crusher. "Boy" that's one thing you need. Maybe you'll take it easy on your teeth.

Well, here we have been kept busy. The "Gooks" hit us again today with mortar and their automatic weapons and we chased them back to the hills. The helicopter with rockets and 60 cal. machine guns are keeping them there now. So we won't have to worry about them tonight. They only hit when they know they can get away. They are really smart. We suffered a few wounded, but none killed. Charlie (Cong) got away without hardly a scratch. The helicopter hurt old Charlie the most. We don't know how many they got. He's hard to find when you go looking for him. He digs in and covers up with the same soil he took out in the first place. Looks just like nothing is there. He's all around us but you hardly ever see him. He hits you with a few mortars and then runs. They can get away with this forever.

Well I'm going to read another letter tomorrow and so on. We get our letters all at once. About every week but keep sending them every day. I'll try to slow my recorder down. I can hear you just fine. You sound so wonderful. I love you very much. Send one about every week. I'll try to send one as often as possible. They are worth a million. Well I guess I'll sign off for now. I've got a little time, so I think I'll write Dad a short one. Kiss Lori for me and tell everybody I'm keeping alert and low.

I've got a lot to live for.

With All My Love Forever
Your Husband Larry
P.S. <u>Sleep Warm</u>
If you hear anything about our territory it was our sister company, they took heavy loss. 4 killed and 60 badly wounded. We were lucky. Charlie got hurt pretty bad on their side of the camp.

Dad's photos from Ca Lu.

JOURNAL

JAN. 13, 1968

345

Today was a little more exciting. Old Charlie hit us on our sister company's side and we were put on the alert. We only had a few wounded and none killed. Charlie is real tricky. Our sister company had D & F but things are under control. Early today we built a shitter (my first). I'm proud of it too. Things are shaping up and should run smoothly. While we're here medically I mean. I received my first letters today and "boy" I really feel better now. I've listened to part of the tape and Marty sounds so good. I love her so much. I also received a picture of my daughter today and she's so cute. I'm really lucky I got a wonderful family. Dad wrote me and so did Bonnie Kay. Feeling real good.

Goodnight.

God bless all and My Family

JOURNAL

JAN. 14, 1968

344

Today I have been away from my wife one month. I missed her so much I listened to her tape today and also sent her one. I just loved listening to her tape. It's just like over the phone. A wonderful invention. Well we were kept on alert all day today but didn't have to go out. The final figures on the convoy yesterday were KIA 16 WIA 6 Corpsman KIA 1 WIA 4. Hope things get better. We are now listening to the tapes of music I have. They really make things better. Chow is supposed to be great tomorrow also. I hope.

Goodnight

God Bless all.

Watch over my Family

JOURNAL
JAN. 15, 1968
MONA'S BIRTHDAY
343

Today was a rather misty day. It would rain a little and then the sun would shine a little. We moved our new shitter up to Texas today and now they got a little privacy. I also wrote my sister a letter today because it is her birthday. No. 24. I sure hope everything works out ok for her. I read another letter from my darling wife. More good news. Also, today we had some steel plates brought in for our bunker and I got a few pictures. They really blow the dirt around. Well I took a shower today in our new shower we put up. It is getting better. Well I'll sign off for now. Will be thinking of my Darling wife and daughter.
Goodnight
God bless all

JOURNAL
JAN. 16, 1968
342

Well today was a fair day it was warm and then in the afternoon it started raining. No action today which was nice. I wrote my darling wife and daughter and told them I was fine and that they are number 1. We are just about finished with our bunker and with our shower and washstand. It is real nice. I also played wash woman today and finished my dirty clothes off. I also got my M16 back and cleaned it. I had loaned it to a corpsman* who went out on a

---

* Years later, I found out that corpsman was Doc Ray Felle. He became a significant part of my search in 1999, when he contacted me for the first time.

2-day recon patrol. It was a little dirty, but I want mine nice and clean all the time. It may save my life someday.

Well good night.

God bless Marty & Lori

I love them Very Much.

Building a bunker for the captain. My dad was in the Command Post, so he slept there too.

*Left:* Dad standing under the shower he helped build at the Ca Lu Combat Base.
*Right:* Dad and platoon members fill and stack sandbags around their bunker.

JOURNAL
JAN. 17, 1968
341

Today was a nasty day. The mud was slippery as ice. I fell on my ass about 4 times and was lucky so few. It rained most of the morning and then misted with a little sun in the afternoon. I made my rounds of 1st and 2nd Platoons today and then worked on our bunker; Filling sandbags and laying them along the sides. It's going to take BUKU sandbags. Its good exercise though. Builds big muscles and lets off your energy. Haven't received any letters since the 13th but there's 60 bags of mail at the Rockpile. It will be here soon, I hope.*

Well I'm going to read a little from my Personal Bible Verses. Goodnight
God bless My Family

LETTER 13
JAN. 17, 1968

Dear Darling,

How are you tonight? I have yours and Lori's pictures in front of me now. I look at them as often as possible. You are very beautiful and Lori in her 3-month-old picture is darling. I love you both very much. I have read all your letters up to Jan 2 now and am waiting for more. I love the way you write. You are so sweet, like you really are. I have your Christmas cards beside your pictures, and I read the verses every day. Tell Grandma that she sounds good over the tape recorder. I think she was a little sad though. Just tell her I'm fine. I want to come home as

---

* Although my mom wrote my dad every day, it took a long time for him to receive the letters.

much as you want me to. I just do my job the best I can and the safest way I can to do the most for everyone involved.

I'm down to 341 days now but ½ that until Hawaii. I know we'll have a great time. It will probably be the only real vacation we will get in a long time. We've got a lot to do before we can settle down. A home and a lot of money in the bank for Lori. Our whole life will be to make a future for our daughter.

How's the bathroom problem? It is probably fixed by now. Tell uncle Russ, he'll just have to build an "outdoor shitter" and burn it out every day or just dig a hole in the ground and cover it up like a cat. It makes the grass grow greener. How's the transmission on the car? I hope it wasn't anything serious. They can run into a lot of money. Tell him that's a bad way to start a new year. What did the boys get for Christmas? I bet a lot. Why did Donna & Dan have to get a new place to live? Tell him not to let that job go to his head. If things go real bad over here I might see him. Tell him I hope not. A man should see his children grow up. War is Hell isn't it. But Love will last forever.

Well not too much has happened today. No Charlie for us. It has been rainy and walking on this dirt when wet it's like walking on ice. Well, we are still working on our bunker and the captain says we will have it done tomorrow or else. He and the Lt and all of us are going to work on it all day tomorrow until finished. We will be tired! It's about ½ finished and it still has about 1700 to go. That's sandbags. I'll get some pictures and show it to you. It sure helps when the mortars come in. Well I can't think of anything else to say. Wait! I wrote Mona yesterday and wished her a Happy Birthday. I'll be writing you too. I hope you waited to open yours (Birthday Card). I thought it was sort of cute. What did you buy yourself from me for your birthday? I'll sign off for now. Kiss Lori for me and tell her daddy loves her very much. I love her Mommy very much also.

Love,
Larry
Your Husband Forever and Always
Sleep Warm!!

This letter contained the most wisdom for me as I reflect on what our lives together would have been like. My dad told Dan to stay humble and be present in his children's lives. War truly is hell, "but love will last forever."

Me at three months old (October 1967).

LETTER 14
UNDATED

Dear Darling,
    How are you doing? I received 2 letters and a tape today. I also received one from Grandma and Mona Sue. I haven't read them

yet. I listened to the first side of your tape. It was really good. Lori was really doing some talking. I could hear her saying Mommy. I think she really sounds cute. We got a good little daughter.

Now to answer some of your questions. I'm not stationed with Stan.[*] I don't know where he's attached. I'm going to write him a letter soon. The pictures I took that didn't turn out was the ones of Alaska and I do think one was of a sunset. The $6.00 I won playing gin. After that I played poker at the Rockpile and lost $5.00. But then I won $4.00 here so I'm still ahead.

I don't exactly know how much I will make but here's an estimate, $260.70 + $65.00 hostile fire pay $15 overseas pay + $25.00 increase on your BAQ which is $365.70 - $40.00 which you get maybe $10 social security? - Insurance $2.00 - bond $18.75 about $295 after 10 Jan 68. They sometimes have a few mix-ups, but they straighten it out in the end.

My rate in the Marines is Sergeant E5.

Thank you for the sports section, but you can just write in your letters the scores of Marion High school Basketball. Who's ahead in baseball. Send the standing in letters. That's about it.

You can send tapes whenever you want but I'll send one about every two weeks, that's okay with me too. I just want to hear your voice really, but I do like good news though. I can't think of anything I need, but I'll tell you when I do. We had turkey for Christmas dinner. Wasn't too bad. Also when you hear things on T.V. it wasn't always the worst so don't get upset. There's a lot of Marines here and they're stationed all over. We are just one small place. I'll tell you when things happen. How about sending me your ear plug from your radio? You don't have to worry about the tapes. I'll send you good ones from now on o.k. Well, I'm going to

---

[*] Stan Burkart and my dad met in boot camp and became close friends in corps school. Stan was stationed near my dad in Vietnam at the same time, but with a different company.

send these pictures back because it's too wet here for anything. I'm also going to send your tape recorder warranty.

Well I guess I'll close for now. I love you very much.

Love,
Larry

JOURNAL
JAN. 18, 1968
340

Today was a nice day. The sun came out and dried up a little mud. I had a long walk to OP Texas this morning with the Chief to check on a Marine who tore some ligaments in his knee. We gave him some Robaxin and wrapped it up and two days of bed rest. The rest of the day was Adm. Getting the blood type of all the men and filling their jungle kits with salt tabs and etc. I received two letters and a tape from my wife today. Mail is sure good. I miss home. Well, goodnight. God bless all.
Marty & Lori

JOURNAL
JAN. 19, 1968
339

Well today started out just like any normal day. I checked my men and had just eaten evening chow then we got the word to go on Operation Sparrow Hawk. We got our gear and headed for the LZ. The choppers were waiting and off we went. The purpose was to help a recon squad who were ambushed by the NVA.[*] We

---

[*] On January 19, a team in Charlie Company was given a mission to conduct reconnaissance on Mutter's Ridge. After reaching Hill 484, the team was ambushed.

got to the valley floor of the hill in which we had to go. This was the place where last contact was made. We got there, but dark settled in quick so we had to dig in for the night. And it was quite a night. Rainy, cold and scary. The mortars were coming close. But we were lucky.

God bless All

Dad standing on the LZ (landing zone).

JOURNAL

JAN. 20, 1968

338

Today is my wife's birthday.* May she have many more. I love her very much. We were reinforced with the rest of our company. Two

---

* It was Mom's 23rd birthday. At the top of Dad's journal, Mom wrote the words: "Hi Honey, I love you, always." She has kept this promise for fifty-four years.

were found. We started towards our objective. It was through dense jungle land and up steep hills. And we had to fight the leeches. We made fair progress but only made about half our distance. We had to settle in for the night. It was another rainy & cold one. We were in better shape, because we were on higher ground but it was still dangerous, because the NVA were out there but where? We were dug in and on 100% alert in ½ hour. We rested and filled our bellies. Then to rest at 50% alert all night.
God bless All

JOURNAL
JAN. 21, 1968
337

Today we started to our final objective Hill 484, where the recon was last known. We made it at mid noon and found the men E[*] of them dead. They had been dead for 3 days and were a horrible sight. We gathered up their remains and covered them with ponchos. And awaited a helicopter for lift off. We didn't know if we would have to stay the night or not. I didn't want to. The copters came at 1630 and we were off to Ca Lu and home. We arrived and had a hot meal and plenty to drink. Then a little clean up and sleep.
God bless, bless all
Thanks for getting me home safe.

JOURNAL
JAN. 22, 1968
336

Today was a day of getting your gear cleaned and to repack your gear for another journey to the bush. I restocked my unit 1 and my

---

[*] The letter "E" denotes that five men died.

haversack with chow and cleaned my M16 and enjoyed evening chow, which was very little but good. I also received mail and a package of film and batteries from my wife. I can now use my razor. I am now getting ready for sleep. I'm still tired from my 3-day adventure so good night and God bless my family and all Marines in the war burned country and the people all over the world.

LETTER 15
UNDATED
OPERATION SPARROW HAWK[*]

We got the word to move out and help a Recon Unit out, who had got hit by the NVA. At first it was going to be a platoon, but it was enlarged to a whole company. We packed up our gear. Mine consisted of a poncho cover, a mosquito net, two canteens of water, 1 meal of chow, 7 full magazines of ammo, my M16, Bible, my unit 1, two grenades, entrenching tool, flak jacket, helmet, a picture of my wife & daughter and finally me. We loaded on to helicopter and started for our objective. We were in copter 3. Only 4 were able to set down. So, we had about 75 men out of our company of 200 at our objective.

When we unloaded, we were down in the valley and jumped into elephant grass about 8-foot-high and sharp as a razor. We proceeded up to a small plateau, where we could hardly defend ourselves. There was no sight of the recon platoon (squad) #8 men. No firing or sounds. The night was coming up on us, so we had to dig in for the night. I prayed to God to bring me through this and to see me through my job, and to do it to my best. As we got our 360° protection set up. It was now dark. My hands were all cut up from the grass, but I didn't care. I just wanted to see morning. So,

---

[*] I inserted this letter here out of chronological order because its content corresponds to the journal entry.

I started digging in. You couldn't hardly see in front of you, but finally I got the job done. Then I dug one for the captain, who was busy setting things up. Mortars, and security.

We finally got settled in and then the rounds started coming our way. Luckily none came into our perimeter. The feeling you get when you hear the rounds coming. It's hard to explain, but you just hit your hole and pray it doesn't hit you. We survived. The night was cold and rainy, and I couldn't sleep at first. I didn't want to. I wanted to be alert as long as I could. But finally, I couldn't hold my eyes open and the next thing I remember was waking up. It was dark and cold with a mist coming down. Everything was quiet, so I tried to go back to sleep. My watch had stopped so I didn't know the time. The night seemed like a year. I thought morning would never come. But it finally did. Nobody was hurt or missing.

We ate our morning C rations and waited for the rest of our company, who couldn't make it the night before, because of darkness. The low ceiling finally raised at about 11:00 and the helicopters brought the rest of our men in. We now had a full company. Ready for battle. We had ammo up the ass. It would take a regiment to take us that is if we got to high ground. We got resupplied with water and C rations and got ready to move out. We had to go down through the valley floor to approach the hill where the recon team was last heard from. As we started off two people were spotted off on a small hill waving a shirt to try and get our attention. We reported into battalion and they sent a copter to check it out. They were two members of the recon team, who had got separated from the rest, when they were ambushed. There were six men still out there somewhere. And we had to find them. Were they dead or what? We didn't know. So, we proceeded towards our new objective.

We started out through the same elephant grass we landed in the night before. That was not bad at all compared to what was ahead. The dense jungle. We started out with a platoon on each flank and us the CP group in the middle. We climbed up and up, then down a little and then back up. Leeches were all over and were trying to get under your bloused trousers and into your skin and their blood meal. I flipped them off my boots and trousers. None got in for a blood meal. They are really nasty things. When they get on you and start sucking. They are hard to get off. Pulling and flipping doesn't budge them. A little insect repellant does wonders, but while humping through the jungle, you don't get time to treat yourself, so they stay there until you stop.

We made about half our distance before dark. No signs of the recon or Charlie. He doesn't fight much during the day. We had a better site for defensive purposes. We were high up on a plateau now and it's easier fighting down than up. We dug in again, getting ready to take mortar. We set up our 360 again, but this time with 200 men. We were setting good as means of fighting man to man, but we were going to take mortars. Charlie only fights man to man when he is ahead 4 to 1. The night was the same as the first. We didn't take any mortars. We were lucky or Charlie was out. Rain and cold and fear of dying. It's always with you. When you are out in the bush and Charlie is just waiting for you to make a mistake. The night was long again. Woke up about every hour again. Sleeping in a hole just isn't what you call living. But it's protection.

The morning came and we started off again. Through jungle and insects. One's about as bad as the other. We left for our objective, which was hill 484 and about four hours later we made it. We found our missing recon. They were dead. It was the most horrible site I've ever seen. They had been dead for 3 days. The odor was something I'll never forget. There were five of them. Four regular Marines and one corpsman. They were shot up pretty bad. The "gooks" have no mercy after they were dead. He still puts a bullet in your head. It was terrible seeing your buddy lying there with nothing left of them really visibly. You learn to hate real quick.

You're now not a statesider, you're out looking for them and with one thing in mind Kill. You're a killer and you hate them all.

We wrapped the bodies up in ponchos and took them to the top awaiting a helicopter. The one that was missing was a Vietnamese scout. They probably wounded him and instead of shooting him in the head, they waited for him to die more painfully and slower. After trying to pump information off of him. They really hate their own kind helping us. Even though one's North and one's South. While all of this was going on with us the NVA were trying to take Cam Lo. So, all the helicopters were busy. They said we might have to stay another night. "Boy" this was not going to get it. We waited, hopefully things will go our way. They called us and said 4 choppers were on their way from Phu Bai. This was about the happiest I've been since I've been in country. They arrived about an hour later. I went out on the ninth chopper. I felt like a million dollars when I knew I was off that hill.

We finally got back to home (Ca Lu). The major was there and the first thing he said was hot chow go get it. I ate my fill and drank until I thought I'd bust. I got back and cleaned up and now I'm ready to see another day. I was doubting it the last three days. This is the toughest job yet. I'd rather fight than wait and worry. At least you know you beat him. Not that he's watching you and maybe his next bullet has got your name on it. Waiting is what really eats you over here. I'm just thankful to God that I made it.

I read these letters and am amazed by the details my dad's writing contained and the honesty in his words. The missing men deserved the effort put forth to recover their bodies. Unfortunately, twenty-four days later, my dad became one of the missing men whose bodies were left in the jungle for twenty-one days. My dad did exactly what he asked God to help him do: his job to the best of his ability. But that time it cost him his life. God did not "bring him through," and from this side of heaven, I will never understand why.

JOURNAL
JAN. 23, 1968
335

Today was a calm one. I got caught up on my washing and straight-ening up my rack and living area. I received 3 letters from my wife and one from my mother. I also need mail and my family sends plenty. I got three pictures that were very nice, and I also sent my wife and mother letters. I also wrote my buddy Stan. I sure hope my letter gets to him. Well that's about it. I'm cleaned up and ready for sleep. God bless my Family goodnight

LETTER 16
UNDATED

Dear Darling,

Received two letters from you today. Also, a newspaper sports page. Also, three pictures, the ones we took before I left stuck together, but not too bad. Also, you sent me the one in your bathing suit. I like them all. I'll keep them for a while and then send them to you. Lori looks real good in the one where we both are in our stateside clothes. She looks so cute in the other one where her head is bent a little. You can put the pictures in the scrapbook of us before my departure and also of the ones I send home. Will sure have a big one.

In the Stars and Stripes today, it said your temperature was 39°. It's getting better huh! I can't think of too much to say since I sent your tape out yesterday. So, if it sounds rough it's because we haven't had any missions since Sparrow Hawk. I'm going to Dong Ha tomorrow on a convoy and I sure hope it doesn't get hit. I'll write you as soon as I get there, so don't worry. I'm going to check on my pay. They paid me $330. I'm going to send it all home by check so you can put it in the bank and pay bills. They owe me about $200 more so I'm going to check on it. Are you getting your allotment OK? I sure hope so. I've also got to sign some papers too about going over two years and also one so you'll keep getting your allotment. I should be back in about two days. I'll write you from there though. I'm going to close early and always remember I love you very much and kiss Lori for me.

Love,
your husband Larry
P.S. I'm just fine, don't worry I'm coming home to you.
Sleep Warm!!

JOURNAL
JAN. 24, 1968
TRAVELED TO THE ROCKPILE BY FOOT
334

Today we started out for Dong Ha. The convoy waited from 1200 to 430 because there weren't any Huey helicopters to support us. We waited through rain and it really felt good but being wet isn't the thing to be. But we dried out quickly. We still didn't have any choppers at 430 so we started so we could get there before dark. It took 2 ½ hours to make the trip which usually takes 45 minutes. We traveled slow and checked the road and back for NVA. We used BUKU ammo and shot up the countryside. We finally arrived and had some good chow. Fresh bread and that's a luxury we don't get at Ca Lu. I stayed the night at BAS in the bunker I built when I was there last time. I slept well.
Goodnight and God bless All

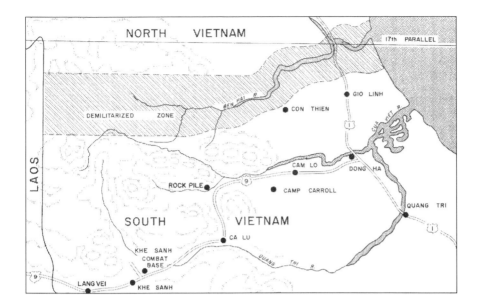

The places my dad wrote about in his letters home.

LETTER 17, THE ROCKPILE

UNDATED [JAN. 24–25, PER HIS JOURNAL]

Dear Darling,

I'm at the Rockpile now. I proceed on to Dong Ha tomorrow. We had a hairy trip from Ca Lu. We didn't get hit but we had to go out looking for him 4 times. That is the convoy stops and everybody gets off and goes into the bush and sees what's there. I didn't go for that too well, but you do it. It took us about 2 ½ hours to make a normal 45-minute drive. I sure was glad to get here.

How's everybody at home? Has everyone gotten a letter? I still haven't written Aunt Marge because I know you tell her everything. But I'm going to. I like the material you made your slacks out of and the hearts were cute. Thank you very much. I know you love me, and I love you just as much. We will have a very happy life together. I hope this year goes by real fast. I want to be home and care for you and make our family grow. How is my darling daughter doing? I really got a kick out of hearing her on the tape. She is really talking. She'll be carrying on a conversation soon. When you come to Hawaii, she'll really be talking.

I'm going to fly back to Ca Lu on a helicopter, so you don't have to worry. I should get back tomorrow or the next day if I'm lucky. It really isn't bad there as long as you're inside the perimeter. The food is getting better and I hope the temp doesn't get too hot. It is hot now and summer hasn't even started. We have to wear long sleeve shirts and our flak jackets. That doesn't help much. Well I guess I'll close for now. We've got to leave early in the morning, so take good care of yourself and kiss Lori for me. I love you very much.

Love,
Larry
Sleep Warm, I'm thinking of you.

JOURNAL
JAN. 25, 1968
333

Woke up this morning and had a good chow (breakfast) which was fresh eggs and French toast. We don't have things like this at Ca Lu. I'm going to travel more. Like R & R. We were supposed to leave for Dong Ha early, but enemy action on the road and near Camp Carroll, which is two miles East kept us here, because we had to go by the place on the way to Dong Ha. We are in a seize and convoys won't be going out for 2 to 3 days until the enemy are disposed of. I hope to get out by chopper tomorrow. I have to get back as soon as possible. I'll go back by helicopter all the way about a 15-minute ride. We are now sitting around talking with electric lights. I wish I was here this beats candles.

Goodnight God bless Martha & Lori

JOURNAL

JAN. 26, 1968

332

Left this morning on a CH 46 helicopter for Dong Ha. Arrived with no sweat at all. Proceeded to BAS and checked in. XO and I went to Delta Med about his physical. Then to the "gook" village and I bought an album for my pictures and a 45-pistol cover and a pair of Ho Chi Min shower shoes. I also went to the (Mars Station) to call home but they broke down. I went back to the PX and bought supplies for myself and supplies for some people at Ca Lu. Then after chow I went back to the Mars Station and talked to my darling wife for three minutes. It was wonderful hearing her surprised voice. I know she got a thrill. I know she is o.k. and happy. I'm taking a shower and hitting the rack.

Goodnight and God bless

All my Family

Phoned Marty

LETTER 18

JAN. 27, 1968

Dear Darling,

How are you doing after that phone call last night? I bet you sure were surprised and happy. I phoned from Dong Ha, where I told you I was going in my last letter. I couldn't hear you very well, but I knew it was you. I could hear your sweet voice but couldn't make out everything you were saying. The way I called was by way of MARS[*] station, it is a radio that can send messages to the states, by way of short wave or something.

How is my darling daughter? I would have loved to hear her last night, but it would have taken too long. I wanted to hear your voice and feel your happiness. I love you very much. Write me and tell me what went through your mind when you found out it was me. How is the rest of the family? Tell them I am fine. I will be here until tomorrow, then I will leave for good old Ca Lu, but by helicopter all the way this time. I've had my fill of convoys they are too dangerous and too slow. The only time I'll take another one of those is in an emergency, a big one.

I can't think of too much to write, because I haven't had a letter because my mail goes to Ca Lu. This will be short, but I will write more when I get back, so take good care of yourself and my darling daughter and I LOVE YOU both very much.

LOVE,
Larry
P.S. SLEEP WARM
GOD BLESS YOU ALL
SEE YOU REAL SOON BYE BYE!!!!!

JOURNAL
JAN. 27, 1968
331

Went to disbursing and got things straightened out, I hope. Then went to the "Gook" village again and bought a lamp that runs on fuel. I then went back and had a delicious dinner and it was really

---

[*] The Military Auxiliary Radio System (MARS) system connected service members in Vietnam with their loved ones back home by using a "phone-patch" telephone connection over short-wave radio. Each service member had a free five-minute personal radio phone call.

great. E-5s have their own mess hall here and no waiting in line. Served on good old plates. First time since I left Okinawa. We have been told "Gooks" are going to try and overrun the place, so we are all ready. They rock this place a lot but do not try to overrun it. It's too big. They would be sorry, and Charlie is not dumb, so I'll hit the sack again then say Goodnight.

God bless Marty & Lori

I love them very much

JOURNAL

JAN. 28, 1968

330

Didn't do too much today. Had another good breakfast. Then we went to the LZ and waited for choppers. We didn't get one so I'm back at BAS. It's real nice. We had another fine meal. I could stay here for the rest of my tour with ease. I got a snoopy blanket today and a 45 pistol yesterday so I'm happy about the results I got here. I hope I can get some soda tomorrow, but I doubt it. I can take Ca Lu with a little luxury. It's been short today, so God Bless Marty & Lori Jo and Goodnight. I also wrote Marty today.

LETTER 19

JAN. 28, 1968

Dear Darling,

How are you? I am fine. I'm still at Dong Ha. I tried to get out by helicopter today but no luck, so I'll try again tomorrow. Should get out without too much trouble. Helicopters were just tied up today. I haven't done too much since I've been here. I bought four more tapes and some batteries for the tape recorder of the captain's. I hope to get another one of my own soon. McDaniel, a guy in my company is on In Country R&R now and he said he would try and pick me up one. I sure hope he does. Then I can listen to your tapes every night before I go to bed. Have you sent your earplugs from your radio yet? I should have plenty of mail when I get back to Ca Lu. I'll read it all and send you a tape soon. How is my darling daughter doing? I bet she's got teeth by now. If she hasn't, she's probably keeping you up nights. I know she's really growing.

I bought a small picture album to put pictures in so if you want any of the ones you sent back, just tell me and I'll send them to you. I've only got one picture on my roll of 20 prints so I will send it in a few days. Then I will start taking slides again. Send the prints back to me and I'll send them back after I look at them, OK! I miss you very much. I keep thinking of poetry to write to you but it's no good so when I see a good one in the paper, I'll send it to you from me OK!

The food here at Dong Ha is great. You eat on plates like back at home. You can eat all you want. I'll be back here in about six months. Then my worries will be over. All I'll have to worry about then is the days not hurrying by fast enough. The time is going fairly fast. I guess when you keep busy it does. I like what I'm doing and it really isn't too bad right now. When it gets worse, I will get by, because I have your love and I just want to come home to you very much. I hope you are getting along OK. If you have any problems, I want you to tell me. You know I don't let anything get me down. I just fix it or live with it. I'm hard to shake up. I know you are a great wife and a damn good mother for one thing so I don't worry there.

How is the family? Has Uncle Russ and Aunt Marge fixed all the troubles? They sure got hit all at once. How is Don and Dan doing? I bet their house is real cute. Grandma said she was doing fine. I sure hope her business works out. I sure wish she didn't have to worry with it. I know how she worries. I'd go nuts if anything happened to her. She's really been a mother instead of a grandmother to me. I'd do anything for her. She's done plenty for all of us and she deserves the best.

Well, call Ronnie and tell him he'd better write or I'll kick him good. About once a week it won't hurt him. How's he and Gay doing. I hope he gets married so he won't have to come in the service. Well tell your family I'm fine and to take care of themselves. Also kiss my little daughter for me and tell her daddy is thinking of her and mommy all the time. I miss you both very much. We'll see you soon in Hawaii. Before you know it will be there.

Love,
Larry
P.S. I love you – Sleep Warm!

My dad's positive outlook and calm demeanor are endearing. He didn't let things shake him or get him down.

JOURNAL
JAN. 29, 1968
329

Today is just like yesterday. Waiting at the LZ. Eating dust and dirt from the helicopters and getting nowhere. It is now 1515 and I don't know if we'll get out or not. The good thing about today was breakfast. Pancakes, sausages, and eggs. Real good. Also had a good dinner. We made it out about 1600 and got back by 1615. A beautiful ride. The country is really beautiful (from the air). It's good to be back. This place has really changed since I left. They now have two lanterns in the bunker. They give out real good light. We bought a generator from Dong Ha for electric lights, but it will be a month or two before they get them working. Goodnight and God bless Lori Jo and My Darling Wife

JOURNAL

JAN. 30, 1968

328

Well today was my first day back on the job. Everything has went well since I have been gone I went and visited the 2nd platoon and OP Texas. They are all doing real good. So, no complaints. I also had mail yesterday from Marty & Lori and also Dad and Bonnie. Then today I got one from Marty and Bonnie. I wrote Bonnie and sent a tape to Marty and Lori. I'm going to write Connie now during my radio watch. It's a good time to get things done. Nobody to bother you. So, I'll sign off for now. Goodnight and God bless my family and everybody.

JOURNAL

JAN. 31, 1968

327

This is the last day of the month. It is hot and sunny. We have had a fairly slow day. A Co. of 3/4 landed today and were supposed to take our place and we were going to the field. Swept the area from here to the Rockpile. But they changed their minds. I'm glad of that. I had everything packed and ready to go but I'll unpack without any sweat. I'm glad we're remaining here. Well I got paid today $330 and I sent it to my wife. I know she'll use it wisely. I hope we can save plenty. We'll need it. Goodnight and God bless Marty & Lori

JOURNAL

FEB. 1, 1968

326

The first of Feb was a very busy day. First of all, everybody got paid and got their W2 forms. Plus, I gave them a foot check which turned out fairly bad. These people just don't care, I guess. So, they see me every day until their feet get cleared up. Also, I did my washing. Doesn't take too long just risk losing your clothes. I worked on my clothes putting my name on them and I also finished my calendar. Made my new desk and that's about all. Goodnight God bless Marty and Lori.

LETTERS 20 AND 21 (ONE ENVELOPE)
UNDATED

Dear Darling,

We were going to move today but they changed our orders. I sure am glad. We will probably be moving in the near future but not right now. I'm on radio watch right now. I'm helping out so everybody else can get a little sleep. It gives you a little time to write letters. I've got yours and Lori's picture in front of me now. The one where she's holding her foot out. I think it's so cute. The other one is where we're both holding her in black-and-white. I change them every few days.

Well I can't think of too much more. So I love you very much and miss you. Also, what time was it when I called from Dong Ha and what day?

Love,
Larry
P.S. Sleep Warm Darling

Dear Darling,

How are you this evening? Well I'm sending you my check tomorrow morning for $330. Also, my tax statement. I'm also sending more pictures of Vietnam. I hope you like them. I just read two letters from you which you wrote on January 19th, 20th, and 21st. They were really nice. I enjoy reading your letters. You write such sweet things. I love you very much. You told me Dad was down and that you had a good visit. I'm glad you like them. They really like you too. I'm glad they had a birthday party for you. Also I'm glad your relatives baked you a cake. They all really like you. It's hard not to. You're so loveable.

Lori hasn't got her teeth yet? I feel sorry for her. I know how uncomfortable it is for her. I hope she still keeps eating. As long as she eats she'll stay healthy. I'm glad you had a good stay at your moms and I'm glad they all got back OK. It was probably a real tough and tiring ride. She'll probably sleep for a week. I'm glad to see Marion beat Lafayette. That will really pick them up. I also got your paper. Thank you. Glad to see you started a scrapbook. It will be good for your future reading. I'm glad you liked your birthday cards.

Well we're going to move to a new location. We don't know yet but we're supposed to leave February 3. I'll tell you as soon as I find out. We usually only stay in one place for 30 to 40 days then move. So, don't worry until I find out.

Well I think I'll talk about my daughter. I know she is really getting big and talking constantly. I bet she is real cute. I'll really enjoy seeing her in July. We'll have a great time. I hope you're doing fine. I know you're lonely like me, but we have to think of the future, don't we. I love you very much. Well see you soon. Thinking of you always.

Love,
Larry
PS. <u>sleep warm keep cool headed though.</u>

JOURNAL
FEB. 2, 1968
325

Well today was another hot sunny day. We didn't do much because we were on 100% alert and had to stay near our holes and be ready for anything and everything. I finished Marty and Lori's bamboo drinking cups. I hope to send them out soon. I wrote my darling wife and daughter today. Haven't received any mail yet, but it's on its way. I sure hope I get my tea soon. Something to drink besides Kool aid all the time. I'm not griping though. It could be worse. We are all ready for our sweep tomorrow. So, Goodnight and God bless Marty & Lori and all.

LETTER 22
FEB. 2, 1968

Dear Darling,

How are you and Lori? I hope this letter finds you both well & happy. I miss you very much. I haven't received any mail for a while, because of the trouble around the area. We should be getting some soon. I've been playing your tapes, so I'm o.k. Just a little behind on the scoop. Has Lori got any teeth yet? I hope she gets them in soon. She'll have many by the time I see her. "Boy" she sure will be pretty. How are you doing on making little girls' clothes? I bet they are pretty. I listened to the tape where Grandma talked to me. The last letter I got was 21 Jan. so I should have plenty on the way. I'm fine here.

Things are picking up now as you've probably been hearing on T.V. We haven't had too much trouble when we go out on patrols. They're out there, but he doesn't want to fight, I guess. To the West he's fighting and to the North also. I hope he stays away from our door forever. The weather here is hot!! HOT. We got our first little rain last night in about three weeks, which lasted for about an hour. It sure is nice to get little spurts like that. It cools the place off a bit. During the day, you can hardly stand it and on patrols and sweeps its almost unbearable. But we move along.

How is everybody else at home? Has your mom gone back to work? Did Joe get a job? I sure hope they don't stay out too long. How is Donna doing? Is she gaining or tapering off? How does Dan feel? Is he nervous like I was? I think this was one of the most exciting times in my life. We do have plenty of good memories. How are the boys doing? Is Lori keeping them busy? Are you eating properly? I am so I don't see why you shouldn't. You've gotta keep full of pep you know. If you want you can keep my tax forms there. I don't have to file until I return home. . .So I will sign off for now. I love you very much. I miss you more than you'll ever know.

Be good and take it easy. I'm thinking of you always. Kiss Lori for me.

Love Forever and Always
Your Husband Larry
Sleep warm XXX

JOURNAL
FEB. 3, 1968
324

Well, today we went on a company size patrol. We started at 8:30 and returned at 6:00. It was an overcast day, so it wasn't too bad. It wasn't hot and a nice breeze was blowing. We didn't see Charlie. We just got some practice. We did get into water up to our ass though. It was refreshing. But your feet are soaked, and it takes time to dry. We got back from the patrol and had chow and then I got cleaned up and am getting ready to rest more. So, Goodnight and God bless Marty and Lori and Family.

Dad on patrol. He is wearing the same gear
he had on the day he was killed.

JOURNAL
FEB. 4, 1968
323

Well today was really a bruiser. We were blowing safe lanes between 1st Platoon and here and 2nd Platoon and here. We had our door on the bunker blow out and our supply bunker was a loss. My shirt sort of got torn a little too. I had a discussion over haircuts today. We don't have them as short as Marines. I fight first. We got it straightened out. I wrote my wife today and sent her some propaganda messages for our scrap book. It's going to be a big one. Lori can use it in school. Well goodnight and God bless Marty and Lori.

LETTER 23
UNDATED

Dearest Darling,

How are you feeling? I hope this letter finds you both well. I received my first letter in 7 days. Things are really getting slow out here we're completely out of food. That's why we got a few choppers out today. Charlie has got all the roads closed but when we go looking for him, we can't find him anywhere. Like I said he fights only when he has the upper hand. If it wasn't for our big guns and helicopters we would be in a <u>hum</u>.

The last two days have been real busy. Yesterday we were out on a patrol all day and today we were blowing a path through the minefield with C-4. It really goes off with a bang. The power that it releases blew our supply bunker apart and wrecked my shitter. They still have another one to blow tomorrow. We go out on patrols every 3 days, because we have 3 companies here. That's one a day. The grass is thick and heavy brush. But it's cooled off a little now, so it isn't too bad. When it's hot you about die. The grass is about 10 feet high and when you're down in there it's twice as hot. I got a few pictures of us going through some burned out villages. Not supposed to but I'm careful. I just take them when I know it's safe. I learned to hug the ground.

Well that's all about me. How about you? Is my tea on the way? How is my darling daughter and her lovely mom? I know you're fine. Also, send a pack of Kool-Aid in every five letters until I say stop. Grape, raspberry, and orange is fine. Just send regular, I've got sugar o.k.? Well kiss Lori for me. I love you very much. I'm thinking of you always. I carry your pictures in my flak jacket pocket with me all the time. You and Lori are with me all the time.

Love,
Larry
P.S. Sleep Warm. I Love You

JOURNAL
FEB. 5, 1968
322

Today was a very boring day. They were blasting the lanes through the minefields and so I stayed close around in case anybody got hurt. I built a chair today for myself. It's not too bad. Real comfortable. I wrote my sister today. I hope we get some mail tomorrow. I hope my tea is in the mail and some pictures. I love pictures. It's something over here. Back home it was nothing but you don't see your loved ones over here 7,000 miles away. Well I don't have any more to write. Charlie is knocking on our door tonight. Good night God bless my family.

LETTER 24
FEB. 6, 1968

Dear Darling,

How are you feeling today? I hope you and Lori both are well. The mail here is almost at a standstill, so your letters are probably all messed up. I received mail on the third. One letter and seven days before that I received three from you. I don't know when mail will come again. I hope tomorrow.

How is the family? Has Lori got any teeth yet? How was her 6 month checkup? I sure do miss you both. The tapes sound so good, but I start missing home that much more. But to hear your voices is worth it. I love to hear you tell about Lori and I wish you'd say a little more about yourself. How about sending me a back scratcher? The one that looks like a hand. Just wrap it up by itself and send it. Okay!! We killed a bear here tonight. Running out by our lines. We have everything here.

Well, today we went on another patrol. It was a long one. We had to go through dense bush and up small hills and then down in the valley by a Montagnard* village. This is the village outside of Ca Lu. These people are friendly (supposed to be). We treat them once a week for sickness. They have it hard. Very primitive. It was another cool day today, so the patrol wasn't too bad. The long distance got to your feet and walking through water again wasn't good. We didn't find any "gooks." They must go up into the mountains during the day and out by night. We are strong (many men) when we go out. They don't like those odds, I guess. I hope I don't see anymore.

Well, how do I sound? I hope you don't think I'm dodging bullets all the time, because I'm not. We see Charlie face to face maybe once a month here. He doesn't fight all the time. He just harasses us all the time. A few rockets here and there. And then an ambush about once a month when we think he's quiet. Well I guess I'll talk about something else. A man is on R&R now. I hope he finds a tape recorder for me. If he doesn't, I'm going to have you send me one. OK. I listen to your tapes on mine. I just have to slow it down with my finger. When you first send it, I listen to it on the captain's, so I can hear you real good. You sound so wonderful. I love hearing your sweet voice. It is like music. Your voice is so soft and it makes me feel so fine. I love you very much so kiss Lori for me and take care.

Love,
Larry
Sleep Warm

---

* "Montagnard" (French for "mountain man") is an umbrella term for the various indigenous peoples of the central highlands of Vietnam.

JOURNAL
FEB. 6, 1968
321

Today we went on another patrol. It wasn't bad because the weather was cool, and we didn't see any "gooks." We went by a "gook" village and it was interesting. The people are very primitive, but they seem happy as long as you leave them alone. The women seem to do all the hard work. The people are very small, probably the tallest one is 5'2" at the most. It was a long tiring, but good day. I wrote my wife but didn't receive mail. That's the only thing that's really bad about this place. So, Goodnight God bless my family [&] Marty.

JOURNAL
FEB. 7, 1968
320

Well today was another cool one. The sun was never out, and it now is cold at night. They have completed the safe lanes between section 1 and 2 so it is real easy to get back-and-forth. I saw an inspection of the area and things look good. I received mail yesterday from my darling wife. Four letters and 2 tapes. That's what I like to see. The tapes were real good. I also received a letter from her mom and Donna and Dan, so I am up on the news. I made her a tape last night so it should go out today if we get any helicopters. So, Goodnight and God bless Marty and Lori and all.

JOURNAL

FEB. 8, 1968

319

Well, today was a busy day. I did my washing and lost a pair of pants. Marines have a hard time getting clothes, so I guess they steal. I have to watch more closely. We built another shitter today and it's not bad. My best yet. I'm getting to be a good shitter builder. At least it was cool today and it rained a little tonight. Cold too. So, take it easy. I wrote Dad & Mom today and I'm going to send Marty's tape tomorrow so Goodnight and God bless all My Family.

JOURNAL

FEB. 9, 1968

318

Well today was an ass kicker. We went on another patrol out by the Little Rockpile and had to cross the river going and coming back. We were wet all day long and the river was real swift, and sometimes knocked you off your feet. The leeches were bad, and they were big ones. We got in late and we were tired and cold. We got mortared with 5 rounds and a man lost a finger too. Pretty rough day I believe. Goodnight and God bless Marty & Lori

JOURNAL

FEB. 10, 1968

317

Well today was a drying out day. All our equipment was soaked from crossing the rivers yesterday. The weather has turned extremely cold here and everybody is catching cold because of being wet. I got my hair cut today with those good old manual type clippers. Leech did a good job I think. Well, we go on C rations three meals a day after tomorrow's breakfast. We are low on everything including mail, but we'll get some soon. Goodnight and God Bless Marty & Lori. I love them both very much.

My dad's last haircut, Ca Lu Combat Base (Feb. 10, 1968).

LETTER 25
FEB. 10, 1968, AT 0500

Dear Darling,

How are you and my darling daughter doing today? I hope you are all fine. I'm tired and cold, but happy we're back from our patrol. We got mortared today by Charlie, but we were out of range, so nobody was killed. A man lost a finger that was about it medically. We had to cross the river down in the valley and it was very swift and cold. We made it but with some difficulty. We were going across by rope and it was hard keeping on your feet. We were wet from armpits to toes. We were in water all day about our feet and then on our way back we crossed the river again. It was something but we are safe and getting warm so I'm happy.

The weather has changed here now. No more hot sunny days. Now cold, rainy, cloudy. Back to the monsoons again. But it's only bad when you go on patrols, so that's only every three days. I can handle that. Well that's enough about me.

How is Lori doing on the teeth problem? I sure hope she gets them in soon. Then you won't mess with her or you'll be pulling back a stub. She sure is talking a lot. I bet she is a real joy. I wish I was there. I haven't had time to listen to your second tape yet, but I'll do it tonight so don't worry. I'm enjoying you on tape. How is everybody else there? Your mom sure has a load. Maybe with help soon she can get on her feet and not have to worry so much.

Well I'm writing a short one tonight. I'm tired and going to hit the rack for another hour and a half. I'm on radio watch if you wonder what I'm doing writing at 5 in the morning. So God Bless you and Lori and family. I love you very much. Thinking of you constantly.

Love,
Larry
P.S. <u>Sleep Warm</u>

JOURNAL
FEB. 11, 1968
316

Well today was another cold day. We are on full C rations now until food arrives. We went to the practice range today and I shot my 45 and a M16 and the two shot guns. Also practiced throwing hand grenades. Three live ones into the river to kill fish for the villagers. Besides, treating everybody for colds I've not done much today. Just getting ready for the patrol tomorrow. I'm going to write Marty so Goodnight and God bless Marty & Lori & Everybody

JOURNAL
FEB. 12, 1968
315

Well today was a real bad one. We had a patrol. It was raining and very cold, so I wore my long johns. We were going up the hill where we got mortared from last time but we heard about 200 Vietnamese people coming our way, so we laid in ambush. They were moving, and they also had Water Bull with them, so they were probably friendly, so we left a spread out there overnight to keep a check on them. On the way back we drew sniper fire and more mortars. It sure is getting interesting. Well I'm going to do some writing so Goodnight and God Bless Marty & Lori and family.

LETTER 26
FEB. 12, 1968, AT 0400

Dear Darling,

How are you and my darling daughter doing? I miss you very very much. I love you both more than you'll ever know. Here the weather has turned from <u>extremely</u> wet to extremely cold. I have my long underwear on now. Having to walk in that cold river up to your armpits and now this cold, everybody is feeling pretty low. Myself, I'm not feeling too bad. I started taking pills before I got anything. The weather makes you feel tired all the time by itself. I hope it warms up a little, just a bit. This should slow ole Charlie down a little.

Yesterday we went to the practice range and fan fired our weapons. This gets you more used to your weapon a little more. Also, you can check for malfunctions. They drill you like if you were walking down a trail and Charlie hit you. What to do immediately. It was a real good drill. I shot my 45, a M-16 rifle and also a 12-gauge shotgun which the captain carries. Also threw a few grenades. Got to keep practicing for the real thing. You're never good enough or too good. Besides that, we've just been getting ready for our patrol today.

Well how is everybody at home? Is Donna getting fatter, only 5 months to go now? Everybody sounded pretty good on the tape you made Jan. 21st I like the tapes you sent. They showed me you love me very much. I know you do, and I love you just as much. I have your pictures in front of me now and I always have one on me. You're with me constantly. So don't worry you're guarding me all the time. I love you both very very much. Kiss Lori for me.

With all my love,
Larry
P.S. Stay Warm!!


Twenty-seven years later, we would find that one of the pictures my dad was referring to was used to identify his remains after his body lay on Valentine's Ridge for three long weeks. This photo of me was still in his breast pocket, close to his heart. It was not until July 1995 that I learned this, and I heard it straight from the man who identified my dad's body, Dr. Jerry Behrens.

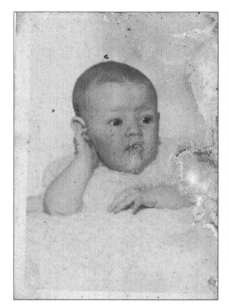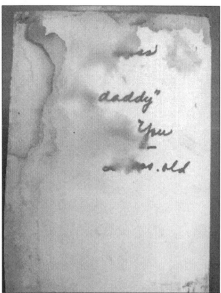

*Left:* My dad had this photo of me in his breast pocket when he was killed (hence the water and sun damage). It was in the box of his belongings that my mom received.

*Right:* The back of the photo.

On Feb. 13, 1968, my dad wrote his last letter to his little sister, Bonnie Kay:

Dear Bonnie,

How are you and the family? I hope this letter finds you all well. I received two wonderful letters from you today. They are wonderful to read. I also got your Valentine. Thank you very much. I hope Marty and Lori get down to see you soon. I know she enjoys seeing you all. She says she calls and writes you often, plus you come and see her too. I'm very glad to see my family writes and keeps me informed. I'm glad you get to be together. It lets me know how much you all care. Knowing you care keeps me from worrying and I know Marty and Lori are in good hands. I received Connie and Tom's letter today, so tell them that I did and I'll try to write soon. I'll write you and dad and you can keep them informed because things are getting more hectic over here now and free time is getting less. Tell them I'll write as often as possible.

I'm glad to see Dick got on the police force. I know he'll like it. Tell them all I'm fine and will write them soon. Things over here are like I said busy. We just got back off of a patrol yesterday. We drew sniper fire and about 17 mortars from the hill we did before. We're going to sweep the hill on the 14th and run Charlie into the ground. He's causing too much trouble with his mortars. He must be dug in good, because our big guns can't stop him, so it will take men to wipe him out. It should be very interesting!! I hope we don't lose too many men, but the job has to be done. Well, I'll write more later. So take it easy and be good.

Love,
Larry

P.S. I'll be fine. Me and the ground are real close. We've got used to each other quick. Tell Dad and Willie I'll write them as soon as we get back. If you haven't heard anything you'll know I'm fine.

That same day, my dad also wrote his last letter to my mom. But it was not in the stack of letters she gave me—she told me later that she had kept it in her purse since she received it, more than fifty years ago.

* * * * *

My mom's perspective was chronicled eloquently in each of her journal entries. She wrote about her faith in God and constant state of praying and pleading with God to keep her Larry safe. On January 14, exactly one month before my father was killed, my mom wrote in her journal:

> Lori woke up at 8:00 and the snow was really coming you could hardly see. She had a bottle and we slept until 10. We had snow until about 2:00 pm and it had snowed all night. We have 12 inches. Read the paper about the helicopter crash below Dong Ha. Three Navy men, 31 Marines. Please God don't let it be Larry. Please keep him safe for us. I love him so. Please don't let Larry be on the helicopter.

My mom wrote in her journal each time she received a tape or letter from my dad. Each one meant he was fine.

JAN. 22, 1968

> Donna and I got Lori to talk to her daddy on the tape recorder. I'm getting ready to finish the tape. Please Lord keep Larry safe.

The only day my mom did not write him was on Wednesday, January 24, when she was sick. She wasn't too sick to pray, though. She wrote in her journal that night:

News today was our ship was captured by Korea. Real scary. I'm so worried about Larry, haven't heard from him since Friday. The fighting is real heavy there. Please Lord, take care of him, please bring him home safe, I love him so much.

JAN. 25, 1968

No letter from Larry.[*] Lori Jo is 6 months old today Lori woke me up at 7:30. Felt real sick all night. President Johnson called up 14,000 reservists to try to get our ship from Korea. Fighting is still heavy in Khe Sanh Valley, lost some Marines. Please take care of Larry. Don't let him be hurt. Real worried haven't heard from him since Friday. His mail probably can't get out. I love him so much.

On Sunday, January 26, my mom received a phone call from my dad at 4:45 a.m. She was so happy to hear his voice. She wrote in her journal:

4:45 a.m. Received a phone call from Larry in Vietnam. We were all shocked. We talked for about three minutes. He said he was fine. Couldn't say where he was. He asked me about Lori, license plates, my allotment, also wanted to wish me a Happy Birthday, six days late. He sounded fine.

She called Grandma, her mom, and Donna to tell them the good news. On Sunday, January 28, she took her mom to Sunday School and church. When she got home, she called Harry and Marie to tell them about my dad's call.

---

[*] The mail was delayed due to the ambush on January 13, 1968, and obliterated when the North Vietnamese Army hit the convoy Dr. Jerry Behrens was riding in.

On February 1, my mom received a letter from my dad and a funny story he wrote about rock apes. It was nice to see that my dad was keeping his sense of humor under such horrific conditions. She ended her journal entry that night with a prayer asking God to keep Larry safe.

Saturday night, February 3, my mom and I spent the night in Indianapolis at Harry and Willie's house.

FEB. 4

In Indianapolis. Didn't go to bed until 4:30 a.m. Had waffles at 2:00 a.m. Harry and Willie and me sat and talked about Larry, Marie and other things. Harry realizes his mistake now and he is sorry. He wants to be a father to Larry. Please Lord give him another chance.

FEB. 5

Made Larry a tape. Lori talked on it too. The fighting is so bad, so Lord please take care of Larry for Lori and me.

FEB. 8

I love you Larry. Please take care of him Lord.

FEB. 11

I miss Larry terribly. Please Lord keep him safe for Lori and me.

FEB. 12

A letter from Larry. Fed Lori her bottle at 7:00, she vomited after that. Fed her cereal. At 10:00 she vomited that. Had a little fever. Took her to Dr. Baily at 4:00. He gave her a penicillin shot and a prescription and 2 kinds of medicine. Said she had intestinal flu. I wrote Larry two letters and sent him some Koolaid and pictures of Lori. I love you Larry.

FEB. 13 [FEB. 14 IN VIETNAM]

No mail from Larry. Lori and I had a rough night. She couldn't sleep so we slept most of today, Mama called at 1:00 to see how Lori was then Fran called so I could call Ronnie and give him Larry's address. Donna and I went to the post office. Mailed Larry a Valentine.

In the left margin, my mom wrote: "Lori waved bye-bye."

# CHAPTER EIGHT

# Life Back Home

My mother poured out her love and devotion for my dad into her letters, and was honest about her fears. The news of the war was extremely troubling, and he was stationed near the worst part, the DMZ. But despite her worries, she cheerfully told my dad of everything happening at home, because she knew he didn't want to miss a thing. As I sifted through my mother's stacks of cards and letters written in 1967 and 1968, some written from her point of view and some she wrote from mine, I found this one at the top.

Love to DADDY at Christmas

Hi Daddy,
    We love you and miss you very, very much. Take good care of yourself so you can come home to mommy and me. We will always need you and love you. Goodbye for now.

Hugs and Kisses,
Your Darling Daughter, Lori Jo

Also at the top was a Christmas card from my mom that my dad received in Vietnam.

Darling,
I miss you more than ever
Now that the holidays are here
But Darling, I am sure you know
In thought, you're very near
And every time I think of you
Within my heart I pray
That God will bless and keep you safe
And bring you home to stay

On the left side she wrote:

Darling,
    I know this is late but I bought them before Christmas so I thought I would go ahead and send them because the card says exactly how I feel. Please take care.
All our love forever and always.

Love,
Marty and Lori Jo

Although the three of us had celebrated Christmas together the day before my dad left for Vietnam, my mom wanted him to receive Christmas cards from us too. Photos of that precious time we shared, though sad, are priceless to me.

My mom wrote my dad fifty-two letters from the time he left for Vietnam until the day his remains were recovered on March 6, 1968.

JAN. 25, 1968

Hello Sweetheart,

Darling, I'm so worried about you. I know they must be keeping you terribly busy, just trying to stay alive. I haven't heard from you in 7 days. I know your mail probably can't go out. There is so much fighting going on.

Everyone here is fine. Lori's asleep right now. She is ½ year old today. Really growing.

I love you darling more than you will very know. Always stay well protected so you can hurry home to Lori and me. Will close now and go to bed, and dream of you. Last night I dreamed you and I were on Hill 861 together.

I love you, Darling.


All My Love
From Your Loving Wife,
Martha and Darling Daughter Lori Jo

SUNDAY NIGHT
JAN. 28, 1968, 12:15 A.M.


Hello Sweetheart,

How are you today? Hope and pray that you are safe. I also hope that you aren't in or near Khe Sanh. They have been fighting there for a long time. Wish you could have told me on the phone where you were located, but I know you weren't allowed to. Sure hope I hear from you real soon. Have you been receiving my mail?

I called your dad today to tell him about your phone call. He could hardly believe it. He was glad you got to call.

Your grandmother went to the shopping center today and she couldn't resist buying Lori something.

Lori and I got up early this morning and went to Sunday school and church. She was real good.

Darling I want to tell you how much I love you. Hearing your voice was so wonderful. You'll never know how much I love you. I'm sending you all my love, forever.

All My Love,
Marty and Lori Jo

Mom sent this picture taken the day of my christening (Nov. 19, 1967) to Dad. She wrote on the back, "Isn't she a darling?" Dad replied, "Yes I agree."

MONDAY NIGHT
JAN. 29, 1968, 12:30 A.M.

Hello Sweetheart,

Lori and I are so tired tonight. We started out at 10:00 a.m. and finally got home at 11 p.m. They all get so excited when I hear from you and I always tell them what you have to say and I always play the tape for everyone, including my family. Everyone enjoys hearing from you, but you'll never know how much hearing from you means to me. Love you so much. The tape you sent was wonderful. I got it at 1:30 p.m. and I have heard it 5 times, and I'll play it all the time.

Honey, on your tape you were telling about going out hunting the 8 men that were on a recon mission, isn't that what you told Stan to sign up for and you were going to too? I thought it sounded very dangerous. You aren't doing that now are you? I hope not honey. At least don't volunteer for anything like that. I love you so much. Tell your captain to take good care of you. I have to have you back.

Donna and I went to the laundromat tonight. Grandma called and wanted to know if she could watch Lori while we were gone. She and Lori had a good time. Lori was asleep when I went after her. She never cried. We really got us a good baby. You knew what you were doing, ha-ha.

Sweetheart I must sign off and end with a mountain of love to you. I love you so.

Please take it easy, so you can come home to Lori and me. We all love and need you. I'm sending you my love.

Forever and ever your loving Wife,
Marty and Darling Daughter Lori Jo

That same evening, Mamaw and Aunt Linda wrote my dad letters too:

Dear Son,

Was surprised but most happy when I got home today to find a letter from you. There's no use asking how you are. But here's hoping you are still o.k. I don't know what we would do with Martha if something should happen to you. I don't think I ever saw anyone love a man as much or miss one like Martha does you. That makes me very happy. That's how it should be. She was here when I got home to let us hear your tape. Those tapes are so nice.

Yes, we had a very nice Christmas though we couldn't forget you and what you were facing. My vacation means a lot to me now. I didn't know I was spending my last days with my mother but now that she is gone I'm glad I had the time off. I enjoyed Martha and Lori very much. She is so sweet. Today when Martha was playing your tape she looked at the tape recorder and smiled as if to say "That's my dad." I asked her if that's daddy. She just smiled the sweetest smile.

The Gipsons are all well. They said a big "Hello."

Thanks for the pocketbook. I sure needed it. It's very nice. God bless you. I hope He watches over you Day and Night and brings you back <u>Soon</u>.

I know you don't have time to write very often but when you do write again please. All my Love to a boy I would pick for a Son in Law any time. I hope the other girls are as lucky as Martha.

Good night Son. God bless you.
Geneva

Dear Larry,

Martha and Lori were here today. Lori just laughed and talked every minute. We really love her a lot, she's such a doll. Martha played the tape she got from you for us today. Your tapes mean so much to everybody, especially Martha. I'm awfully glad you make them as often as you do. I guess it sounds silly to tell a guy fighting in Vietnam to be careful – if he's not going to be anything else, I'm sure he'll be careful. But I want you to be extra careful because I don't know what Martha and Lori would do without you.

God Bless You – We all love and miss you.
Linda and all

I knew my dad was an incredible man, but reading Mamaw's words made it more clear. My dad received these letters eight days before he was killed. He needed to hear his mother-in-law call him "son." What a blessing she sent him. And my Aunt Linda was right—my mom and I needed him. He made our life great and he planned to spend every day doing that for the rest of his life.

TUESDAY NIGHT
JAN. 30, 1968, 12:50 A.M.

Hello Sweetheart,

Just finished writing to your dad and Willie telling them that I had received two letters and a tape from you. When I talked to him Saturday, he told me to let him know. He told me to call but it only takes a letter one day.

Hope you are fine. The news today was frightening. The Viet Cong attacked almost every city in Vietnam. Also damaged over $25 million dollars of planes and helicopters. Sure hope they didn't get near Ca Lu. They mentioned several battles near Camp Carrol, so I know you are near but I don't know how much.

Everyone here is fine. Lori is asleep. Last night for the first time, she slept in her bed all night until 9:30 a.m. this morning. She didn't even cry when she woke up. I woke up because I heard her playing with her bells. She sure is precious and lovable. Just like her dad that I love very much. You'll never know.

Grandma came down 3 times today. She is almost always here when the mailman comes. She's always anxious to hear from you. She looks real good. Lori Jo loves her too. When Grandma walks in Lori smiles so big. She sounds like she says bye-bye. Today Grandma was telling her bye and Lori waved her arm and said bye-bye. Your Grandmother got the biggest kick out of it.

Sweetheart I will close for now and have sweet dreams of you. Take care and may God Bless You and Keep You.

All My Love,
Marty and Lori Jo

With Grandma Bradford in Marion (January 1968).

WEDNESDAY NIGHT
JAN. 31, 1968, 1:00 A.M.

Dear Darling,

Got two wonderful letters from you today. One you had written in Dong Ha. Sure hope you didn't have any trouble getting back to Ca Lu. We know now how you got to call us, and we know you aren't hurt. Please call whenever you can. You'll never know how shocked and happy we all were. I could hear you real good, wish you could have heard me better.

Today has been a really busy day. I got my allotment and honey it was $7.50 more. I would give a million to talk to you anytime anywhere. I had the car filled for $3.15, needed 9 7/10 gallons. Almost empty wasn't it. Lori is fine. Donna, Marge, Lori and I went to one of Grandma's Tupperware parties. We didn't need anything. She just wanted me to bring Lori so those women could see her. She was a little doll. She sat on the floor and played most of the time.

Honey, the fighting over there is getting worse and worse. I hope you get back to Ca Lu and inside your perimeter before it gets real bad. What did you have to do in Dong Ha? Is it a very big place? How close to Ca Lu is Khe Sanh? Sweetheart you are on my mind constantly, in my dreams nightly and in my heart always.

All my love for you. I love you. May God Bless and keep you.

Your loving wife and darling daughter,
Marty and Lori Jo

Aunt Marge called herself "Anny Granny."

SATURDAY NIGHT
FEB. 3, 1968

Hello Sweetheart,

Sitting here thinking about you and how much I miss you. Lori is asleep. I mailed your package today Honey, and I know you'll be mad at me but the next time I'll send it SAM. I asked the man at the post office and he said that since it was cake we shouldn't, because they have so many airmail packages going to Vietnam. The SAM packages might sit and wait. Please don't be mad. I love you very much.

We didn't hear from you today. The fighting over there is so bad. From the DMZ to Saigon. Please be careful darling.

Sweetheart I will close for now and tell you how very much I love you. You mean so much to me. Please take care, I Love You.

All My Love Always,
Marty and Lori Jo

Inside my mom's diary, she kept track of every penny that came in and every penny that went out. Although money was very tight, and at one point she was down to a single dollar. Still, she made supporting her Larry overseas her top priority. By sending the above letter and Grandma Bradford's delicious carrot cupcakes through regular mail rather than by SAM, my dad was able to enjoy them the night before he was killed.

The last letter my mom wrote prior to receiving the news that my dad was missing was dated February 22. Included in the envelope was one package each of raspberry and grape Kool-Aid and part of our local newspaper with the sectional basketball scores.

THURSDAY NIGHT
FEBRUARY 22, 1968, 1:00 A.M.

Hello Sweetheart,

You have been over there in that terrible place two months now. Seems like a year and I know it must seem much longer than that to you. I love you so much. We are all terribly worried. All the news has been about 40,000 Viet Cong being dug in surrounding Khe Sanh. Said reinforcements have been flown in. Honey I'm scared that you may be there. I hope and pray that you are not. I love you so much. Please take care.

Our little daughter is really progressing. She can almost pull herself up in her bed and when I do stand her up, she holds onto the rail and walks around the end of her bed from side to side. She doesn't like to sit down. She also says huh all the time whenever you call her name or say something to her, she answers huh. Sounds as though she is really talking to you. Also, today for the first time she clapped her hands for "patty cake."

I am fine. A little sleepy. Marion beat Fairmount by about 28 points tonight. I can't remember the exact score. I'm sending you a few clippings from the paper. Will send you a few every night until the sectional is over. I love you, I love you, and I love you. So very, very much.

All our love Always,
Marty and Lori Jo

I was down to just two more envelopes in the stack. I opened the first. It was the birthday card my dad sent my mom from Vietnam. I don't know how he did it, but it was a testament to me of his giving spirit and loving heart. The outside of it read "Open Jan 20, 68."

The front of the card pictured a beautiful lady that looked much like my mom. She was wearing a blue necklace, my mom's favorite color. Inside the card was a plastic pink rose. Even though my dad was careful with money, he was generous with my mom. He wanted her to be prudent but wanted her to have what she needed.

On that lonely day in March when she received news that her Larry was never coming home, the sadness overwhelmed her, but in the days that followed she realized that he had left her things that no one could take away. It had been more than fifty years since he gave that little plastic rose to her, and it was still inside the card. When I opened the card, the rose had dropped onto my lap. I held it to my cheek and cried.

*　*　*　*　*

My mom was in our upstairs apartment at Aunt Marge and Uncle Russ's house when the phone rang. Something told her to pick it up. It was something she had never done before because it was their phone. On the extension from the other end of the line she heard the voice of Harry Goss, my dad's father.

My dad's half-brother Dick was a detective for the Indianapolis Police Department. He was pulled out of training to receive the news that his brother Larry was missing in action. Dick called his dad, who then called Uncle Russ so he could relay the news to my mom before the dreaded knock at the door.

As soon as she heard Harry's words, she screamed and dropped the phone. The noise scared me and I started crying too.

That knock at the front door came, hours later. Men in uniform came to deliver the news that my father was missing in action and to express their remorse.

My mom was in shock. She had to tell Grandma Bradford and her mama. She needed them to pray that her Larry would be found alive. That he would return to her and to me. She had to believe he was safe.

She went through the daily routine feeling numb. I still needed to be fed, bathed, and loved; it's all that got her through. She waited daily for the mail, hoping for letters he had written that might contain clues.

On Tuesday night, February 27, she wrote to her husband.

Hello Sweetheart,

The past four days have been a nightmare for all of us. You have been reported Missing in Action since Feb 14. I was notified in person Friday (Feb 23) at 4:00 p.m. and then notified by telegram Monday (Feb. 26). Received my 2nd telegram tonight (Feb 27) telling me that the patrols so far have found nothing.

Darling I hope and pray that by the time you get this you will be back in your company. I had to write you letting you know that I love you no matter where you are. My life is empty, and I don't know what to do. Lori and I know that you will be found safe so you can come home to us safe. And we will love and take care of you forever and ever.

I love you darling and dream of you constantly.

Your mother and family got in today; Tom brought them then he went back. They will be here for two weeks.

I love you darling, I miss writing to you every night. I mailed you two letters Saturday. I tried to write Friday night, but I just couldn't. Every time the phone rings I hope and pray that it is you calling from some Mars station. We are all praying for your safe return darling. Everyone that knows us in the Marion, Gas City, Jonesboro, Fairmount, Indianapolis and other places are all praying and thinking about you. I love you darling, please come back darling.

Love Forever,
Marty and Lori Jo

This is the last page of her letter:

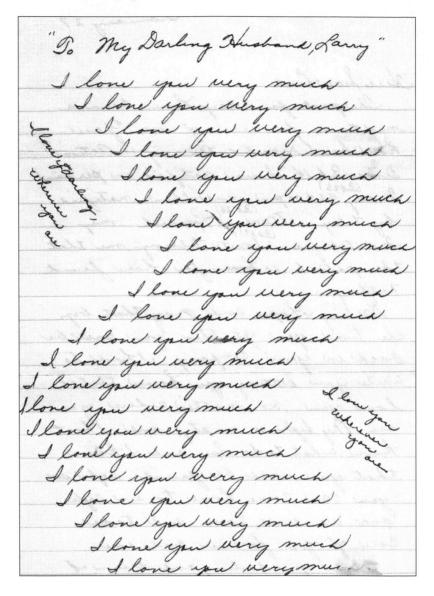

Her devotion to my dad was unwavering. His love for her was the same.

As I sifted back through the stacks, other cards caught my eye. There were Valentine's cards from her and me that I don't think my dad ever received. It was the only Valentine's Day when I had a daddy to wish a Happy Valentine's Day to. I looked at the postmark of each letter, wondering which ones he received. I found sixteen letters that had my dad's address marked out. They were stamped "return," then postmarked April 22 and May 3. The last envelope in that stack contained a birthday card she had sent with him. He was to open it on July 7, 1968, on what would have been his twenty-second birthday.

My dad's last letter, which until now has been safely in her purse, arrived the day my mom received the news that he was missing in action—I believe that was a tender mercy from God, not a coincidence.

Letter 26 [his last letter]
Feb. 13, 1968

Dear Darling,

How are you and my darling daughter today? I miss you both very much. I received your package yesterday. You sure paid a price to send it. S.A.M. gets here just as fast and costs ½ as much so please ask for S.A.M. I know you wanted me to get it real soon. Thank you very much.

The cupcakes are fine, and I didn't need the sugar, but I'll use it for my tea. It's probably better than we get in our C rations. I don't need anything else right now. The next time also put it in the smallest box possible. You don't need paper. They don't get torn up that bad. I haven't eaten any cupcakes yet, but they look real good. I'm going to eat them tonight a couple and pass some out to the guys here in the bunker. I'll let them eat them and then tell them what they're made of. They'll be surprised. You can send cookies but just a small amount about the time you get this letter. About a dozen is all. Small package please.

On the slide film just send the slides. I'm going to send a few of your tapes back soon. Keep them for our old days. They are worth a million. Tell Grandma thanks a bunch for her carrot cake cupcakes. They are nice and moist. Grandma's the BEST cook ever. She is the greatest grandmother a guy could ever have.

Well here we are getting ready for a sweep. We went out yesterday and got mortared and snipered at again from the same place. So we're going to go find him. And blow his ass off. It should be interesting, and I'll write you about it when I get back. You don't have to worry, because I got through it OK if you haven't heard from anybody. Me and the ground are real close friends. So he'll have to be real good to get me.

Well that's enough of that. How is my darling daughter? Has she got any teeth yet? How was her 6-month check-up? Are you taking pictures of her <u>and you</u> regularly? I mean when she does something new. I don't want you to take them just to be taking them. It costs a plenty. I'm still an old <u>scrooge</u>. I'll never change. I hope you are eating regularly and doing exercises. I want you shapely but firm not a bean pole. OK!!

Well I'll sign off for now. Kiss Lori for me <u>I love you</u> very much.

Love,
Larry
P.S. <u>Sleep Warm</u>

I am glad my mother did not send the package "S.A.M." If she had, my dad never would have received it.

It brings me comfort to know that my dad got to enjoy his Grandma Bradford's carrot cupcakes one last time. He knew how much she loved him and his devotion to her was immense.

My dad was optimistic about the patrol, yet he knew his life was in danger. He saw up close on Mutter's Ridge what happened to dead bodies in the jungle if the NVA got ahold of them. My dad's words—"Me and the ground are real close friends"—never left my mind when I searched for answers about his death. His words helped me keep searching until I finally found the truth.

\* \* \* \* \*

On the day my mom received the news that my dad was missing, she wrote the following in her journal entry that night:

FEB. 23, 1968

> Got a letter from Larry. Said he was going out on patrol. I was going to the post office to mail Larry 2 letters and Marie her picture, but we got news he was missing in action. No other details.
> Please God, Please let Larry be safe.
> Please, Please
> I love you and I love him, please keep him safe.

FEB. 24, 1968

> Mailed Larry two letters (51 & 52) and sports clippings.
> Please Lord let the news we get today be good news. Please find Larry safe for Lori and me. We need him and love him so much. Please take good care of him and find him safe. I love him so.

Mom wrote "Larry missing" on
the back of this photo (March 1968).

171

WESTERN UNION
TELEGRAM

DEA265 PA485 DE

P WB102 XV GOVT PDB 4 EXTRA=FAX WASHINGTON DC 26 455P EST

MRS MARTHA NELL GOSS, REPT DEL, DONT PHONE=

1020 SOUTH PENNSYLVANIA AVE MARION IND=

I DEEPLY REGRET TO CONFIRM ON BEHALF OF THE UNITED
STATES NAVY THAT YOUR HUSBAND, HM2 LARRY JO GOSS,
USN, B50 42 75, IS MISSING IN ACTION AS OF 14 FEBRUARY
1968 IN THE VICINITY OF QUANG TRI PROVINCE, SOUTH
VIETNAM. HE WAS LAST SEEN WHEN HIS PATROL WAS AMBUSHED
BY THE ENEMY. YOU MAY BE ASSURED THAT EVERY EFFOR T
IS BEING MADE WITH PERSONNEL AND FACILITIES AVAILABLE
TO LOCATE YOUR HUSBAND. YOUR GREAT ANXIETY IS THIS
SITUATION IS UNDERSTOOD AND WHEN FURTHER INFORMATION

WESTERN UNION
TELEGRAM

IS AVAILABLE CONCERNING THE RESULTS OF THE SEARCH
NOW IN PROGRESS YOU WILL BE PROMPTLY NOTIFIED.
I WISH TO ASSURE YOU OF EVERY POSSIBLE ASSISTANCE
TOGETHER WITH THE HEARTFELT, CONCERN OF MYSELF AND
YOUR HUSBAND'S SHIPMATES AT THIS TIME OF HEARTACHE
AND UNCERTAINTY. IF I CAN ASSIST YOU PLEASE WRITE OR
TELEGRAPH THE CHIEF OF NAVAL PERSONNEL, DEPARTMENT OF
THE NAVY, WASHINGTON, D. C. 20370. MY PERSONAL
REPRESENTATIVE CAN BE REACHED BY TELEPHONE AT
OXFORD 42746 DURING WORKING HOURS AND OXFORD 42768
AFTER WORKING HOURS. THE AREA IN WICH YOUR HUSBAND
BECAME MISSING PRESENTS THE POSSIBILITY THAT HE COULD

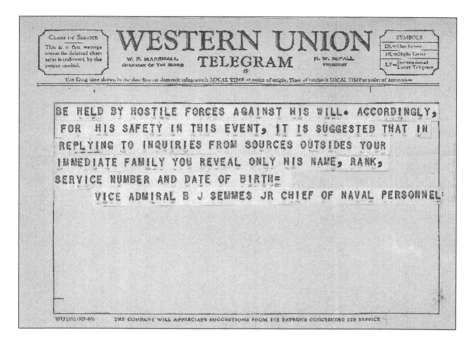

First telegram, received Feb. 26, 1968.

There was so much to do. Although she was in shock, Mom's brain took over and she began making calls: her family, Dad's family, her church congregation. She found a way to function because she had to—she had a baby who needed her. She was strong, but this devastating news knocked the wind out of her. She knew that if my dad were alive, he would find a way to make it home to her. She was sure of it.

She held me tightly as she prayed. Shock, denial, and hope all jumbled together inside her. She believed in her heart that her Larry was OK. He had to be.

FEB. 25, 1968

> Please God bring Larry back safe to us. I love him so much. He will have been gone 11 days today if he hasn't been found. Please find him safe.

Harry and his family stayed with us that day, and Marie called. She had received her telegram.

FEB. 26, 1968

Larry missing 12 days.

Still no word from Larry. Larry Lincoln HM from Anderson called. I called Lt Hinkle from Anderson. Harry called. I received my telegram at 7:15. I called Harry.

Took Lori to the doctor $6.00. Constipated.

Dear Lord I hope and pray that you find Larry safe for us. We all love and <u>need</u> him so. Please don't let anything happen to him.

Mama, Linda, Donna and Grandma spent most of the day with me.

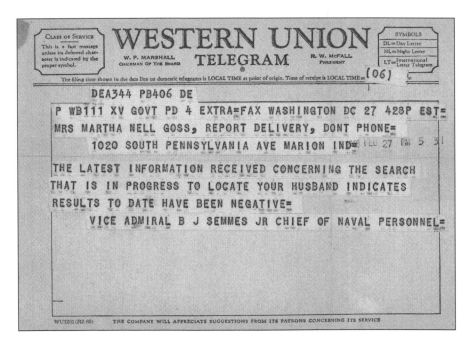

Second telegram, Feb. 27, 1968

The next day, a third telegram gave more information, but no news regarding whether my father was alive, missing in action, or deceased.

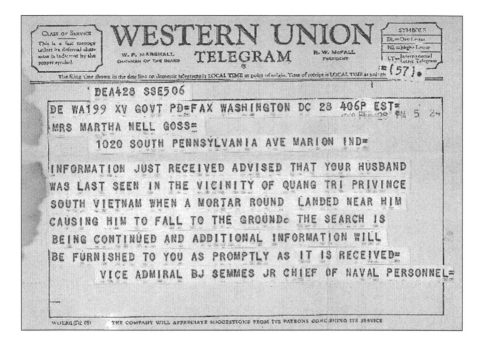

Third telegram, Feb. 28, 1968.

Two days later, my mother received the following letter from Lt. Col. Edward J. LaMontagne, the lieutenant colonel who commanded the Third Battalion, Ninth Marines:

HEADQUARTERS
3d Battalion, 9th Marines
3d Marine Division (Rein) FMF
FPO San Francisco, California 96602

29 February 1968


Mrs. Martha N. Goss
1020 South Pennsylvania Avenue
Marion, Indiana 46952

My Dear Mrs. Goss:

It is difficult for me to express the regrets and sorrow felt
by the Marines and Navy Personnel in this battalion over the
disappearance of your husband, Hospitalman Second Class Larry
J. Goss, U. S. Navy, who has been missing in action since
14 February 1968.

Larry was a Hospital Corpsman in Headquarters and Service
Company attached to Company K. On 14 February 1968, Company
K was engaged in a patrol search and clearing operation west
of Ca Lu Combat Operating Base, Quang Tri Province, South
Vietnam. At approximately 4:30 p.m., the company came under
intense enemy fire consisting of small arms, machine guns,
antitank weapons and mortars and became physically split.
Larry was last seen at 6:00 p.m. on 14 February 1968. The
remaining elements of the company were reorganized and a
night defensive position was established in the area of engagement. Larry did not reach this defensive position. On
the morning of 15 February the company departed from the
defensive position and began searching for Larry. While in
the process of searching for your husband, the company again
made contact with the enemy on the afternoon of 15 February.
The search continued throughout the day but with negative
results. The company still under intense enemy fire sought
assistance from another company from Third Battalion, Ninth
Marines and was forced to withdraw to the Ca Lu Combat
Operating Base arriving there about midnight on 15 February.
A search in the general area of engagement continues daily
for your husband.

Larry's cheerful disposition, uprightness, and devotion
to duty have won for him the respect of all who know him.
Although I realize that words can do little to console you,
I do hope the knowledge that every effort is being made to
locate Larry will in some measure alleviate your anxiety.

If you feel that I can be of any help to you, please do not
hesitate to write me.

Sincerely yours,

Edward J. La Montagne
Lieutenant Colonel
Commanding

My mom stopped writing my dad letters, but she could not stop praying for his safe return. In a different colored ink, she backdated her journal two weeks and started writing.

FEB. 14, 1968

Larry went out on a patrol and now he's missing in action.

FEB. 17, 1968

Please dear Lord don't let Larry be gone. Please, please take care of him. He doesn't deserve this. Please God let him be safe.

FEB. 18, 1968

Please God let Larry be found safe you know I need him. Please take care of him. He is a good person. I love him so.

FEB. 20, 1968

Please find Larry safe, Please, please Lord. I'll do anything if you will just bring Larry back to Lori and me. I love him so much.

FEB. 21, 1968

Please dear Lord don't let Larry be gone. Please find and look over him so he can come back to Lori and me. I love Larry more than life itself. Please find him safe. Please.

FEB. 22, 1968

Please God find Larry and bring him back to us, I love him so much.
Please God, Please, Please take good care of him.
Lori started Patty cake.

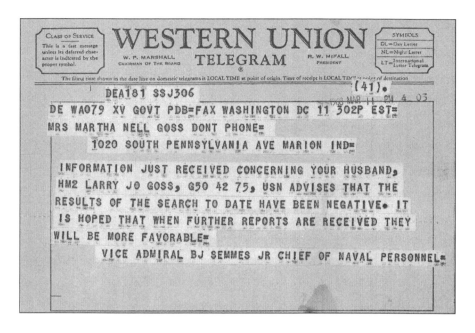

Fourth telegram, March 11, 1968.

Mom held onto hope but did not make any more journal entries, until a fifth telegram confirmed her worst fears.

| CLASS OF SERVICE | WESTERN UNION | SYMBOLS |
|---|---|---|
| This is a fast message or a letter telegram unless its deferred character is indicated by the proper symbol. | W. P. MARSHALL CHAIRMAN OF THE BOARD   TELEGRAM   R. W. McFALL PRESIDENT | DL=Day Letter NL=Night Letter LT=International Letter Telegram |

The filing time shown in the date line on domestic telegrams is LOCAL TIME at point of origin. Time of receipt is LOCAL TIME at point of destination.

DEA804 PC256                                                           EST:

DE P WB111   XV GOVT PDB 4 EXTRA=FAX WASHINGTON DC 20 418P

=MRS MARTHA NELL GOSS, REPORT DELIVERY DONT PHONE=

1020 SOUTH PENNSYLVANIA AVE MARION IND=

IT IS WITH UTMOST REGRET I CONFIRM THAT YOUR HUSBAND,
HM2 LARRY JO GOSS, B50 42 75, USN PREVIOUSLY REPORTED
MISSING IN ACTION HAS NOW BEEN REPORTED TO HAVE BEEN
KILLED IN ACTION ON 14 FEBRUARY 1968 IN THE VICINITY
OF QUANG TRI PROVINCE, SOUTH VIETNAM WHEN A MORTAR
ROUND LANDED NEAR HIM CAUSING HIM TO FALL TO THE GROUND.
=HIS REMAINS WERE RECOVERED.=
A LETTER FROM YOUR HUSBAND'S COMMANDING OFFICER
SETTING FORTH THE CIRCUMSTANCES OF DEATH WILL FOLLOW.

WU1201(R5-60)        THE COMPANY WILL APPRECIATE SUGGESTIONS FROM ITS PATRONS CONCERNING ITS SERVICE

| CLASS OF SERVICE | WESTERN UNION | SYMBOLS |
|---|---|---|
| This is a fast message unless its deferred character is indicated by the proper symbol. | W. P. MARSHALL CHAIRMAN OF THE BOARD   TELEGRAM   R. W. McFALL PRESIDENT | DL=Day Letter NL=Night Letter LT=International Letter Telegram |

The filing time shown in the date line on domestic telegrams is LOCAL TIME at point of origin. Time of receipt is LOCAL TIME at point of destination.

IF YOU DESIRE AND AT NO EXPENSE TO YOU WE WILL PREPARE
AND CASKET THE REMAINS AND TRANSPORT THEM WITH AN
ESCORT TO ANY PLACE YOU DESIGNATE. ALSO WE WILL ALLOW
YOU AN AMOUNT TOWARD FUNERAL AND INTERMENT EXPENSES
NOT TO EXCEED FIVE HUNDRED DOLLARS IF INTERMENT IS IN
A PRIVATE CEMETERY OR TWO HUNDRED FIFTY DOLLARS IF
REMAINS ARE CONSIGNED TO A FUNERAL DIRECTOR PRIOR TO
INTERMENT IN A NATIONAL CEMETERY, OR SEVENTY=FIVE
DOLLARS IF REMAINS ARE CONSIGNED DIRECTLY TO A
NATIONAL CEMETERY. PLEASE WIRE COLLECT THE BUREAU OF
MEDICINE AND SURGERY, DEPARTMENT OF THE NAVY,
WASHINGTON, D. C. 20390, THE NAME OF NATIONAL

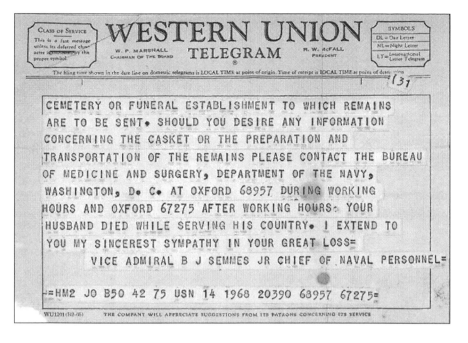

Fifth telegram, March 20, 1968.

MARCH 20, 1968

1st C, Larry Linton and a Lt personally came and told me that
Larry had been found. Killed by mortar fire on Feb 14th. Found
him March 18th.

Another report said he was found on March 6 at 1730.

MARCH 21, 1968

Harry called and said the Lt in Indianapolis received word that Larry
was in the states. In New Jersey. No details on when he would be
brought home. The news was on all radio stations all day. Also his
picture and article in the morning and evening papers.

# Marion medic dies in Vietnam

The death of a 21-year-old Marion sailor, earlier reported as missing in action in Vietnam, was confirmed Wednesday by the Defense Department.

Hospitalman 2-C Larry Jo Goss, 1020 S. Pennsylvania St., was reported killed by mortar

**LARRY JO GOSS**

fire on Feb. 14 while he was serving in Quang Tri Province in South Vietnam.

Goss was the 17th Grant County man to die in the Vietnam war.

Goss enlisted in the Navy in April, 1966. He had served in Vietnam since December.

He was a 1964 graduate of Marion High School, and was employed at General Tire and Rubber Co. before he enlisted. He attended Jonesboro Wesleyan Methodist Church.

Survivors include his w i f e, Martha; a daughter, Lori Jo, at home; his father, H a r r y Goss, Indianapolis; his mother, Mrs. Marie Shore, W i c h i t a, Kan.; a sister, Mrs. Mona Dollar, Noblesville; four half-sisters, Tina and Bobbie Shore, both of Wichita, Kan., and Mrs. Connie Trimmer and Bonn i e Goss, both of Indianapolis; four half-brothers, Billy and Jimmy Shore, both of Wichita, Kan., and Dick and Jack Goss, both of Indianapolis; his patern a l grandfather, Vernon Goss, Fishers; maternal grandpar e n t s, Mr. and Mrs. Jesse Rogers, Upland, and maternal grandmother, Mrs. Ruth Bradf o r d, Marion.

Funeral arrangements a r e pending at Needham and Son Funeral Home, 814 S. Adams St.

On the front page of the Marion *Leader-Tribune*, March 21, 1968.

This newspaper article made me believe my dad was a medic. I did not learn the difference between a corpsman and a medic until I was an adult.

Flipping through my mom's journal, I found no more entries.

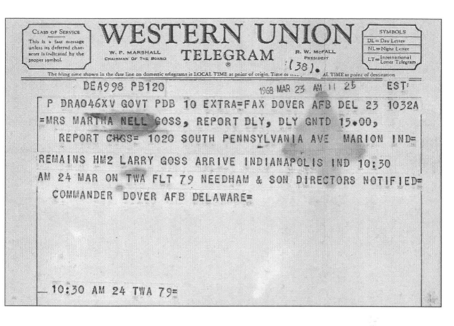

Sixth telegram, March 23, 1968.

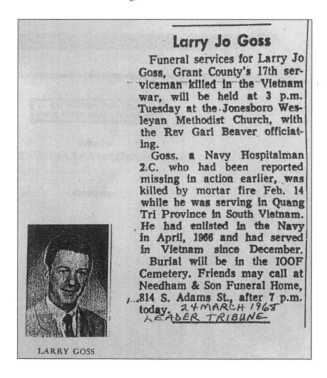

Marion *Leader-Tribune*, Mar. 24, 1968.

My dad's body returned inside a sealed casket, arriving at the same airport from which he left exactly one hundred days before.

The Indianapolis Police Department issued a bulletin that same day:

```
                    INDIANAPOLIS POLICE DEPARTMENT


    BULLETIN                                DEATH NOTICE
    NO. 68-63                     CORPMAN-USN-LARRY JO GOSS
                                  BROTHER OF RECRUIT OFFICER
    ISSUED: MARCH 21,1968         HARRY RICHARD GOSS
    _____

    CORPMAN LARRY JO GOSS, BROTHER OF RECRUIT OFFICER HARRY
    RICHARD GOSS, WAS KILLED IN ACTION FEBRUARY 14,1968, IN
    THE VICINITY OF QUANG TRI PROVINCE, SOUTH VIETNAM.

    SERVICES WILL BE HELD AT THE NEEDHAN FUNERAL HOME,
    MARION, INDIANA.

    FUNERAL ARRANGEMENTS ARE PENDING AT THIS TIME.



                                  WINSTON L. CHURCHILL
                                  CHIEF OF POLICE


                                  BY: THOMAS W. HARLOW
                                  DEPUTY CHIEF OF POLICE
                                  INSPECTION & TRAINING
                                  DIVISION

    DISTRIBUTION:

    ALL DIVISIONAL & BRANCH COMMANDERS
```

My dad and Harry Richard were not raised together, but they had a father in common. My dad would have liked knowing he was officially claimed as a part of the Goss family now. Had he lived, he and his Goss siblings would have become good friends.

My mom turned back the pages in his journal to March 6th and wrote:

Larry's body was found at 1730 on 3/6/68. The report said death was instantaneous – from massive tissue damage.
I pray to God that he didn't suffer.

My mom was still praying. She was taught not to question God, to trust that He was in control and that all things, good and bad, crossed through His hands. She would need His strength to make plans for the funeral, which was held at a little church in Jonesboro, Indiana. I was nine months old and did not attend. My mom left me in the care of Aunt Marge's co-worker, whom she did not know. She was barely making it through each day and welcomed Aunt Marge's willingness to drive me to her friend's house.

Decades later I drove to that church, imagining what had occurred inside. I felt the sadness, and my mother's shock and grief. The Navy paid the funeral home $542.50; she paid the balance of $119.20. My dad would have been fine with just the basics covered by the Navy's allotment. My mom, however, wanted more for him. She paid an additional $356.20 for his gravestone, which bore the image of a heart. One word was engraved on the ribbon surrounding the heart: "Wife." She would forever be a part of his heart, and hers would never be the same.

I've heard stories about the viewing from many people. While agonizing over painfully difficult decisions, Mom also had to deal with her mother-in-law. After arriving in town from Kansas City, Marie had all her teeth pulled, hoping for sympathy. She also contacted my mom's church and told them to take all the food the parishioners prepared to Grandma Bradford's house, where she was staying. Marie knew full well that my mom and I were still living with Aunt Marge.

The afternoon of the viewing, as a big crowd was lined up, waiting to pay their respects, Marie made a scene. She went to the funeral

KISS LORI FOR ME

home director and demanded that he open my dad's casket. Since my dad's dog tags were not returned, Marie did not believe anything was in the casket and doubted that he was dead.

Marie knew my mom was the only one who had the right to make that call. Mom found the strength to hold her ground while the guard stood resolutely by the casket. She had been highly discouraged from opening the casket and believed there was a good reason for this government recommendation. She also knew my dad's body had lain in the jungle for three weeks. She had no desire to see her Larry this way.

My mom still had many unanswered questions, and dates in the telegrams didn't match up with other military papers she received. She had a checklist of my dad's items that were stored at Camp Hansen Okinawa: shirts, trousers, caps, and so on, everything but his dog tags. They were all in a cardboard box and accounted for on March 7, 1968—three weeks after he had been listed as MIA. My mom couldn't help but wonder: *Couldn't they possibly have been wrong?*

My dad was buried at the IOOF Cemetery (now called "Estates of Serenity") just three miles from where we were living, and we went there almost every day. It was quiet there, and no one would see her as she wept over his grave.

One day, everything my dad had kept in his bunker arrived in a box. My mom bundled me up and we took the box to his gravesite. As she looked through each unopened letter, his diary, his briefcase, unused stationery and stamps, all she could do was sob. *The stationery and stamps were all supposed to be used!* she thought, devastated. She had sent enough for an entire year. Overwhelming sadness overtook her, and she didn't know how she could go on.

But as she looked at me sitting nearby, she knew she had to for me—and for her Larry, too. Although she had lost the love of her life, my mom believed her beloved husband had lost so much more. He would never feel the warmth of her touch again, never hear her say "I love you" again, and never receive hugs from his baby girl. As she gazed at me, she clung to this thought: *Larry lost everything, but I still have Lori.* She would go on for me and make sure that he remained a part of our lives. That was the least she could do.

Mom and I at my father's grave after the funeral dinner (Mar. 26, 1968).

When it seemed that my mom could not possibly be sadder, an invoice came from the U.S. government for the cost of shipping my father's remains. The bill was a slap in the face—hadn't she and Larry already paid enough? —but she paid it because she thought she had to. Later, she received an apology and a refund. Not long after, when my father's insurance money arrived, Harry asked her for a loan. She gave the money to him because she felt like it was the right thing to do. It took him four years to pay her back.

On April 10, Lt. Col. Edward J. LaMontagne sent my mother another letter:

HEADQUARTERS
3d Battalion, 9th Marines
3d Marine Division (Rein) FMF
FPO San Francisco, California 96602

10 APR 1968

Mrs. Martha N. Goss
1020 South Pennsylvania Avenue
Marion, Indiana 46952

My dear Mrs. Goss:

The untimely death of your husband, Hospitalman Second Class Larry J. Goss, U. S. Navy, on 14 February 1968, near Ca Lu, South Vietnam, is a source of great sorrow to me and his friends in this battalion. Please accept our deepest sympathy in your bereavement.

Larry's remains were recovered on 6 March 1968, in the area west of the Ca Lu Combat Operating Base, Quang Tri Province, where his company had engaged the enemy on 14 February 1968. Medical authorities have determined that his death was caused by fragmentation wounds to the body from an enemy explosive device.

A Memorial Service will be held for Larry as soon as the tactical situation permits and I assure you his many friends will attend.

Larry was one of the finest Corpsman I have ever known. His exemplary conduct, leadership and singular determination to do every job well were qualities all of us respected. We will miss him and hope you will find some comfort in knowing this.

If there is anything I can do, please feel free to write me.

Sincerely yours,

EDWARD J. LA MONTAGNE
Lieutenant Colonel
Commanding

On April 11, my mom received a letter informing her that Dad had been posthumously awarded a Purple Heart and service medals.

DEPARTMENT OF THE NAVY
BUREAU OF NAVAL PERSONNEL
WASHINGTON, D.C. 20370

IN REPLY REFER TO:
Pers-G25-MB/db

APR 1 1 1968

Dear Mrs. Goss:

As Chief of Naval Personnel I am privileged to inform you that the Secretary of the Navy has awarded posthumously to your husband, Hospital Corpsman Second Class Larry Jo Goss, United States Navy, the Purple Heart. In addition, he earned the National Defense Service Medal, the Vietnam Service Medal, and the Republic of Vietnam Campaign Ribbon Bar during his naval service.

These awards have been forwarded to the Commandant, NINTH Naval District, Building I, Great Lakes, Illinois 60088. He will communicate with you in the near future regarding your wishes for a presentation ceremony.

I realize that medals are small consolation for the loss of a loved one and that they can do little to assuage the grief which you have experienced. However, I hope that they will serve as symbols of your husband's devotion to duty in the service of his country.

Sincerely yours,

B. M. STREAN
Rear Admiral, U. S. Navy
Acting Chief of Naval Personnel

Mrs. Larry Jo Goss
1020 South Pennsylvania Avenue
Marion, Indiana 46952

My mom received his medals at a quiet service on the courthouse lawn. She wore a simple knee-length black dress and held me in her arms. In the photo below right, she bites her tongue, holding back the tears as she holds a pacifier in my mouth.

TRIBUTE TO SERVICEMEN
Mrs Martha Goss, widow of Larry Goss, United States Navy, who was killed in Vietnam in February received the Purple Heart, National Defense Medal, Vietnam Service Medal and Republic of Vietnam Medal awarded to her husband. She was given the awards Tuesday August 20, During the Serviceman Recognition Day Program held on the south side of Marion Courthouse square.

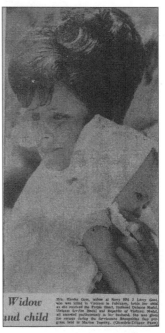

*Widow and child*

Mrs. Martha Goss, widow of Navy BM1 J. Larry Goss, who was killed in Vietnam in February, holds her child as she received the Purple Heart, National Defense Medal, Vietnam Service Medal and Republic of Vietnam Medal, all awarded posthumously to her husband. She was given the awards during the Servicemen Recognition Day program, held in Marion Tuesday. (Chronicle-Tribune Photo)

From the Marion *Chronicle-Tribune*, August 23, 1968.

MARION'S POPPY GIRL — Lori Jo Goss, Marion's 1968 Poppy Girl, clutches a flower for Mayor Gene O. Moore. Lori is the nine-month-old daughter of Mrs. Larry Jo Goss of Marion. The infant's father, Larry, died of combat wounds Feb. 14 in South Vietnam. The annual Poppy sale will be conducted here Friday and Saturday under the sponsorship of the Veterans of Foreign Wars Auxiliary. (Chronicle-Tribune Photo)

She sent a letter to the Navy on April 15, pressing them for more details about my dad's death. She received this response:

DEPARTMENT OF THE NAVY
BUREAU OF MEDICINE AND SURGERY
WASHINGTON, D.C.   20390

IN REPLY REFER TO
BUMED:3143:ET:et

2 6 APR 1968

Mrs. Larry Goss
1020 South Pennsylvania Street
Marion, Indiana 46952

Dear Mrs. Goss:

As requested in your letter of 15 April, a copy of the official death certificate in the case of your husband, HN Larry Jo Goss, USN, is enclosed.

We regret that we have no information concerning his death other than that which was given to you by the Bureau of Naval Personnel and by Lt. Colonel Edward J. LaMontague, Commanding Officer of the Third Battalion, Ninth Marines, Third Marine Division, Reinforced, in his letter of 10 April 1968.

After recovery on 6 March, your husband's remains were transferred to the U. S. Army Mortuary at Danang. His identification tags were found on his remains. In addition, in order to verify identity, the dental and physical characteristics were compared with the dental and physical characteristics recorded in his health record and found to be in excellent agreement.

The Bureau of Naval Personnel is responsible for matters relating to disposition of personal effects. A copy of your letter is being sent to that Bureau for reply to your inquiry concerning non-receipt of your husband's effects.

Once again we wish to extend to you our sincere sympathy in your great loss. If you have any further questions, or we can assist you in any other way, please do not hesitate to communicate with us.

Sincerely,

R. B. BROWN
Vice Admiral, MC, USN
Surgeon General

Encl:
(1) Death certificate
(2) DD Form 1300

Enclosed was the death certificate and DD Form 1300, a report of casualty:

| Name | Age | Religion |
|------|-----|----------|
| Goss, Larry Jo | 21 Yrs. 7 MOs | Protestant |

| Color of Eyes | Color of Hair | Complexion |
|---------------|---------------|------------|
| Hazel | Brown | Ruddy |

| Height | Weight |
|--------|--------|
| 68 ½" | 140 lbs. |

Time of Death
February 14, 1968, 1730

Disease or condition directly leading to death
Massive Tissue Damage

Approximate interval between onset and death
None

Summary of facts relating to death
While engaged in action against hostile forces in the vicinity of Quang Tri Province, RVN, subject suffered massive tissue damage causing instantaneous death.

NO AUTOPSY PERFORMED

Positive identification made by dental comparison.

Prayers offered by F. J. Urbana, CDR, CHC, USN
Transferred to U.S. Army Mortuary, Da Nang, RVN
Signed 16 Mar 68
Court of inquiry or board of investigation will not be held.

My mom had dreams about Dad being alive. The statement "Positive identification made by dental comparison" opened up the crack of doubt even more. My father had false teeth. The other thing that troubled her was that his dog tags were not returned. Was it possible Dad was still missing? She held on to that hope for many years.

Visiting my dad's gravesite on Memorial Day (above) and Christmas, 1968.

# CHAPTER NINE

# My Growing Years

The contrast between the life my mom and I had and the life my dad would have given us is stark. For eight months after my dad was killed, we continued living with Aunt Marge and Uncle Russ. My mom paid rent faithfully during that time, but felt she had imposed long enough when their daughter, Donna, mentioned that the house two doors down from her was available to rent. My mom took that to mean we should make the move.

But she didn't want to live alone—it had just been seven months since my dad's funeral. During the days she felt sad and lonely, and during the nights she felt afraid. Her little sisters, Rhonda and Sandra, were only six and ten years older than me. She had them over often to play with me and to help her feel less scared at night. My mom's twenty-fourth birthday, her first without Larry, was hard. Her mama tried to make the day special but all she wanted was her Larry. They had always talked about having a boy and girl that they would name Lori and Larry. She had their little girl but the rest of their dreams were shattered.

With Mom in January 1969, when she was 24 and I was 18 months.

"Reading" a book to my dad (July 1969).

On the first anniversary of my dad's death, she still had a shrine for him set up in our living room. I was only eighteen months old and have no memory of that painful time, but I wonder if my body absorbed the sadness. Each day for her was filled with loneliness, grief, and fear. Mom continued to faithfully attend church and Sunday School. She took to heart the messages she received about not questioning God. From the time my dad left for Vietnam, she prayed to God daily to please keep Larry safe. After she received word that he was missing in action, she begged God to help the Marines find her beloved husband alive. Though God did not answer her prayers with a "yes," she somehow still believed in Him.

Before my dad left for Vietnam, he told my mom that if he didn't make it home, he wanted her to remarry—but stressed that he did not want her to live with a man before then. Throughout his childhood, he had watched his mom bring home various men, and he did not want me to experience the trauma he endured. With his words in her memory, she got remarried when I was two. Her sadness was replaced with joy when she later gave birth to the little boy she dreamed of. But her new husband was nothing like my dad. After their wedding, he moved us across town, and my contact with my dad's family radically decreased.

Mom took great care of Dad's grave and
decorated it beautifully (July 1970).

Mom made sure, however, that I still spent time with my dad's Grandma Bradford. She loved me deeply, just as she had my father. I knew he was very special to her. My dad's family gave me the nickname "Oreo Cookie Jo," but strawberries were my favorite treat. Grandma Bradford always had a strawberry pie waiting for me in her refrigerator. When I was four, I started spending the night at her house. I still recall the lump in my throat at night because I missed my mom. I was not used to being away from her and needed to know she was safe.

My birthday party was at Grandma Bradford's house that year. Mom always made a big deal about my birthdays, but this one was extra special. Dressed in a yellow plaid dress, I smiled sweetly at the camera. Surrounded by dad's family and my mom, I felt adored, loved, and safe.

Celebrating my fourth birthday at Grandma Bradford's house (July 25, 1971).

My mom channeled her grief into taking care of my little brother, Shawn, and me and in remembering my dad. She vowed to do everything she could to make sure her beloved Larry was never forgotten. Though her last name had changed, her love for him never wavered.

In 1972, she sent his photo to News Channel 6 WPSD-TV for a Memorial Day program and received this letter back:

Thank you so much for sharing your loved one's picture with us. We're glad we could share it with our viewers. We appreciate your willingness to help us remind everyone of the huge sacrifice these soldiers made for our freedom.

I wish everyone could have had the experience I did in opening all of the letters and emails we received. Each picture had such a moving story behind it. Many were young men who had just graduated from high school and were barely beginning adulthood. It made me wish I had listened to my grandpa's war stories much more when he was alive.

Memorial Day can be a painful time for people who lost a loved one in war, so again I appreciate the fact that you were willing to share your picture with our viewer. Perhaps reminding people of the past will help to keep us from repeating it.

Sincerely,
Andrea Underwood

My mom's second husband was an alcoholic and, just a few years into their marriage, his abuse had taken a toll. Unbeknownst to him, she had been saving portions of my dad's Veteran's benefits during this time and finally had enough to cover a deposit on an apartment. One day he complained about me again and she'd had enough. When he left for work, she moved us out. Though I was young, I clearly remember my Uncle Joe coming during the day to help us move. As I walked up the stairs to Apartment C, our new home, for the first time, I didn't understand what was happening, but I trusted my mom. The apartment was in a little town called Fairmount and only a few blocks away from my Mamaw.

A few months later, I was headed off to my first day of kindergarten. I looked forward to going to school and talked about it often.

Mom rolled my hair in curlers the night before and took pictures of me in my new outfit before we left Apartment C. My teacher, Miss Gibson, greeted me with a smile as I entered my classroom at Park Elementary. Yet when she did, the same lump I felt in my throat at Grandma Bradford's house unexpectedly appeared.

I was embarrassed by my tears and found a way to manage them, but thoughts of my mom dying like my dad sometimes filled my head. If my mom was late to pick me up after school, my fear worsened. I wondered what would happen if she died. Who would take care of my little brother and me? Where would we live? Mamaw loved us dearly but she did not have enough room in her house for us and she had her own children to care for.

The following year, still holding onto a sliver of hope that my dad was alive, my mom's heart was shattered again when she watched all the POWs walk off the airplane and did not see my dad. The war in Vietnam was over. Her Larry was really never coming home. I sat beside her on the couch but had no understanding of the significance of that event or that there were families whose nightmares were over.

The look on my face shows that my understanding of our loss increased as I grew older (December 1972).

\* \* \* \* \*

Before I started grade school, I didn't realize that everyone else had a dad. In first grade, when kids were telling stories about their fathers, I told them about my Mamaw—the strongest person, physically and mentally, that I knew. Valentine's Day that year was especially difficult for me. We had a party at school. As we were walking about the room putting Valentine's Day cards in our classmates' mailboxes, I started to cry. I didn't know how to feel happy like everyone else, because this was the day my dad had died. On a day when love is celebrated, I was reminded of my greatest loss, and I had no idea what to do with those feelings. I didn't know anyone else whose dad had died, let alone on a holiday.

My teacher that year, Mrs. Smith, took a special interest in me. Although her intentions were good, her actions made me feel even more different than I already felt. She often called me to her desk to ask about my feelings. She even took me to her house one day at lunchtime—just me, no other kids. I didn't like people feeling sorry for me; I just wanted to be like everyone else. Mrs. Smith told my mom that I needed to see a counselor, but I never did. Back then, there was no such thing as a grief counselor at school.

My second-grade teacher, Mrs. Harvey, was a blessing. Her husband was a pastor with a big smile and a hearty laugh, and he often came to our classroom to say hello. He would ask us all to close our eyes so he could kiss his wife goodbye. We sometimes peeked and giggled. It was the first time I had seen a loving relationship between a man and a woman—something I would have seen daily had my dad lived.

I don't remember my exact age but I distinctly remember grieving the loss of my dad as I lay in bed and listened to music in our new house on Second Street. It was the fifth place we had lived since my dad was killed, and it was my favorite. Our two-story house felt like a castle to me because we had plenty of love and laughter. Mom worked the second shift at Kmart to make ends meet and had trouble finding good babysitters for Shawn and me, but we weren't aware of the stress she felt. Our sweet next-door neighbor, Mrs. Templeton, watched us sometimes at our house. My brother and I would hide in the compartment of our sofa-bed couch and surprise Mom when she walked in the door.

Mom made sure Shawn and I said our prayers every night (1973).

During our time on Second Street, two of my favorite songs were "Billy, Don't Be a Hero" and "Run Joey Run." The word *Daddy* was not one I said often, but as I listened to the music, I reflected on mine. Where was he? Did he really live in heaven like Mamaw said? Could he see me? Did he really die? As I blew out the candles on my birthday cake each year, I wished the same thing—that he would come home. I remember crying when "Billy, Don't Be A Hero" played on my record player. I didn't want my dad to be a hero! I wanted him to come back to my mom and me.

None of the places we lived were near a military base, and we didn't know any veterans. My mom ended her search for my dad after becoming a single mom of two. The only thing military-related I remember growing up was the song "America (My Country, 'Tis of Thee)." When we sang the words in music class, I always felt sad. There really was a land where my father had died, and that was not true of anyone else in our school. I also thought of my dad every morning in school when I put my hand over my heart and said the Pledge of Allegiance.

By third grade, I no longer felt worried when I was away from my mom. I loved school and made friends easily. One friend came home with me every day because my mom provided after-school care to him and his sister. Each day, Mom had a snack waiting for us when we walked in the door. I was proud of our little family and loved going to Park Elementary School. My maternal grandma lived a few blocks away and life was good.

Fourth grade was my best year ever, thanks to Mr. Garringer. I don't know if it was my wise principal or God who assigned me to his class, but a male teacher was exactly what I needed. He called me "Jo," which I loved. *Charlie's Angels* was a popular television show at the time. Mr. G (as we all called him) picked my two best friends and me to be "Mr. G's Angels." He was always appropriate, always affirming, and always fun.

We memorized the states and capitals that year, and Mr. G picked me every time he said Hawaii. I would stick my right index finger in the air, point my nose to the sky, and say "Honolulu." When I got to "lulu," I would howl like a wolf, and Mr. G would smile from his desk. My classmates would laugh, and my self-worth grew from his approval. Mr. G saw my strengths and believed in me. They say that little girls first fall in love with their daddies. I never had the privilege of experiencing that, but through Mr. G's eyes, I saw my value and worth.

That year, I wrote an essay titled "My Wish."

## My Wish

*My dad got killed in the war. I was six months old. Mom didn't get back the dog tags. He may have been captured because he was a doctor. I have just about stopped wishing that he was just captured and come back. My grandma still believes he's alive.*

*We have his diary, pictures, slides, and tape recordings in a lockbox. I will go through it someday. It doesn't bother me to talk about him. It's the letters that upset me.*

*If he came back it would help all our family. Especially Mom. They were only married a year. My grandma has cancer and he's about the only thing she has to live for. I don't know what it's like to have a real father. So, if I had one wish that would come true, it would be that dad was just captured and would come back soon.*

Fifth grade brought many changes. My mom's remarriage to her second husband, a move to a town away from Mamaw, and a new school. That same year, Grandma Bradford died. My mom told me as soon as I got off the school bus. Her funeral was the first I had attended, and the first time death became more to me than a word associated with my dad, or a childhood pet. Marie came up to me as soon as I walked into the funeral home, hugged me, and told me she loved me. I didn't really know her, so that felt strange. How could she love me if she didn't know me? She took me right up to the casket and placed my hand on Grandma's hand. I will never forget how hard and cold it felt. That experience has stayed with me.

My sixth-grade teacher, Mrs. Hubbard, had an indelible impact on my life. I told her I was going to be a doctor one day because of my dad, and Mrs. Hubbard never forgot. She had me sign "Dr. Goss" on all my papers that year. By writing it, I came to believe that I would truly become Dr. Goss one day. Not a medical one—the sight of blood makes my stomach hurt—but some kind of doctor. My dad never realized his dream of becoming a doctor, but I could live out his dream for him. I wanted to honor him with my choices and behavior, to make him proud and bring honor to his name.

When I got older, my mom had an idea of how we could remember my dad, and make sure others remembered him, too. My mom knew I loved to write, so she said that each year, on the anniversary of my dad's death, we could place a tribute in the local newspaper. Mom wanted to make sure my dad was never forgotten, and she knew I would know just what to say. I sat down and penned words to a poem my mom placed in the newspaper on the fourteenth anniversary of my dad's death. She paid to print the same poem every year on Valentine's Day.

As I entered high school, my belief in Christ gave me hope that I might see my father one day. After my baptism at age thirteen, I faithfully read the Bible each night, and though I knew very little about theology, I believed in the sovereignty of God. I didn't want to dwell on the sad parts of my life; I wanted to enjoy high school and all the exciting opportunities that came my way. My focus was on being strong and living each day to the fullest. My dad had only twenty-one short years and I wanted to make sure I enjoyed life enough for both of us. It seemed to be the least that I could do.

During my sophomore year, I joined my classmates for a trip to Washington, D.C., on Veterans Day—the same day my dad's battalion doctor, Jerry Behrens, marched in a grand parade down Constitutional Avenue to the Vietnam Memorial. Though our paths did not cross, we were in the same city. If my dad had been able to look from heaven to earth that day, he would have realized the significance Jerry and I would have in one another's lives. The time was just not right yet.

The following article about this trip that would become the catalyst for my search appeared in the school newspaper:

Local Students Took Washington D.C. Trip

Veterans Day was a day full of American history for 88 students and adults from Oak Hill who, with Madison Grant and Tipton, took a tour of the nation's capital. Leaving Oak Hill at 4:50 a.m., the group arrived in Washington at day's dawn.

Principal Larry Stoner accompanied the group and noted that the flight alone was worth the trip's cost to 2/3 of the Oak Hill tourists who had never flown before.

Tour buses greeted the students and chaperones at the Dulles International Airport to usher them to the Hiroshima Memorial and Arlington Cemetery.

Stoner noted that the only disappointment of the trip came during the visit to the cemetery because the group could not witness the usual changing of the guards due to a ceremony at the Tomb of the Unknown Soldier.

The Lincoln Memorial and the Vietnam Memorial were the next two stops on the whirlwind sightseeing tour. Stoner said both memorials were perhaps the most impressive of all the sights, certainly the most sobering.

Stoner added that the Vietnam Memorial had a certain poignancy for the Oak Hill visitors because one student, Lori Goss, located the name of her father, lost in her infancy, on the Vietnam Memorial.

The memorial to soldiers lost or missing in Vietnam was officially dedicated on Saturday Nov. 13, a ceremony which drew a large crowd to Washington days before.

The Oak Hill residents got a chance to draw a breath as they stopped at a souvenir shop and ate lunch in a downtown cafeteria. The brief respite over, the group moved to Capitol Hill and the Smithsonian Institute. The American History and Aerospace Museums each drew a number of residents.

Finally, the Oak Hill tourists were whisked back to the Dulles airport where they experienced a two-hour delay due to a stubborn engine, which refused to move.

The excited but weary students returned home at 12:15 a.m. Stoner said he was exceptionally pleased with the trip and would like to sponsor another in a few years.[*]

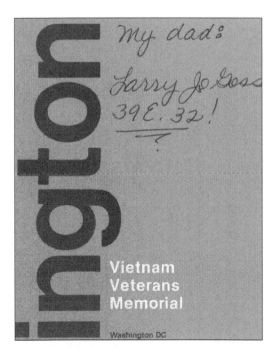

Vietnam
Veterans
Memorial

Washington DC

---

[*] Oak Hill High School newspaper, *The Oak Bark*, Nov. 11, 1982.

The brochure I wrote on at the Wall, indicating where I could find my dad's name.

As my sophomore year continued, I found that I was well liked by my teachers and my peers. They saw me as a leader and I happily accepted the role. With that came awards and honors, which imperfectly filled the space where my dad's praise would have been. It was enough to get me through, though I greatly missed his presence. This was especially true one night in July when a boy came to take me on my first date. My mom made sure I had a new outfit and took a picture before he arrived, then greeted him warmly. I thought of how my dad might have grilled him with a series of questions or made him pass a litmus test. That boy, Eric Reaves, would later become my husband. He's always had profound reverence for my dad's memory. And years later, I realized that he needed my dad, too.

The next year, my mom again placed a memorial in the local newspaper, and this time it caught the attention of a reporter, who asked to interview me. That morning, before the school bus picked me up, I carefully placed a framed picture of my dad in my backpack. It made me smile to think he was going to school with me, something I had wished for many times.

The photographer, Kim Kolarik, asked me to pose with the photo of my dad. I didn't know if I should smile. How could I? The feelings of that little girl who sat on her bed and listened to the words "Billy Don't Be A Hero" still resided inside. I thought I should probably smile because I loved my father, but I missed him so much.

When the article came out, the caption under the photo read "Lori Jo Goss holds a photo of father, Larry Jo Goss, she has never seen." That was not true. I *had* seen my dad. In fact, he spent three months with me—one of the months I was alive he spent at Field Medical School. I was four months old when he last held me. Even though I can't remember him, I did see my dad. Nevertheless, the

following article accompanied my picture in the local paper, the
Marion *Chronicle-Tribune*:

Lori Jo Goss speaks of her father-a man she never
knew-in a clear, strong voice.

It never waivers, it never cracks.

Maybe that's because this 16-year-old Oak Hill High
School junior has had 16 years to deal with her loss,
to understand it and to try to make what happened
to him in some way useful to her during her life.

Maybe it's because the only way she knows him is
through his diary, his letters, and the things people say about him.

And maybe it's because Lori is a very together,
very mature teenager who views life for what it is,
and makes no pretenses about what it is not.

Larry Jo Goss, her father, was killed in Vietnam
16 years ago Valentine's Day. She was six months old
then. For the last three years, Lori has published a
Valentine's Day poem in the Chronicle-Tribune classified ad section as a memorial to him. It is her
own very personal, yet very public tribute.

"I write poetry a lot. Mom mentioned the idea to
me, to write a poem and put it in the newspaper as
a memorial to him. It was the hardest thing-I have
no memory of him.

"Before I write, I always pray. I prayed and this
is what came out."

In Loving Memory of My Dad,
who was killed in Vietnam on Feb. 14, 1968

Dad died sixteen years ago today,
What he was like I really can't say.

I was only six months old,
But many great things about him I have been told.
He had a lot of love deep within his heart,
But it was God's will that he and
the world should part.
I used to lay in bed at night
and think of him and cry,
Then the Lord made me realize it was for the
best so I should hold my head up high.
And be proud of my Father for
giving this country his all,
Then giving his life when the Lord came to call.
To tell my Dad "I love you" was
a chance I never had,
So I wrote this poem to dedicate
it to Larry Jo Goss, My Dad.

"I don't remember a certain time that my Mom told me my Dad was dead. I just kind of knew. We had always gone and put flowers on his grave. I guess I just realized that death happens. God promises us that all of this is done in His will."

Goss kept a diary during his two-month stay in Vietnam. When he died, it was returned to his wife, Martha, along with letters and tapes she had sent to him.

"Dad kept a diary. The first page of the diary is Jan. 1. He writes, "This year is going to be one I'll always remember. I hope I can tell my grand-children about it."

"My kids will never know their grandfather. The only thing that still lives of my dad is me."

She says people tell her she looks like her dad and acts like him. But she says, she really doesn't know.

"My name is a lot like his."

Actually, Lori looks and acts like an average teen – her peaches and cream complexion accented by a smart-looking gray and lavender outfit. Her light brown hair is perfectly brushed back away from her face, every hair in its place.

She's active in school affairs – a member of the student council and secretary for her class, co-chairman for the prom, member of the drill team, a member of the Fellowship of Christian Athletes choir and a member of the Fellowship of Christian Athletes.

On the inside, however, Lori is perhaps a little older than most teens.

"A lot of people especially at this age resent their parents. I would just be glad to have a dad. It really hurts. I've had to grow up more, I think."

"Mom and I are super close. She's always trying to be a mom and a dad to me. No one can ever take Dad's place."

Her mother has since remarried and Lori says she accepts her step-father for the person he is.

"Before, I thought I should be sad. I think I miss him more the older I get. I have a boyfriend now, and there are just things I'd like to share with him."

But all Lori can share her thoughts with are pictures and letters. "Mom and he wrote every day. She has all these letters and tapes she sent him. We have a big barrel full of them in the barn, full of tape recordings and stacks of letters. When I read those letters I learn more about Dad. I haven't listened to the tapes yet, not yet."

She says her religious beliefs have helped her deal with her dad's absence.

"Mom and Dad used to go to church together. I think Mom always prayed to God that he would bring my dad home, and when he didn't, I think her faith was tested. Mom put a shell around herself, it really made her wonder."

"I've always said my bedtime prayers but something always made me want to know more about God."

"When I was in the seventh grade I went to this summer camp and I became a Christian. I just realized that you're nothing without Him."

The last day Goss wrote in his diary was Feb 12, two days before he was killed by mortar fire.

He wrote, "Today is a really bad day . . . Things are getting interesting."

He was 21 years and 7 months old. Lori knows this because she has his death certificate, and the telegrams notifying her mother of his death, the newspaper articles written when he died, the painting which was placed on his casket during the funeral, the one picture of the three of them together, the diary, the letters, and the tapes.

She has no memories.

She does, however, have a legacy of sorts. And it's a sad legacy, especially for a teenager.

"The one thing I've learned is you can't take life for granted. I look at me and my boyfriend and we're really happy now, but so were my parents. Life could end at any minute and you just have to make the best of what you have. There may never be a future."[*]

After the article ran, I received a letter from a member of the Indiana House of Representatives, P. Eric Turner, praising me for the article about my dad. I also received a letter from Sen. Richard Lugar of Indiana, congratulating me on being Rotary Student of the Month. Did my dad know? I didn't think so, but I knew I was at least honoring his name. The dream of becoming a United States senator had not yet been built in my mind, but it did the following year when I ran for office and was selected to that position at Hoosier Girls State. That week instilled in me feelings of patriotism and a deeper understanding of the things my father died for: freedom and our democratic way of life.

Could my dad see me marching each morning at Girls State? Did he know that with each step I thought of him and the marching he did at boot camp? Without his assurance that I was beautiful, valuable, or smart, I built my self-worth on the accolades I received from others. Each one I tucked away in the "my dad would be proud of me" portion of my heart.

Throughout the remainder of high school, I deeply felt my father's absence many times. Though my mom faithfully attended all my activities, it was hard for me to see her sit alone. She made friends with my girlfriends' mothers, but my friends' dads were there too. I longed for normalcy. Although I no longer wished on my birthday cake that my dad would come through the door, I still needed him as much as ever, and maybe a little more. As I performed on a piano, in the Fellowship of Athletes Choir, and on an athletic court as a dancer, I wanted him to be near.

---

[*] Sue Weber, "My Dad," Marion *Chronicle-Tribune*, Feb. 19, 1984.

*Left:* With my mom on Senior Night, March 1985.
*Right:* My Senior picture (1985).

People said he was watching over me, but I had no assurance of that being true. The one thing I was keenly aware of was that my mom and I had each other. The tragic events of February 14, 1968, had caused us to become a team of two. Though some things had changed, my fear of losing her remained.

During my senior year of high school, I attended my former school in Fairmount on a Student Council Student Exchange Day. As school was about to end, I was called to the office. The principal gave me the terrible news that my mom had been in a car accident. Thankfully, she was alive, but she had suffered a crushed ankle. My high school graduation was approaching, and she would need my help to get through it. Both sides of the family were in the audience as I sat on the stage with the other officers of my senior class. As I took my turn at the podium to read a poem I had written, I was mindful of another proud moment without my dad. Though my mom hid it well, many years later she confessed that it had been one of the saddest days of her life.

My boyfriend, Eric, presented me with a gift at my graduation open house that deeply touched us all: a colored pencil drawing depicting my dad in his forties, proudly standing by my side on my high school graduation day. It was Eric's way of acknowledging the pain of my father's absence while at the same time saying that my dad would have been very proud of me. While my head always believed that to be true, my heart needed to hear those words on that special day.

Eric's art portraying my dad standing beside me at my high school graduation.

As I fell in love with this boy, I wondered what my dad would think. Would he approve? What advice would he give me? Several months later, on a snowy day in December, we visited my dad's grave. Eric got down on one knee and said, "I wish your father were here so I could ask him for your hand in marriage. I would tell him that I promise to take care of you always. Lori, will you be my wife?"

Eric had my mother's engagement ring in his hand. She had saved it for me in the hope that one day I would wear the beautiful wedding set she and my father had picked out together, the day after he asked her to be his wife. With great joy, I said yes. It was another moment of happiness sprinkled with a dash of sadness.

I saved my father's veteran's benefits to pay for my wedding day. Although the benefits came at the cost of his life, I knew he would want my mom and me to feel his love in that way. By paying for a decorator and caterer, my mom and I got to spend the day relaxed, taking in each moment to the fullest. My father was our provider that day, the way I knew he would have been had he lived. I wanted a man to walk me down the aisle, so I chose my father's Great-Uncle Tom.

Uncle Tom and I had connected through his love of music. My dad's cousin, Nancy Hutchison Maddox, had attended one of my Fellowship of Christian Athletes choir performances and sent Uncle Tom a recording. Our connection also centered on our faith. Tom had spent many years in prison prior to becoming a follower of Christ, and now had a prison ministry in Kansas. He was a blood relative of my father's and an emotionally healthy male, two things I had little exposure to in my growing years. Uncle Tom loved golf and wanted me to enjoy it too. To improve my game, he gave me private golf lessons. Being cared for by a male was something I had not experienced since fourth grade, and it felt good. He enjoyed my company and Eric's and treated us like we were his kids.

As I placed my arm inside of his as the wedding march played, I hoped my dad was looking down from heaven. He would have been very grateful that his Uncle Tom stood in his place. My uncle walked me down to my mom, who stood alone just like she had at my school events. I put my sadness away, for a young, handsome man was waiting for me at the end of the aisle, and he wanted to make all my dreams come true.

On our wedding day, Dec. 19, 1987, with
Great-Uncle Tom Hutchison, my mom, and Eric.

# PART II
## *The Search*

With Eric at the Vietnam Veterans Welcome Home
parade in Chicago, June 13, 1986.

# CHAPTER TEN

# Looking for Clues

E ven before we got married, Eric was a part of the search. The respect he showed for my need to know my dad was just one of the
many things I loved about him. Along with the graduation picture, he and his beloved teacher, Mr. Pete Beck, made me a shadow
box of pine that held my dad's picture and his Purple Heart. I knew
we would proudly display it in our home for many years to come.

Eric also made me a scrapbook. Mom helped by sharing all the
items she had saved and protected for years. Included were things
Dad sent home in his letters, such as newspaper clippings, propaganda, and Vietnamese money. He wanted us to know about the
things he experienced during the year we were apart. He told Mom
to save them so he could make a scrapbook for me to take to school.
My kind and caring father was in the middle of a deadly war, yet he
was thinking about his little girl's future. As I looked through every
item he sent home, I found evidence of what he valued, how he
felt, and who he was. He even wrote in the margins of the cartoons
and poems, providing another window into his heart. He hoped he
would be there to tell us the stories. His absence left so many unanswered questions.

I did take the scrapbook to school, but not to my own history class. Alan Coats, a local Vietnam Veteran, invited me to speak with him at local high schools. I told the students about my dad as his audio tapes played in the background. You could hear the choppers overhead and the cheerful voice of my dad telling us how much he loved us.

That was his legacy. He deeply loved us and needed to make sure we knew. He had almost two years to express his love to my mom, which gave him the assurance that she knew. But I was a four-month-old baby when he left. The moment he received his orders to serve with the Marines on the front lines, he knew the probability of making it home was slim. This would leave my mom with the difficult task of making sure I knew the depth of his love for me. Often at the end of his letters he told my mom, "Kiss Lori for me."

For most of my life, I understood the meaning of those words, but it wasn't until I completed the search that I truly understood the depth of his love. It seemed fitting that the search officially began in the Windy City, where I was born, at the Chicago Vietnam Veterans Welcome Home parade with Eric in 1986. I had not been to Illinois since my dad moved my mom and me back to Indiana when I was two months old, but I had photos of the three of us outside the apartment where we lived. We had spent two wonderful months together there before he received his orders for Vietnam. Though my mind did not remember our time together, my heart did—he and I were bonded spiritually and emotionally. I had to find out if he was still alive.

Eric and I arrived early on June 13, 1986. We found a group from Kilo Company and walked with them. An estimated 300,000 spectators cheered for our Vietnam Veterans and finally welcomed them home as the parade of Vietnam Veterans and their families passed by. I had mixed emotions. My childhood sheltered me from the harsh reality that they had not been welcomed home after the war. I respected the men I walked with and they respected my dad. Not because they knew him personally, but because he was a corpsman. I asked everyone I met if they knew Larry Jo Goss, but no one did. I believed one day we would find someone. It would just take more time. Eric and I wore POW/MIA shirts because, in my heart, my dad was still missing. His MIA status had changed to KIA eighteen years before, but I needed to find someone who knew for sure. His Grandma Bradford died believing he was still alive. Could she have been right?

My dad's mom, Marie, did not believe he was dead either. Almost three years before the parade, she took me to a local restaurant, Rosie's Little Italy, for my sixteenth birthday. I had very few memories of spending time with her—and none on my birthday. My dad's youngest brother, Jimmy would be joining us. My dad loved him and wanted to make sure someone took good care of him. I had a lot of compassion for Jimmy, whose life was spent confined to a wheelchair without the use of his arms or his legs. I agreed to go to dinner with Marie because Jimmy would be there.

Sitting in the dark restaurant as I enjoyed my favorite Italian food, Marie said, "You know, your dad is not really buried at the IOOF Cemetery." I listened intently as she went on to say, "Your mom would not have the casket opened so your Grandpa Tom and I went back to the funeral home after the viewing and demanded that the funeral home director show us what was inside. When he opened the casket, there was nothing in there."

I did not know what to say. Could it be that my dad really was alive? I wanted to believe her story, but something inside me did not trust her. As soon as I got home, I told my mother what Marie claimed. She was angry. I was hurt and confused. I knew Marie was selfish, but to tell me a lie—and that lie, of all—on my birthday seemed cruel beyond comprehension.

My mom told me that Marie was mad at her for not having the casket opened. Mom said she wanted to remember my dad the way he was. She gave me the name of the funeral home director and the name of the funeral home. The funeral home director was still living but retired. The receptionist offered to give him my phone number. It seemed like weeks as I waited on his call.

Images of my dad living in Vietnam came back to my mind. In those images, he was working and saving his money, waiting on the chance to escape the country and make it back to my mom and me. I envisioned him coming to our house. I replayed in my mind the picture of him embracing me first and then he and I walking hand in hand together as he went to surprise my mom. I had thought of their reunion many times. With those thoughts fresh in my mind again, I finally received a call from the funeral home director.

"I remember your grandmother and her husband coming to the funeral home after everyone else had left," he said. "He had been drinking. They demanded that I open the casket but I assure you that I could not. There was a Navy escort guarding the casket and my instructions were that it could only be opened at the request of your mom."

His voice was kind and assuring. I believed him, but my disappointment with Marie remained. I wondered if her guilt over spending my dad's money made her believe her own lie. If it weren't for her, he would not have been drafted. My mom blamed her for his death and still does to this day.

Marie's story, while false, created more doubt in my mind that my dad's remains were truly buried under his tombstone. I looked through the government letters my mom received and found the two from Lt. Col. Edward J. LaMontagne. If he had been in charge* on February 14, 1968, maybe he could help me find Stan Burkart, my dad's good friend from boot camp, and other men who had served with my dad. Surely one of them knew the answers to the questions that spun in my head, like: "Was my dad really killed in action in Vietnam? Since the papers say he was identified by dental records, but he had false teeth, were his remains really recovered? Is it possible my dad was taken as a POW and still alive? Since my dad's dog tags were not returned, couldn't it be possible that his body wasn't

---

* In 2020, I found out that Lieutenant Colonel LaMontagne was not the battalion commander on February 14, 1968. He took the place of Lieutenant Colonel Cook, who rotated out while my dad's remains lay on Valentine's Ridge.

recovered? Could my dad have escaped imprisonment, infiltrated the country of Vietnam, and be waiting for the time when he can return to my mom and me?"

I know the last question seemed farfetched, but it was a dream I had played in my mind several times since I was a little girl.

I read each line of LaMontagne's letters over and over and wondered what caused my dad to "disappear." Why was he not found when they went "searching" for him? Did they really find him on March 6, 1968, as the telegrams said? If so, what happened to him during the time he was MIA?

\* \* \* \* \*

I grew up talking about my dad to anyone who would listen, but I had no connection to the military. Finding the men who knew the truth about what happened to my dad was a goal I believed I would one day achieve, but I had no idea how. That all changed on my twentieth birthday, when I received a letter stating that the Third Marine Division had awarded me a scholarship.

The notification letter provided me with a veteran's contact information, and I excitedly sent him a letter with a question. Could he help me find Stan and Lieutenant Colonel LaMontagne? His reply was discouraging. He had no information on Stan Burkart and suggested that I discontinue the search:

Insofar as your father's Battalion Commander, Lt Col La Montagne, my very honest opinion is that you should not even try to locate him, Lori Jo.

I can understand your feelings about wanting to know everything you can about your father. It has to be difficult to have never known him. BUT please understand that he did something very special for you and your mother, and for his Country and his Corps. It is never a pleasant thing to live with, but it's something you can be very proud of! And I'm certain that had he lived, he would have been very proud of you, as you've grown into a loving and caring adult.

I appreciated his kindness but would not give up. I continued to tell the story about my mom and dad, hoping that someone with information would surface.

On the twenty-first anniversary of my dad's death, I changed the memorial poem to reflect the things I knew about him. It was my hope that those who knew more would contact me. Soon after it ran in the newspaper, I received two letters from my dad's fourth-grade teacher, Mrs. Bailey. I also received a note from another person who encouraged me in my search:

Lori,

There really aren't words to tell you how deeply this touches my soul! To say it is wonderful isn't enough!

So many children see their daddies every day and yet never find this kind of love!

I can only imagine how your mother must have felt! She deserves so much admiration for helping you to know your dad—for keeping him alive!

And, as you share his life with your children, you can let him live on for years!

Over the last six years I've tried very hard to put into prose or poetry my feelings on "Daddies and death." Your love is just one more proof of my feelings that Daddies don't die.

He's looking down and smiling proudly at his little girl. "Though he is dead he still speaks." Hebrews 11:4

Lois

Eric and I were not yet parents, but we had so much love to give. Nothing could contain our excitement on that summer day in June when our baby boy, Christopher Eric Reaves, was born. He was named after his father, but he also carried my father's genes. I think that's one reason I wanted so many children: so a part of my dad could live on. We would teach our children about their wonderful Grandpa Larry.

In 1990, a contest was held to elicit designs for a Vietnam Veterans monument in Marion, Indiana, my father's hometown. Eric's design was selected out of the seven that were submitted. I had never felt prouder of him. His vision was a seven-foot-tall monument made of black granite that looked like a slice of the Wall in Washington, D.C. It was unveiled on Veterans Day that year.

Christopher was four and a half months old. As I held him in my arms at the ceremony, I prayed that he would grow to understand his grandpa's sacrifice and be blessed by the legacy his grandpa left behind. My mom, maternal extended family, and Eric's parents also attended that day. Eric had the opportunity to speak and honor the thirty-two Grant County men who were killed in Vietnam:

| Army Spec. 4 Rollie Lee Bolden<br>Nov. 17, 1965 | Army Spec. 4 Joseph D. Guerrero<br>Feb. 6, 1966 |
| Marine Cpl. Thomas Jefferson Fears<br>March 2, 1966 | Marine Sgt. Marvin Glassburn<br>March 21, 1966 |
| Army Spec. 4 David A. Scott<br>May 6, 1966 | Marine Cpl. William F. Clover Jr.<br>May 12, 1967 |
| Army Pfc. Ralph W. Blackerby<br>May 23, 1967 | Marine Staff Sgt. David Dixon<br>June 2, 1967 |
| Marine Pfc. Larry Lee Morris<br>June 7, 1967 | Marine G/Sgt. Emmett Lee Booth<br>June 11, 1967 |
| Marine Cpl. Edmund "Bill" Travis<br>June 27, 1967 | Marine L/Cpl. Mark Black<br>August 14, 1967 |
| Marine Pfc. Terry V. Leach<br>Sept. 2, 1967 | Army Pfc. Donald Cutler<br>Sept. 3, 1967 |
| Army Cpl. Carl Dingus<br>Feb. 3, 1968 | Navy HM2 Larry Goss<br>Feb. 14, 1968 |
| Army Pfc. Terry L. Weaver<br>March 2, 1968 | Army Spec. 4 Larry Dee Sherman<br>March 13, 1968 |
| Army Spec. 4 Lynn Allen Pierson<br>April 23, 1968 | Navy Tmcs Harry Mitchell<br>May 6, 1968 |
| Marine L/Cpl. Michael Travis<br>June 7, 1968 | Army Spec. 4 Stephen Wright<br>July 9, 1968 |
| Marine Cpl. Steven Brandenburg<br>Aug. 19, 1968 | Marine Cpl. William Berry<br>Sept. 21, 1968 |
| Army Cpl. Donald J. Smith<br>Jan. 19, 1969 | Army Spec. 4 Robert H. Parcher<br>Feb. 8, 1969 |
| Army Spec. 4 Jack C. Lee<br>June 11, 1969 | Navy HM3 Steven Poe<br>Aug. 20, 1969 |
| Army Sgt. Kenneth Alan Richey<br>Dec. 7, 1969 | Army Pfc. Danny Fankboner<br>Dec. 7, 1969 |
| Army Spec. 4 Daniel N. Heater<br>March 12, 1970 | Army Sgt. Keith Lochner<br>April 22, 1970 |

Juanita Travis was also at the memorial dedication. She lost two sons in Vietnam.

*Left:* Behind the monument on the right, I'm holding baby Christopher in my arms with Eric, his mom, and my maternal family (October 1990).

*Right:* The shadowbox that Pete Beck and Eric made for me (March 1984).

* * * * *

Fifteen months later, our second son, Cody Lawrence Reaves, was born. It was important to me that we name him after my dad. As I labored in the hospital, my obstetrician helped us come up with the name. "Larry" sounded too old-fashioned, but Lawrence sounded just right. As our boys grew, my mom often talked about how much of my father she saw in them: Chris's love for George Carlin and the way he loved to make others laugh, Cody's determination and the smile he always had on his face.

As my husband and I raised our young family, joy filled our days.

# CHAPTER ELEVEN

# Grieving Times Two

In 1995, our world came crashing down around us and I needed my dad more than I ever had before. I had known God as my Heavenly Father since 1980 and believed that He only wanted what was best for me. My view of a father was of a perfect being who embodied complete love. I believed that although God allowed me to experience trauma in my childhood, He was going to bless me in adulthood with a healthy family and children who were living parts of my dad.

But the events of 1995 changed me. Although my faith remained intact, God no longer fit the image I once had of Him. He was bigger, unpredictable, miraculous, and in control—yet willing to allow my heart to be broken beyond what I could understand. I knew God was love but I did not feel loved by Him. I wrestled with God, but never let go. I am thankful that He did not let go of me either.

The rollercoaster started with an unexpected call from my dear friend Ed Pereira. He met a man named Bill who said he served with Larry Goss in Vietnam. Ed asked if I wanted to talk with him. I was excited to think that the man who held the answers to my questions had lived in my hometown the whole time. The man was unwilling to meet me in person but would talk with me on the phone. Late one afternoon, we finally talked. He told me my dad had been taken as a prisoner in Vietnam and that they found him weeks later, hanging from a tree and shot between the eyes.

Something inside me doubted his honesty. Before grieving with this new picture in my mind, I needed to do some digging. I found out where his wife worked and went to see her. As soon as I told her who I was, she said, "My husband served in Vietnam, but not with your dad. He wanted to be connected to a hometown hero, so he made the whole thing up." I was disappointed and dismayed, but simultaneously relieved.

Weeks later we hosted friends for dinner, and I shared that story with them. They were equally appalled. My friend Beth said, "You know, I think my dad can help you."

Her father was Col. Wayne Ellis. I had no idea my friend's dad had served in the military. He had lived in my hometown my whole life, but we had never met. He offered to write a letter to *The VVA Veteran** and screen each response.

I did not allow myself to feel much hope after my disappointment with Bill, but I was thankful to have someone offer to help. Though finding the men who served with my dad was important to me, my focus was on raising my two boys and giving them the life my dad would have given me.

Then on April 24, 1995, our second son, Cody, got his neck stuck in the power window of our SUV. I was sitting in the back seat right beside him when it happened, and yet he nearly died. In fact, he was lifeless for some time when a nurse who happened to be driving by while I carried his body into a local car dealership stopped to assist me in doing CPR. My sense of security was shattered. I needed my dad and he was not there. Little did I know that my dad's friend from Home Corner, Gary Mayo, worked at that dealership and was aware of the accident. He told me later that he

---

* This bi-monthly magazine is a publication of Vietnam Veterans of America, Inc.

had prayed my dad would help me that night. He felt my family had suffered enough.

I don't know if God gives power to those in heaven to help us on Earth, but I believe wholeheartedly that God saved our little boy that night. I believe He was also at work in Casper, Wyoming, orchestrating interactions that allowed me to find a man who knew my dad in Vietnam.

* * * * *

Dr. Jerry Behrens, an orthopedic surgeon in Casper, Wyoming, did not subscribe to *The VVA Veteran*, but New Jersey police officer Ed Salau did. Ed had been a tank platoon sergeant stationed at the Rockpile in 1968. Ed had called Jerry in March about the request he had read in the magazine, but the note to call Ed back had been misplaced. By the time Jerry responded, Ed no longer had the magazine.

Linda Watson, a former Army nurse in Vietnam and friend of Jerry's, ran the local Veterans Center. She went through each issue of the magazine until she found the right one. She circled Colonel Ellis's request and placed it on Jerry's desk at 8:00 a.m. the next day. Her act of kindness, along with Ed's, helped Jerry find a way to me. Jerry contacted Colonel Ellis by mail:

Tuesday, 16 May, 1995

Dear Col. Ellis,

I am responding to the request for information about the death of Larry Jo Goss, one of my corpsmen, placed in the March issue of the V.V.A. newspaper.

Larry was a friend, and although I was not on the Kilo Co. patrol West of the Ca Lu combat base when he was killed on 14 Feb.

1968, I do know some particulars of that action that took about 11 lives and I did personally handle Larry's remains when the bodies were recovered about one month later and brought back inside the perimeter at Ca Lu.

I would be honored to help you, Lori, and her family with what I know of his death. It was a terrible day—made worse because we couldn't recover the bodies until one month later.

Colonel Ellis mailed Jerry's letter to me and told me to expect a call. When the doctor's call arrived, I walked down to my basement with a paper and pen in hand. I did not want to miss a single word. These are the notes I took of what Jerry told me:

Company commander killed with your dad was the son of a Navy admiral.

Marine Captain (Conger) did a heroic thing that night. Dad was a senior corpsman, killed, they were leaderless. Bill Conger in India Company volunteered to go on a helicopter and he slid down a rope at night in the dark and took over survivors and brought them off the hill with North Vietnam Army all around them. Works for National Car Rental.

Your dad talked about medical school, he was realistic and had his head really screwed on. I said "Wow, I hope this guy makes it through."

Valentine's Ridge is burned indelibly in our minds. What the bodies looked like after they had been in the jungle for one month. I threw up in my mouth and swallowed it and said please God get me through it.

Your dad had his personal ID in utility jacket in his left-hand pocket over his heart. It was slimy. His own picture ID. I said, "Oh God, Larry."

The bodies were torn up, but they were definitely identifiable.

Killed by mortar rounds. Company commander and executive officer and Dad were looking at a map and a mortar round came in and literally hit right on top of them.

All 11 men killed that day and couldn't bring any of them back. Bodies stayed up there for one month. Very demoralizing knowing we couldn't go up there to get them. Recon Marines. Bodies all right there. North Vietnamese had not done anything to them.

Originally, a small party was going to sneak in and load bodies on plastic. When they got up there and got the bodies loaded, they were exhausted. People providing security had to come in and load bodies. Over 100 degrees. They were falling down from heat exhaustion. Brought them down to the bottom of the road to where we had an LZ. Chaplin Richard Black, the major, and I put on gloves. Went down and got ID to record who they were. No way to tell otherwise. We put them in body bags and an honor guard stood there with them.

I remember I was at the Rockpile. Your dad came in and stayed for a while at the Rockpile. A lot of the corpsmen were not E5s. When he got into Vietnam, he was automatically made company corpsman because of his rank. Same as a sergeant. He was their senior corpsman. I remember the time he spent with me, he was a very bright guy. I was 26 years old.

I asked Jerry why they went up the ridge. My mind needed to make sense of why my dad was killed. He said he did not know.

"I was an MD just out of internship and I was a battalion surgeon," he explained. "I was five or six miles away at the Rockpile.

Battalion surgeon is the head of all corpsmen at the Battalion Aid Station. Then each company had several corpsmen."

"Can you tell me about my dad's training?" I asked him.

"They deliberately gave some corpsmen more training," Jerry replied. "Your dad was a rank or two higher than most corpsmen that came over there. There were other corpsmen lower than him. I assume other corpsmen were out on the ridge that day. He was the only corpsman to die that day."

I had so many more questions.

"How many men went up the ridge?" I asked.

"Three platoons in a company," Jerry said. "A company would have been 100–200 men. I took his personal ID out of his pocket and it said Larry Goss. It was so hard. It was so putrid. There were at least three radiomen with that command group."

Jerry also talked about heroism and said that my dad did not run from danger. I didn't understand what all of that meant. As I listened to Jerry describe his brief relationship with my dad, I was struck by his belief in my father's abilities and his dreams. I had always heard that my dad wanted to be a doctor but had no idea whether he truly would have pursued that dream. Jerry knew. He believed my dad would have made a fine doctor had he made it home. I could hear the sadness in his voice.

"You are doing a good job and we are proud of you, Lori," Jerry said. That meant so much to me.

Before I had the time to grieve and digest this new information, I was confronted with devastating news. The baby boy I was carrying had duodenal atresia and, 30 percent of the time, this is present in babies who have Down syndrome. As I had done many times in my life, I tucked away the information Jerry gave me and focused on the here and now. I needed my dad like never before.

I spent my twenty-eighth birthday getting an amniocentesis. Days later, my mom came to our house to care for the boys while we awaited the call. As the nurse confirmed the diagnosis, Eric and I clung to each other and sobbed.

One loss on top of another—I was grieving times two. My dad really had been killed in Vietnam and the baby I had written to daily (in a journal) seemed to have just died, in a way, as well. We named our third son Colton Michael. He spent two weeks in the hospital, hooked up to tubes after having lifesaving surgery to repair his duodenum. He also had a small hole in his heart. I had trouble wrapping my mind around God as our creator. Was this His will too? The little boy we had dreamed of only existed in our minds.

I loved working with individuals with disabilities. I believe that they deserve excellent care, and I've seen firsthand just how important good care is to families raising a child with a disability. I just did not want our son to be made fun of, to struggle, or to feel pain. I knew we would need a good support system but I was used to being on the giving end. Two years later, we learned that Colton also had autism. While this new diagnosis provided a sense of clarity, it also compounded my grief.

Cody, Colton, and Chris in November 1995

# CHAPTER TWELVE

# My Dad's Corpsmen

God knew of my desire for a daughter. I needed to see a little girl of my own receive the love of her dad. The month after my thirtieth birthday, God made that dream come true. Courtnee Jo Reaves was born in August 1997. She was everything I prayed she would be: healthy and full of joy. Watching her grow was a great blessing. Years later, my heart overflowed as I watched her study for hours so she could get into dental school—just like her grandpa had studied for exams in corps school.

Courtnee was only six months old when I received an email that re-opened the search, just two days before the thirtieth anniversary of my dad's death. It was from one of my dad's corpsmen, Ray Felle. He received my contact information from Jerry. He wanted to give me a copy of an 8mm tape that he took on a patrol four days before my dad was killed. Ray ended his email by offering to tell me about the day my dad was killed.

My head was filled with questions mixed with elation. I wanted Ray to tell me everything he knew about that day. I hoped that the questions I had been turning over in my head would be answered by this man who was a corpsman like my father. I wanted to see footage of the place where my dad had spent his last six weeks on this earth.

When the video arrived, I waited to play it until after my children were asleep. Tears softly fell as I watched my dad look at Ray for approximately eight seconds and then wave and smile before he walked away. There was a skip in his step that spoke of an urgency to get to his next task—he was a man on a mission who exuded joy in the midst of horrific conditions.

That was the last video taken of him. His smile to Ray is forever engrained in my mind. Ray also sent me a military record that showed entries from the battle on Valentine's Ridge. Reading each entry caused my heart to beat heavily.

A screen shot of the last video taken of my dad,
February 9, 1968. *Photo credit Ray Felle.*

DECLASSIFIED

UNCLASSIFIED

JOURNAL

UNIT OR SECTION
3d Battalion, 9th Marines

PLACE
THON SON LAM, RVN

FROM (Date and hour)
140001H

TO (Date and hour)
142400H Feb 1968

| TIME IN | TIME OUT | SERIAL NO | DATE TIME GROUP | INCIDENTS MESSAGES ORDERS | ACTION TAKEN |
|---|---|---|---|---|---|
| 1003 | | 1 | 140945H | Approximately 200 civilians arrived at CA LU 008 this morning. MEDCAP is being held, and the refugees moved down to the village. One of the refugees claims to be a popular force soldier who escaped from the NVA. He will be sent to Camp J. J. CARROLL on the first available transportation. | S-2, 4th Mar. |
| 1645 | | 2 | 141645H | Company K at XD 992451 receiving small arms and .50 caliber fire followed by 60mm mortars, 81mm and artillery missions returned fire. AO in the area. Probable enemy positions XD 987456 and XD 975462. | S-2, 4th Mar. |
| 1847 | | 3 | 141500H | Company L found two (2) M32 fragmentation grenades at YD 001564, apparently had fallen off returning convoy. | S-2, 4th Mar. S-4 |
| 1900 | | 4 | 141900H | Company K still receiving mortar fire. Estimate new position at XD 993450. The Company commander and the Executive Officer both are wounded seriously. | S-2, 4th Mar. |
| 1933 | | 5 | 141935H | Company K, 3d Plt with CP group unable to move because of heavy casualties. Enemy strength and positions still unknown. Artillery being fired at XD 975458. 1st, 2d, and 3d Platoons are separated. The Battalion Executive Officer moved to YD 005455 with a platoon security from Company I to coordinate communications with Company K. The 1st Platoon then moved down to Route #9. | S-2, 4th Mar. |
| 2106 | | 6 | 142106H | Casualties brought to CA LU 002 by motor vehicle from 1st Platoon Company K position on Route #9. | S-2, 4th Mar. |
| 2134 | | 7 | 142134H | The S-3A moved to Company K, 3d Platoon at XD 987448 assumed command as The Company Commander of Company K. Received incoming mortars while being inserted. Wounded medevaced by chopper. Company K 1st, 2d and remnants of the 4th Platoon are | |

ENCLOSURE (1)
B

DECLASSIFIED

Ray and I communicated by email and he answered my questions the best he could. I wanted to know more about my dad's rank and why the other corpsmen on Valentine's Ridge survived. I also wanted to know if it was Ray who took over my dad's position as senior corpsman after he was listed as MIA. Although this question may have seemed insignificant to many, my mind was trying to make sense of my dad's death. Was it really his time? If he had somehow survived that one battle, would he have made it home?

Ray served under my dad and was a "hospitalman" (E-5). Ray survived the battle of Valentine's Ridge and safely made it home. Could it be that my dad's determination to do all he could in some way contributed to his death? I wanted to make sense of all I was learning. If my dad had been in Ray's rank and platoon, I thought, he might have survived the battle on Valentine's Ridge and possibly made it home from Vietnam. I remembered the audio tape my dad sent my mom: "Don't worry about me. I am bunking with the captain so I will be safe." That thought was logical to me. My dad had worked hard to earn the position of senior corpsman. He was in the leadership group called the Command Post (CP). One year later, I found out my thoughts were not far off from the truth.

On February 27, 1999, I emailed Ray:

I understand that they left the KIAs for three weeks, but what I wanted to know was did they leave them in the spot they died or move them all together before you guys were ordered to leave them?

Ray replied:

No one died in the portion of my platoon that made it off the ridge on the 14th so my guess is that they were all grouped together. This is customary after a battle to keep track of KIAs, so they don't become MIAs. When we went back three weeks later, they were all in one general location. I did not go back on the hills. It was very painful and a corpsman was not necessary on the ridge. I waited with Lt Holladay on route 9 and the Marines went up to get them. They brought the remains down in ponchos that we all had. They are like a big square of rain proof material with a head hole in it.

I did not know what to make of this. Marines are not supposed to leave their men behind.

Until Jerry's call in 1995, I did not have a picture in my mind of how my dad died. After our call, the image I now saw was one of my father, the CO, and the XO all looking at a map. They were distracted by their need to understand their location and come up with their next tactical move. A mortar landed in the middle of them and they were all instantly killed. But this image changed after Ray connected me to Doc Marty Russell, another one of my father's corpsmen. Doc Russell, Third Platoon, was one of the men who spent the night on the ridge and fought the NVA the next day.

My heart beat with excitement when Doc Russell said he would talk to me. Was this the person I had been looking for, the one who knew what had happened to my dad? As we spoke, I did my best to capture every word on paper:

Doc Russell: Your father was a brave man. I saw him run from one battle to the other. I saw his body and I was sure he was shielding someone from the way his body was shaped. He was shielding this Marine.

Me: You don't know if my dad died later?

Doc Russell: He was OK after the battle. He was with the CP group. He was unharmed. The afternoon when India Company came up to get us off the hill, Don E. Carter was standing over me with a M16. My thoughts I remember thinking was that Larry deserved some kind of recognition because he was so brave and was shielding that guy. I don't know his name. He was also killed. Your dad deserves a Bronze Star for valor. That has been my thought for years. The only one that could do that was the officers and they all died. He came over to help me treat a guy. A guy was shot in the upper arm three times. I was starting to treat him, and your dad came over and I know your dad was with the CP group so to come over to help me was a long way in that. He came over and helped and they took the guy away to the side. The executive officer was on his knees saying the Lord's Prayer. Blood would go out about a foot every time his heart would beat, and another corpsman was paralyzed. We had to leave him. He was scared to death. There are parts of it I don't remember. Some went back to the perimeter back at Ca Lu and some went to the other perimeter. When I awoke it was about twilight. I was standing at a line of Marines and two or three were dead. Then I went up the hill and saw your dad and another Marine and they were both dead.

Me: Was my dad with the CP group?

Doc Russell: Where I saw his body, the CP group could have moved away from your dad or your dad could have gone off to help another Marine. He was not far from the CP group. There was line of Marines at the bottom of the hill. I was on the left side and your dad was on the right side. I remember orders to pull out.

Me: Can you help me understand why they left the bodies?

Doc Russell: They decimated the whole company, hurt or wounded. We were so decimated, every one of us were wounded or killed. Kilo went on a day patrol and they sent India up the next day. The truth is I was so depressed for years after I got out of there and I drank heavily and stopped three years ago. I got off of antidepressants. The battle was two days. Ray went with a group that went back to the perimeter at Ca Lu. I was with the Third Platoon and we stayed there that night and had another battle. I only remember bits and pieces. The corpsman with the CP group was paralyzed and we left the corpsman there — it terrified him. We took the CO over and had to leave the XO. The XO fell silent and we checked him, and he died, and we put him off the trail. He was recovered the next day.

Me: Why would this corpsman be with the CP group?

Doc Russell: In general, a corpsman would stay with the wounded until someone comes to get them. I don't know if your dad had him taken somewhere or what. He was uphill laying parallel with the body and a foot above the guy. A radioman, Wentzell—your dad was about ten feet up the hill from him.

Afterward, I sent Ray this message:

I called Martin Russell. Would love to talk to you about my and your conversations with him. He said that the radioman, Don E. Carter, survived and would possibly know more about my dad's death.

Thank you for linking me to Martin. I'm not sure if it was good for him but it was helpful for me.

Any ideas on how to find Don E. Carter?

From talking to Martin Russell, it sounds like my dad was not killed at the second entry (when the mortars came in). Sounds like he wasn't killed right away like I thought. I wonder where the story of the captain and my dad reading the map comes in here? I know I may never get a complete story, but the pieces seem to be fitting together and the puzzle more complete. Tell me about this idea that my dad's body was positioned such that this guy thought he was shielding someone's body when he was killed.

How do we get a list of everyone who survived the two-day battle? I think someone has to know more details about my dad's death. I really want to keep searching for more.

My training as a licensed clinical social worker gave me empathy for Vietnam Veterans. I did not want my questions to cause them to relive their trauma, but Ray wanted to talk on the phone that evening.

"My thought was that your dad was killed immediately," Ray said, "but Russell said your dad came down and talked with him, so I'm gonna go with what he said."

Ray gave me the name of the corpsman who took my father's place as the senior corpsman of Kilo 3/9: Doc Dennis White. I sent Doc an email and he replied:

Dear Lori,

While I was in your father's unit, I did not arrive there until a few days after he died. Unfortunately, I did not know your father. Strictly from my own perspective as a former Navy Hospital Corpsman who served with the Marines and other places over a thirty-year career, we corpsmen (your father included) were a group of young men who received schooling in keeping people alive under the most extreme circumstances known to man. We were also told time and time again that WE were charged with the responsibility of keeping "everyone alive." We were young and as a group believed not in war but in a sort of sacred trust that saving life was the expected. Any death was a personal failure. Corpsmen have and continue to take risks to save lives without regard for their own personal safety. Not because we think of ourselves as heroes, but because it is that sacred trust and belief inside of us.

While I do not personally know your Dad, I know him as my brother! I know who he was that terrible day because I know us as a group. That day your father was terrified, initially confused about the entire situation but singularly focused on one thing above all else. As soon as the first cry for "corpsman" was heard, your father essentially disassociated with everything but that wounded man's needs. With strength and resolve deep within him, he did everything and anything possible to keep as many Marines as possible alive. While I do not know exactly how he died, I am as certain as I can be that his last ounce of energy was spent trying to keep another man alive.

His death that day was not fair to you or to him. Too many people died over there. You and your dad were cheated out of a relationship that cannot be undone. And there is no answer to why he had to die that day, or at all. No one can answer that for you, certainly not me. Although this may seem insignificant to you next to your loss, because your dad was there during his tour, there are many, many men who he kept alive that survived and were able to go home—because your father was there to stop the bleeding and to keep them breathing. Be proud of what your father was and did for humanity in the face of the inhumanity of war. Honor him, not the war that took him from you.

I am not sure whether what I have written is of any help to you, Lori. I hope in some way it is. If there are any other questions you may have or ways in which you feel I can help, please let me know.

I treasured Dennis's email because it spoke so eloquently of corpsmen and their important role in war. I realized that Dennis was right about my dad keeping men alive who got to go home. I'm sure there were many. And I got to meet one, Camron Carter, in 2015.

Ray continued to answer many of my questions via email. I wanted to know who was in charge on February 15 as my dad's body lay on the ridge. Was this the explanation for why his dog tags were not returned? Ray told me that a Lieutenant Wszolek was the lone lieutenant there on the night of the 14th and day of the 15th. I wanted to contact him but didn't have his information and didn't have any time to search—I had four children ranging in age from two to twelve and a baby boy on the way. They needed to be my focus now. Thanks to Jerry, I knew my dad was dead. Nothing could change that reality, so I put it all away once more.

Around Christmas 1999, Jerry sent me a tribute he wrote to my dad. He placed it at the Moving Wall, the half-size replica of the one in D.C., when it came to his town.

> Larry, you died on Valentine's Day 1968, two months to the day after you left for Vietnam. You and the ten Marines of Kilo Co who perished were close together on the Wall like you died on the ridge west of Ca Lu. I told your daughter whom I spoke to several years ago about your dreams of becoming a doctor. She was surprised that anyone outside the family knew about why you had to drop out of pre-med and enlist and the painful memories associated with that. I know it helped her to talk to me. You have three wonderful grandchildren.

Jerry loved his corpsmen. When he lost one in Vietnam, he lost a piece of his heart. I was thankful he chose to send this to me. It confirmed the story I was told about Marie spending my dad's admissions deposit to Ball State and the money he had saved for college. Jerry did not know I'd had a fourth child since the last time we spoke. Eight years later, he would meet that child when we met for the first time at a Vietnam Veterans reunion in Orlando, Florida.

Our fifth and final child arrived in early January 2000. Casey Jordan Reaves filled our lives with laughter and looked like the spitting image of my dad. The first sign was his dark brown hair—his siblings all had either red or brown hair.

We spent his first Christmas at Aunt Mona's house. I gave her a picture of Casey and Courtnee that reminded her of a photo of her with my dad, and she brought it out to show me. I had never seen it before, and I could not believe the resemblance. Oh, how that picture brought me joy! God knew exactly what I needed. Though I did not know yet how much Casey would look like my father in adulthood, I had evidence that my dad would live on through his grandkids.

*Top:* Mona and Larry Jo (October 1946).

*Bottom:* Courtnee Jo and Casey Jordan (November 2000).

# CHAPTER THIRTEEN

# Pieces of the Truth Revealed

I did my best to maintain a balance between the family Eric and I were raising and the pull of the past. I was now a mom of five and I wanted to give my children the best of me. While I had set aside the search and pushed my questions about my dad's death to the back corner of my brain, pieces of the truth continued to fall into my lap. Perhaps it was God's provision and His placement of clues in my life exactly when He knew I needed them. I juggled my roles as a mom, wife, and daughter as I kept one foot in my family and the other in embracing each new wave of the search.

I did not know what to make of the things Doc Russell told me, because they were different from what Jerry was told. I felt like I was trying to put together a puzzle without the help of the picture on the box. Doc Russell had no reason to make up the things he told Ray and me, and Ray trusted the accuracy of Doc's story. Doc Russell had also sent Ray a letter in addition to the email that included a drawing of the location where he saw my dad's body. In my mind, Doc Russell's story changed everything. My dad was not killed instantly. He may have suffered. He really was a hero—not just because he died in battle but because he spent his last hours on this Earth treating wounded Marines. I wanted to know the name of the Marine my dad was shielding. Doc Russell said that Marine was dead too, when he observed their bodies lying side by side. Did the explosive device hit my dad when he was tending to the wounds of this Marine? Did my dad need a corpsman to come to his aid but none were available to help? While these questions changed nothing about the outcome of my dad's fate, I needed to know. I believed someone else knew, and I needed to find him.

The main questions I now had were: Did my dad suffer? Did he know he was going to die? For me, these questions had spiritual ramifications. As his daughter, I found it awful to think of him lying alone in pain. I would feel better if he had died instantly, but the more important issue was that I would see him one day in heaven.

If Doc Russell's account was true, my dad did deserve another medal. He had received a Purple Heart for dying in battle, but what about putting his life in danger to protect someone? I was not familiar with the requirements for military decorations, but my husband did some research. My dad's commanding officers were the ones who would have made medal recommendations, but they had all been killed in the battle. In order for a medal to be awarded without a commanding officer's recommendation, two witnesses had to provide written accounts. I hoped to one day find a second person, but that would have to wait. Being a good mother was my priority.

I had not spoken to Doc Russell since our one phone conversation in 1999, but on April 30, 2001, I received this email from him:

> On the morning of Feb. 15, 1968, I observed the body of HM2 Goss and a Marine whose name I do not know. HM2 Goss was immediately behind the Marine's body. Because of the positions of the bodies, it appeared to me that HM2 Goss had used his body as a shield for the Marine.

Seven months later, Doc Russell emailed Ray:

> I want it to be known that HM2 Goss was moving about the field of battle on the day of ambush known as Valentine's Ridge. I saw this. He did good.

On January 25, 2002, Ray emailed me:

> Lori,
>
> What I had heard, the day after we got back to Ca Lu, Feb 15, was that the captain was wounded and medevac'd and your dad was KIA. The first time I talked with Marty Russell a couple of years ago he said your dad was dead and lying on another Marine as if protecting him. Lately, Marty has sent me emails stating your dad was alive when he got to the captain.

This was consistent with what Doc Russell told me on the phone.

Soon after Ray sent me this email, he invited me to a Kilo 3/9 reunion. He wanted me to meet his commander, Zeke, and his squad leader, Jed. He told me Jerry might be there, too. I appreciated his kind invitation, but at that time my kids needed me at home more than I needed to go to the reunion. My baby had just turned two and my other children were four, six, nine, and eleven. I could not imagine anyone else handling their schedule that week. The kids had baseball games and Eric was the assistant coach—and I needed to cheer for them. The past was important, but the present was essential. My dad would want me to focus on giving my children all my love and time.

The next email I received from Ray was very unexpected and left me with deep regret. Doc Marty Russell passed away unexpectedly on February 15, 2002. I responded to Ray:

> I printed out all of the communication you and I have had concerning Marty's story. Please help me understand. I wanted to call him again

so badly but did not want to stress his health. The day I talked to him on the phone he seemed so traumatized to talk about the battle and told me how poor his health was. I did not want to jeopardize his health, but I sure wanted to talk to him again. I tried to leave that in your hands, and I appreciate you communicating to him for me. I really thought you could filter it better than me because I would have no way of knowing if what he said was true or not.

Are you comfortable sharing with me any of his emails about my dad? I know I may never know, but I really want to know at what point during the battle he died. I don't understand why he did not pull the captain to safety instead of going to help other Marines. In my mind, if he had pulled the captain to safety and stayed with him until he was medevac'd, then he (my dad) would have been safe too. Were they able to get the captain out during the battle? My assumption is yes.

I thought that Marty told me that he saw my dad "running" up and down the hill helping other Marines and then later found him dead. I know he told me that my dad was alive after the CO and the XO were hit. He also told me that my dad was helping him take care of other Marines. Marty told me he found my dad's body a distance from the CO and the XO. Is that consistent with what he told you? Do you think there are other people you may find who may be able to tell us more about this? I don't know why this means so much to me but it does. I know the XO died. Was he medevac'd too?

I really appreciate the time you have spent on this and you sharing with me about Martin's death. I am so saddened to hear about it. I think it is odd that he passed away on 2–15.

I'm sorry I wrote so many questions tonight. I think I thought that with Martin alive I would eventually find out, and now I feel like with his passing that my opportunity to find out may be gone. Thanks again for your time.

Prior to Doc Russell's passing, he wrote his memories of the battle in response to the questions Ray had asked him. Specifically, whether he had seen the body of HM2 Goss and if he had known Jerry Porter, a corpsman who had served under my dad. Doc Russell spent the night on Valentine's Ridge and fought the NVA the following day. Below are the portions of his account that pertain to my dad:

Dear Ray:

I really don't know which platoon I was with. I only know that I was with the Marines on the observation post just outside the perimeter of Ca Lu.

Yes, I was in sight of the CP group. I saw the dead body of HM2 Goss. I know that I knew Porter before I went to Vietnam. I think I went to Corps School with him also. Maybe he was stationed at NTC with me.

This is how I remember the battlefield. I heard a shotgun go off 2–3 times. The XO who was with the CO yelled for corpsman up. I went from A to B, the Marine line of men ended there & then looped downward from B to C to D. When I got to B, I took off running, unaware that I was running between the lines. The XO yelled, "Doc you crazy SOB, get down here." At that point I looked down, saw the way the Marine line was headed downhill toward them. The broken line from C to D was my path. I reached the line of Marines and faced uphill. There were Marines above the looped line B, C, D.

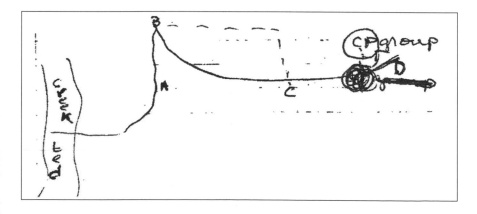

They yelled for a corpsman so I started crawling uphill toward them. I could not tell where they were. I finally had to yell to them to bring whoever was wounded down the hill. They did. It was PVT Camron Carter. He had three bullet wounds in his right upper arm. HM2 Goss appeared & together we treated him. He was removed. The letter E is approximately where we were when we treated Carter. They also said that a Cpl Schneider from Ohio had been killed. An undetonated M79 round in his forehead. They also mentioned an NVA that was in a hollow stump. I don't know if they said they had killed him or not.

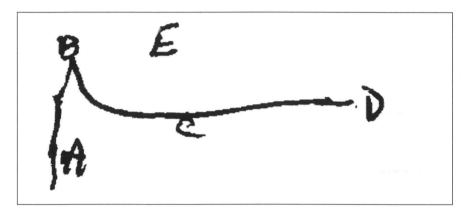

After that, I am not sure the chronology of events. I remember all the mortar sounds and firing on the 14th. I seem to remember people yelling to pull back, to return to Rt. 9 or the perimeter at Ca Lu. At any rate, I didn't go with them. About 10 Marines set up on a hill to the left of where I was. I didn't know that then. I guess I stayed there by myself. The next time I was aware of enough to know something it was twilight. I was standing by myself at letter D. There were 2 or 3 Marine bodies around me, all dead. Jeffrey Wentzell, radioman, was on his back in front of me; a bullet hole between his eyes. A few feet above me were HM2 Goss and a Marine—both dead. A few more feet up the hill was the CP group. The CO, the XO, and a corpsman, I think his name was Jackson, from Montana?, and Don E. Carter, radioman.

Doc Russell also sent Ray a handwritten note:

Dic Narty
DD

After Doc Russell passed away, Ray sent me an email he received from James Nat Lloyd. He was the captain's radioman who survived his injuries on Valentine's Ridge. Lance Corporal Lloyd did not remember seeing my dad during the battle. Ray also sent me an email from Corp. Don E. Carter:

> I was the radio operator for 3rd Platoon with Second Lieutenant Dan Wszolek, and the company CP was with my platoon on 14 February 68. I can only relate what I think happened as the position of the other two platoons has to be determined by the accounts of others. I wasn't really concerned about any 50 Cal fire; our position was hit with mortar, machine gun automatic fire, and grenades. From the accounts which I have received, the 1st and 2nd platoons retreated from Valentine's Ridge after dark and returned to our base at Ca Lu. In the morning of 15th of February 68 we assaulted the ridge, took it, and waited for evacuation choppers. The choppers came in and were hit by a wave of fire as they were about 100 feet off the ground. I could see the holes in the windshield of one chopper and could see that a pilot had been hit; the choppers left and never returned due to the hot LZ. In the late afternoon we received reinforcement who walked from Hwy. 9 up to the ridge and who carried or assisted the walking wounded back to Ca Lu. There wasn't enough manpower to carry the dead, and looking back, and from what I was told later, the LZ was too hot for choppers.
>
> Looking back, I know we should've done everything possible to bring out our dead that day regardless of the circumstances; for this I am truly sorry. As a 19-year-old at the time, my opinion did not mean much. As a matter of fact, I cannot remember anyone in our command doing a debriefing on this patrol, or at least with junior enlisted. I think the Corps was so stunned at our losses and inability to extract our dead that they tried to suppress what happened. The only thing which I remember from our command, after the ridge, was that a directive was issued about 10 days after this incident in that "no one was to send any more letters

to dead Marine relatives." The fact was that some "last letters"*
were mailed for the dead Marines at their request and others
wrote to express their sorrow to the families, not knowing that the
Corps had delayed the notifications until recovery of the bodies; a
complete body count had been made and the dead were grouped
together prior to departing the ridge on 15 Feb.

My husband, Eric, responded to Don with this critical question:

If you were able to take the hill on the 15 Feb 68, why weren't the
bodies, HM2 Larry Goss included, able to be recovered until 06
Mar 68?

---

* Some Marines (and other service members) wrote letters to be read by their loved
ones if they were killed.

# CHAPTER FOURTEEN

# Welcomed into the Marine Family

Grieving without memory is complicated. Your heart has nothing to attach to except stories, but you long for so much more. In 2006, Ray once again invited me to a Kilo 3/9 reunion. I did not want to go because my children were still young and they needed me at home. In 2007, however, Eric decided that now was the time for me to go, and he surprised me with airplane tickets for Courtnee and me. My fortieth birthday was quickly approaching, and our daughter was turning ten.

While I was excited and grateful to be attending, I was not searching for a relationship with the men who served with my dad. My goal was simply to find out the truth. Nevertheless, Ray was waiting for us at the airport. My heart was touched. We had corresponded only through email and letters, and it was nice to meet him face to face.

When Ray introduced me to his close friends Zeke and Jed, they and their wives treated my daughter and me like we were one of their own. I did not anticipate their inclusion, but it felt wonderful. They offered to tell me about the day my dad was killed while their wives spent time with Courtnee.

They told me that Valentine's Ridge was in the shape of a horse-shoe and that when you look at the ridge from Ca Lu you can't tell there are two ridges instead of one. I asked about the mission of the patrol.

"It was supposed to be a one-day patrol," Zeke said. "We were to make a loop out and come back. We were trying to see where the NVA were firing eighty-two mortars from. We knew contact with the enemy was imminent."

As they shared detail after detail, my tears fell gently. No matter how much I tried, I could not stop them from falling. They suggested we meet again later as there was still more they felt I needed to know.

That evening, I heard two Marines talking about being left on the ridge all night. They expressed anger that I did not understand at the time. I also learned that an order was not obeyed and wondered whether if it had been, would my dad have lived? I quickly put that thought away.

The next day, the men of First Platoon told me that my dad was killed in the valley between the two ridges. Although they were not with my dad when he was killed, they treated me like family—a gift I did not expect.

* * * * *

During the closing ceremony, Jerry presented me with a framed photo of a corpsman in the field with angel wings. Again I could not contain my tears. After the ceremony he introduced me to Corp. Don E. Carter, Lt. Dan Wszolek's radioman, the one who had emailed Eric.

Dr. Jerry Behrens hugs Courtnee Jo as a Vietnam corpsman holds the framed photo they presented me at the closing ceremony of the Kilo 3/9 reunion (August 2007).

"Three rounds came in that day," Don explained. "The first one put everyone to the ground. I can recollect hearing three mortar rounds. You only have a few seconds after you hear thump, thump, thump. When you hear the whistle you know they are close. We could tell they were coming down on top of us. The first one hit in the middle of our group."

He described his group as consisting of the CO, my dad, two radio operators, the XO, Lieutenant Wszolek, and him. "There were other people present," he said, "but the first one exploded, knocking everyone to the ground."

Don explained that the CO was to his left when the second mortar round hit his body.

"There was only a second between the first and second, but it felt like a lifetime," he said. "If you know the mortar is coming, you're terrified because you don't where it's going to hit. The third one hit the XO's left side and the CO as well. I got up and saw three bodies that were on the opposite side where the mortar rounds came in."

He sketched a picture that looked like this:

**\*radioman**

**\*XO**

**\*CO**

He was not sure of the order but knew it was three bodies within five feet of each other. Don said he was told the radioman was a corpsman, because of the story passed down about my dad looking at a map with the XO and CO when the mortars came in. Years later, Dan Wszolek told me that it was *he* who was looking at the map with them.

The reunion was ending, but my gut said there was someone else I needed to talk to: a Marine named Richard Foster. I found him sitting at a table with two other Marines and introduced myself. We talked for about an hour. I wrote down his memories and left the reunion feeling like I had finally found a person who was near my dad when he was killed. On the airplane, I wrote these notes:

> I'm exhausted but can't let this day end without writing what's in my head.
>
> 8-10-07—a day I've waited for my whole life—I found a man who was with my dad the day he died. He doesn't remember being with him, but I know they were together. I'll write his account one day. I wish he would write it, but I just feel fortunate that he would talk to me. It was unreal. I was sitting at the banquet and he came up to me. He said something like, "Did you get one of these?" and showed me a Kilo 3/9 lanyard. I smiled and said, "No." He said, "Here, this is for you, don't take it off."
>
> Earlier that evening he came up to me and said, "I knew your dad but I don't have any information that could help you." His daughter made eye contact with me later during the banquet and I noticed he was not at the table. He was pacing in the back

of the room. Something told me he had information I needed. I waited all night and then asked him to talk with me. He still didn't think he had anything to say, but he did. It's what I waited for my whole life. I still can't believe it at all.

What I learned today requires of me forgiveness, the choice not to be bitter, not to wallow in self-pity, to be thankful for what I have and who I am, and for the man who gave me life. I now know my dad. He was an amazing man. He loved my mom and me so very much. He cherished me. Thank you, God, for this weekend and all I've learned. I don't know what happened between some of the men. Part of me feels angry but that will do me no good. Please help me know what to do now—how to best spend my time. How to honor my dad with this information and leave his legacy for my sons and daughter. I know he would have been amazing, and I believe heaven will allow me an opportunity to be loved by him.

The song "You're All I Ever Needed" makes no sense to me. I have you, God, but I still need to meet my dad. I ask you Father to please give me that blessing in heaven. I love him so much. I can't even put it into words.

When I returned home, I shared what I had learned with my husband and oldest sons. One son said, "I know now how he died; now I want to know about his life. Funny stories and things he did." I loved that they were interested and that they were so close to my mom. She was always willing to tell us their stories. Later, my dad's friend Stan Burkart and his classmates from Home Corner helped too.

While they were fresh in my mind, I typed up the notes I took at the reunion. Each man saw the battle from his own place on the battlefield. I hoped one day to put all their stories together and come up with one account. At the time, it was just too much to process. Then, as I had done many times before, I put the notes in a file folder and focused on my family.

Ray, Jed, Jerry, and Zeke stayed connected to me by email. They invited me to their next gathering that they affectionately called "the Rendezvous." Did I really have a new family? They joked about who adopted me first and my heart felt so much joy. I thought of how much I wished my own dad was still a part of their group and wondered if he would have rendezvoused with them. I knew he and Jerry would have had contact after Vietnam. There was no doubt in my mind about that.

Jerry, Zeke, me, Jed, and Ray at the South Dakota Rendezvous (July 2015).

Shortly after returning home from the reunion, at Shawn's suggestion I created a post on the Vietnam Veterans Memorial Fund (VVMF) website for my dad. I posted a remembrance and two blessings followed—one from Rick Foster and the other from Stan Burkart.

I was at a track meet getting ready to watch my fifth-grade daughter run when my phone rang. I couldn't believe my ears when the man identified himself as Stan Burkart, the man my mom always suggested I try to find. He lived about ninety minutes away in Lafay-ette, Indiana, so we set a time to talk—there was no way I was going to miss my daughter's run. It would be the first of many conversations with this kind and generous man. I learned several things about my dad as he spoke to me. I wrote down every word:

Larry was an MAA [master-at-arms], which meant he was kind of an officer in boot camp, so I didn't get to know him that well but in Corps school I did. I met his wife, Marty, and baby in Corps school. I was in VN when I heard that he had got killed. I wanted to go where he was and help out—we were young. I had a plaque in my garage. Larry and I marched together. We'd march along and he'd tie my shoes. He was more like a brother to me.

We loved sports. He told me he played basketball. At the end of Corps school, if you got a 90 or above you got a coin. He got a 90.5 and I got an 89. He tried to give it to me. I said no. We helped each other so much. He was just a really good friend of mine.

Larry was a leader and go-getter. In boot camp I was the kind of guy that our chief disliked—he was a hard-nosed guy. Larry and I were both from Indiana and liked sports and stuff. We were so close that we talked about death and stuff. When I went to the Wall and was almost crying, I threw a $10 bill on it. We bet that—figured one of us probably would not make it home. I would have given anything to have traded him places; it was just meant to be.

So many corpsmen were dying. He was a great dad, believe me. He sure would have been. He would have been a great dad, I know he would have. Covered that guy's body in battle. I had done that once. I heard someone yelling and I knew being a corpsman I had to go to him and I shielded his body and it was just meant to be for us to live. A helicopter landed. His hand was blown off. I thoroughly truly believe that Larry was protecting someone and patched him up. Things happened so quickly.

I didn't talk about any of it for twenty years. Agent Orange and Type I diabetes. I even feel funny doing it now. I always wondered what really happened. So many people talk about the Vietnam Veterans. [Before the war] I always felt like a winner. I know what it felt like to not be welcomed home. I don't want anybody I love to feel that. The worst thing someone could tell me was that we lost the war in Vietnam. I knew the boys that fought, and they did their best. It was the government back here. They drew lines on what you can do and can't do. The Vietnam people experienced freedom for a while. Larry sure was a hero. He certainly is in my mind.

I go to the games at Harrison High School. Every time I see Marion I think about where you live. I think of your mother. To me, you are still a baby. My shoelaces kept coming untied. Your dad stopped and tied them for me. He did that once just to be nice. We marched together a lot.

When Stan told me more about the coin my dad earned in corps school and how my dad wanted to give it to him, my heart skipped a beat. A month or so before I spoke with Stan, I had found a bag of coins. I didn't notice anything special about them, so I put them in my car to spend as needed. When Stan described the academic coin my dad had earned and tried to give him, I knew I needed to look through those coins. Could it possibly be in there? I went to my car and dumped the coins out. In the midst of regular quarters, dimes, and nickels, there was a coin that was more bronze in color. Upon examining it closely, I realized it was the coin Stan told me about. My dad's academic coin! Was this God's timing? It sure seemed so. Had Stan not found me at that specific time, I might have mistaken the coin for a quarter and spent it without realizing its real value—nothing to a cashier, but everything to me.

Stan's stories confirmed ten things I had heard repeatedly in my search to know my dad:

1) He was very smart.
2) He was a leader and very determined.
3) He studied a lot and cared about his academic performance.
4) He was competitive.
5) He was giving.
6) He was extremely kind.
7) He had compassion and empathy for those in need.
8) He loved sports and was athletic.
9) He loved my mom and me very much.
10) He would have continued to be an excellent husband and dad.

My dad's academic coin is now one of my greatest treasures. The story about my dad stopping to tie Stan's marching boots is now a cherished mental picture I carry of my hard-working, compassionate, loving dad.

Front and back of Dad's academic award coin, given to those who received a score of 90 or higher in Corps school.

On October 25, 2008, Stan posted this remembrance on my dad's virtual wall:

Your Corps School friend
by Stanley A. Burkart

You were my best friend in the Navy. You were so good at looking after me. All of our studying, marching, talking sports, and just spending time together.

After being together in boot camp and Corps School, we always hoped that we could have ended up in Vietnam together.

Larry, you made the greatest sacrifice of all for your Country, and all of America is very proud of you.

I know that we would have gotten together after the war, and would have been good friends. Well, you will always be on the top of my list of friends. I miss you and will see you in the next world.

God has revealed to me time and time again that He not only knows what I need even before I do, but He also provides. His answer to my prayers might not always be a "yes," and His provision might not be what I asked for, but He always provides. He showed me that again the following February, on the fortieth anniversary of my dad's death. Like Stan, Rick Foster wrote on my dad's virtual wall. He posted this on Feb. 13, 2008:

Serving a year with Kilo Company, 3rd Battalion, 9th Marines in 1967–68 was a challenge even for an 18-year-old Marine in perfect physical condition. We got scrapes from rocks, cuts from elephant grass, itchy holes from leeches, infections galore, and of course those bullet and shrapnel holes. We ran to the Corpsmen like a kid runs to his mom. "Hey doc, got anything for this?" And during battle, the dreaded scream of "Corpsman Up!"

Larry Goss was a corpsman in my unit, and although I don't remember him individually, I know that at the time I knew him by sight and went to him with many of my ailments.

It was him and others like him that patched us up and kept us going. It was him and others like him that said: 'Don't worry. You'll be fine." And we usually were. It was him and others like him that risked their lives to reach us on the battlefield. "Don't worry. You'll be fine." Just like mom, only better.

And it was him, I now know, that died a few feet from me on Valentine's Day 1968 from two mortar rounds fired by the NVA near the end of a long battle. He was there, doing his job, and exposed. The Company Commander was killed with him, and many more were wounded.

But now I know. It was him that gave us hope. A clean bandage in the mud. A tube of antibiotic gel for our infections. A pill for pain. God bless Larry Goss, and all the other Corpsmen that served in hell with us Marines. And to his daughter, Lori, who never got to touch him, but loves him beyond words, I say what her dad would say: "Don't worry. You'll be fine."*

I emailed to thank him:

Rick, thanks for having me in your thoughts today. I must admit that I've had a rough day. I tell myself every Valentine's Day that it is silly to let one day bother me so much, but it does. I still do the Valentine thing with my family because I don't want my kids to have to struggle like I did (between normal positive emotion, school parties, etc., and grief). It is just that my mind is always at least partially somewhere else. That somewhere is

---

* Rick did not realize that I was four months old when my dad left for Vietnam. He also did not know how my dad was killed but had heard the same rumor as Jerry had. The CO died two days later in a hospital.

imagining what happened 40 years ago and all that comes with those thoughts.

I do feel very blessed by my husband and children's love. God's love has sometimes been hard for me to grasp, I think because I did not get to express love for my dad. I became a Christian at age 13 and really felt like God drew me to him. My commitment was very strong until 1995. That is the year that my third son was born with Down syndrome and two years later developed autism. I was so disappointed with God. I needed my dad and felt abandoned by God. I grieved deeply for about two years. I don't doubt God's love for me anymore. I actually believe that without God, life has no meaning and we have no help. I'm looking forward to the next reunion. I'm still so thankful to you for agreeing to talk to me that night.

In the years that followed, my family and I made many beautiful memories with Ray, Jed, Jerry, and Zeke. Zeke sent me supportive emails that made me laugh out loud and gave me excellent advice when I left my job as a licensed clinical social worker to become a college professor. Jed never failed to tell me he loved me every time we talked on the phone. Ray supported me with his words and shared hundreds of documents with me that he had collected about the battle. One year on my birthday, I received a phone call from all four of them. I thanked God for the blessing of my dad's Marine brothers who lived out the Marine motto, *Semper fidelis*.

\* \* \* \* \*

The rendezvous that took place every year allowed us to know one another outside of conversations about the war. On June 19, 2009, we gathered with Jed and his family to celebrate him receiving a Purple Heart. It was our oldest son's nineteenth birthday, an event I would never want to miss. Eric drove us to Kentucky and back in the same day so we could make it home in time to throw a party for Chris. In 2010, we gathered again in Kentucky with our entire families. Jed and his wife were wonderful hosts.

In 2011, Jerry invited our family to visit him and his wife, Mary, at their condo in Jackson Hole, Wyoming. Ray and his wife, Ginny, were invited too. I called Jerry to check in the day we were to arrive. I couldn't help but imagine my dad checking in with Jerry the week he spent with him at the Rockpile. Dad would never have dreamed that his little girl would be doing the same thing forty-four years later, or that his battalion surgeon would embrace his daughter and welcome her into his home.

In 2012, the group decided the rendezvous would be in Indiana. I was amazed they cared enough to come all this way. The newspaper ran an article which pictured me comforting my twelve-year-old son, Casey, after he sang "God Bless the USA."

The purpose of the ceremony was to dedicate the footstone Jerry had purchased for my dad. I needed to thank him and let him know how much his kindness meant to me. Jerry was out of the country for his daughter's wedding, so Ray taped the service for him.

It was important to me that my mom hear firsthand what I learned from the men who had served with my dad. I wanted extended family to hear too, along with anyone else who loved and knew him. Mom was seated in the front row at his grave that day, just as she had been forty-four years before.

My heart was touched when Colonel Ellis arrived, along with some people I did not know. All my children were there, along with a dear man, John Johnston, who attended our Bible study, and Jack Marshall, a man who graduated from high school with my dad.

The service began with a prayer by Eric, followed by Casey's song. Zeke, Ray, Stan, and I all spoke, along with my dear Aunt Rhonda, who told beautiful, funny stories about the month my dad got to play her dad.

There were no dry eyes. The night before, the Holy Spirit prompted me with a thought. Jed, one of the men who had carried my dad's body off the ridge, was there, and we needed to honor and thank him. I asked Jed, Ray, and Zeke to stand, and told them I hoped they could feel the magnitude of our gratefulness for what they had done. Below them was the casket of Larry Jo Goss. Not empty, as his mother had argued, but filled with some remains of our beloved father, husband, brother, and grandfather. His grave had a new meaning for me now.

Cody gave the closing benediction on that hot summer day in July, and I gave my mother a blue hydrangea and then gave her a long hug. My dad knew blue was her favorite color. He would have given her many blue flowers had he lived.

Ray visited Indiana again in 2013, this time to see Casey in a play. We talked a lot about my dad and enjoyed our time celebrating my son and his unique gifts. Ray showed the utmost respect to my mom, escorting her to the performance and driving her home. I was careful to not let my mind go there often, but as I observed his care for her, I knew my dad would have treated her the same way. That was something significant she and I had missed.

The following year, Mary Behrens invited me to speak at a surprise event she was holding in Jerry's honor. Through her generous donation and Jerry's medical partners, the Dr. Jerry Behrens Orthopedic Surgery Center was being dedicated, and Jerry had no idea. Eric painted an acrylic portrait of Jerry, which included him working on a Marine in Vietnam. Sen. John Barrasso of Wyoming was another speaker. I smiled as I thought about how much my dad would love this—being spoken of in the presence of a U.S. senator!

A news station from Casper, Wyoming, featured the story and contacted me for an interview. Construction at the surgery center was completed and there was much excitement. The interviewer asked me to talk about the impact Jerry had had on my life. What an honor it was for me to tell an audience that knew Jerry personally and professionally about the hero he was in my eyes.

In May 2015, I was invited to speak in Wyoming at a fundraising event for the Central Wyoming Rescue Mission. It was a wonderful opportunity to spend time with Jerry and Mary and share the wonderful things God had done.

Mary and Jerry graciously offered to pick us up at the airport and invited us to stay in their home. They treated us like family, which at times brought tears to my eyes. They had a ranch stay planned for us after the event. I had never stayed at a ranch before and felt like a daughter for a few days. Walking with Jerry and hearing stories about his time in Vietnam filled my heart with pride. Out of all the people my dad could have chosen to connect with in Vietnam, how did he pick someone so wonderful? When Jerry talked about his corpsmen, it was evident that this brave man loved deeply. My dad judged Jerry's character well. Mary is just as lovely—the time I spent with her in the car was therapeutic for me. As we shared personal experiences from our childhoods, we connected in a way that I knew would last a lifetime. She reminded me of my mom in her looks, and of myself in her actions.

Over dinner one night, as Mary and Jerry treated us to a meal fit for kings and queens, they encouraged me to write this book. I knew one day I would start it. Their confidence in my abilities made me think the time was soon.

The words I spoke at the fundraiser still hold true today: Jerry, Mary, Jed, Aggie, Ray Ginny, Zeke, and Cass chose to love me for my dad. Through my relationships with them, I found healing and will forever be changed for the better.

Two weeks later, Ray and his wife took an RV trip across the United States and made their final destination the Goss-Reaves house for two months. We spent the weeks talking about Vietnam and making memories. We rode bikes, made strawberry freezer jam, and took daily walks. Their visit spanned over Father's Day, and it was nice to celebrate Ray and Eric and not feel sad.

Ray got sick during his stay. As I advocated for him at the VA hospital and prayed for him to get well, I realized that it was not just a father's love I had missed out on—I had also missed the opportunity to show love to my dad. Loving and being loved. Both are so important and part of God's perfect plan.

Six days after they left, we all met in South Dakota for another rendezvous. It was my favorite reunion. Mary invited us to stay with her and Jerry in their camper, and listening to Casey sing while Jerry played the guitar soothed my spirit. One evening at Mount Rushmore, a flag-lowering ceremony was held. Jerry and Ray took my hand and led me to the stage. I felt pride in my father's service and thankful for Jerry's and Ray's respect for him.

Casey, Eric, me, Jerry, Ginny, and Ray in South Dakota (2015).

In early November 2016, my husband said he could not wait to see me receive the gift that was coming my way. I assumed he was referring to a Christmas present, since December was approaching. I have never been one who desired big gifts, so I could not even begin to imagine what Eric was referring to. There was nothing tangible I wanted. And there was no material item he could buy me that could create the kind of excitement he was describing.

Three weeks later, with no thought of the surprise, I met Eric after work in the Walgreens parking lot. I walked over to his car and found two people hunched down in the back seat. Jerry and Mary Behrens! My heart was overflowing with joy. They were in Marion, Indiana, for the first time, and there was so much I wanted to show them.

Our youngest son was performing in the play *Scrooge*, so Mary had suggested to Jerry that they come see Casey's show and surprise me. Eric was in on the plan and it was truly the perfect Christmas present. Those were four days I will never forget. I took Jerry and Mary to my dad's grave, the Vietnam Memorial designed by Eric, and one of my favorite places, Indiana Wesleyan University, where I still work as a professor. As I passed the office of the provost, I stopped to introduce Jerry and Mary to her and to our CEO, Dr. Newman. Both had heard my dad's story and the impact the Behrens, Felles, Holladays, and Girtens had on my life. I was so proud the Behrens were there. Their visit meant so much to me.

The evening of Casey's show was extra special. Stan Burkart and his wife, Carol, often traveled from Lafayette to see Casey perform or to take part in other special events with my children. I was so happy as I looked down the row to see my mom, Jerry, and Stan sitting together. They were all enjoying each other's company as they sat waiting to watch my dad's grandson perform. My dad would have loved this moment so much! I could envision him sitting in the middle of Jerry and Stan, laughing and talking with his friends.

The next morning, the Behrens joined us in church and afterward we ate lunch at the restaurant where Marie took me on my birthday so many years ago. My mom enjoyed her time with the Behrens, and they found her to be delightful. As we drove them back to the airport, I was not ready to see them go. I was not prepared to leave them when my husband pulled up to the curb. I cried on our drive home. Leaving the men who served with my dad always tugged at my heart. To me, Jerry represented a part of my dad, and I did not want to say goodbye.

After they left, I wrote in my journal:

I've always been an encourager to others but I'm a better encourager to myself because Mary and Jerry cared enough to come visit. I am still tearing up (OK, crying) when I think of our time together. I always grieve for my dad when I leave those men but this time the grief is lasting longer. Mary said emotions are good. This time I know they are healing. I want to go back to my dad's grave. To write there. To take a nap there. I can finally feel his love. Before I could read about it. Now I can feel it. What a gift Jerry and Mary gave me.

I wonder if my dad knew, when he selected Jerry to share his emotional wound with, that I would need him some day in my dad's absence. Could it be that he had that forethought? He clearly wanted me to have a father figure. Oh, how he must have loved me. When I was younger his absence felt like abandonment. I knew he didn't purposely leave me, but my reality was that he was gone, and I didn't have a dad.

I didn't want pity. No thank you. Instead I would work to need no one. When I focused on making him proud, I felt confident. The problem with that was that it was performance-based. While on the outside I looked accomplished, on the inside there was a void that no degree or position could fill.

The Bible taught me that my Heavenly Father loved me, and I believed and continue to believe that is true. Why did that love not fill the void? What was I doing wrong? I could pray more, read the Bible more, practice spiritual disciplines but still that void remained.

We all have strengths and weaknesses and often find there is a crossover between the two. My strength of being very determined became a negative when I sought out to find a dad.

I don't remember being aware of my need to study fathers and daughters, but I clearly did. When I was in my late thirties, I observed my friend Mark walking out of church with his pre-teen daughter. She had her arm linked in his as they walked happily to their car. That moment stuck with me, as I believed that is what all young girls should experience: the safety of their fathers' arm as they begin the journey to young adulthood and boys enter the scene.

When I think of my growing years, there were no men who played that role in my life. I realize now that it was not because I did not deserve it. Through those years, however, my dad's love— passed on to me by my mom—saw me through. Learning how much I was like him positively affected my development. Knowing a part of him lived on through me gave me a zest for life that was unquenchable.

As a young adult, I was hired to work part-time with licensed clinical social worker Ed Pereira and licensed psychologist Dr. Don Hickman. Both men were instrumental in shaping me into the clinician I am today. Through their love and mentoring, I was able to experience a little bit of what being loved by a dad might have felt like. And I felt the same love from Jerry and the men who served with my dad.

In 2017, Eric, Courtnee, and I visited Mary and Jerry at their home for the solar eclipse. It is one of my many treasured memories. One evening we went into town and stopped at a restaurant for dinner. Jerry ran into some friends and brought them over to our table. His children knew them and so Jerry introduced me. He said, "Lori is like a third daughter to Mary and me." What an incredible blessing their love has been in my life.

Stan, Jerry, Mary, and Mom watch Casey's performance at the
Richie Walton Auditorium in Marion (December 2016).

Mary, Mom, Jerry, Eric, Colton, and me after lunch the next day.

With Jerry at the monument Eric designed to honor the men killed in Vietnam.

# CHAPTER FIFTEEN

# "Dr. Goss"

My dad's desire to become a doctor inspired me. Just like my sixth-grade teacher, Mrs. Hubbard, said, I was going to become "Dr. Goss" one day. Although my degree was necessary to teach at my university, and I love teaching there immensely, the truth is that I did it for him.

In 2012, I attended a dissertation colloquium in Northern Virginia. Sitting in my hotel room, I Googled "events nearby" and found, much to my surprise, that they were reading the names of all 58,282 men and women who were killed in the war in Vietnam. I knew I had to catch a cab and go. Still wearing my university name badge, I wished my dad could look down and see me. They had already read his name when I arrived, but I sat and listened to the other names. I could tell that one of the readers had lost someone dear to her in the war. I waited until she left the podium and then approached her. She told me that her father's name was on the Wall. We had an instant connection and she told me about other events at the Wall for sons and daughters. I looked forward to one day attending and meeting others like me.

Before leaving, I stopped at my dad's panel. The feelings were surreal. I felt compelled to write him a note but only had my trifold name badge with me. I found a pencil and carefully penned this note on the back of my nametag, using every inch of available space, much like my dad did in his letters during the war:

Dad, I came here to write but never dreamed it would be here. I'm at your Wall. I wish your name wasn't on it, but it is and so we all must find a way to make it without you. Some say that you look over me. I would love to believe that, but I don't know what we do after we die. I believe in God's word that says that we go to heaven, but it is not clear on time and whether we go there before the rapture or just sleep until then. Even if you can't watch over me now, you have propelled me to do so many things. Thank you. Your example in your short life taught me to love deeply, work hard, chase my dreams, set goals and do what it takes to reach them, be resilient, never give up, have and go for Plan B with a cheerful disposition, and I must say again (because you modeled it so well) to love deeply!

All of these names. They just said Larry again. My heart dropped. I love you, that I know. You made it so clear that you loved my mom and me so much. We were always in your thoughts. That can be seen in your letters and audio tapes. In 5 more years, I hope to come here and read your name, my father, Larry Jo Goss.

Guess why I'm in DC? Because of you! You inspired me to become a doctor. Not a medical doctor but a Doctor of Social Work. Maybe that is a good combination of you and my mom. She has the heart of a social worker. She would give the shirt off her back to anyone in need. Thank you, Dad, for doing what was right on that battlefield. I used to wish you had run for cover. I met a man who told me he did just that the night you died on Valentine's Ridge. You instead did the job you were called to do. You went to the aid of a wounded Marine and shielded his body with yours. I am so sad that you died, but so proud of you.

It was the first time I had "told" my dad that I was seeking my doctorate and that he was my inspiration. I went to bed that night feeling peace about the degree I was pursuing. It seemed God found a way for me to know that I was within His perfect will.

In August 2014, at the age of forty-seven, I finally accomplished a childhood goal by becoming Dr. Lori Goss-Reaves. I earned a doctorate because my dad had wanted to, but his opportunity was snatched away. Mary and Jerry sent a bouquet of flowers to me at the hotel. Those flowers, to me, represented the presence of my dad at our celebration. Mom stayed with Colton while my other children and Eric cheered me on.

That same year I received another blessing: a surprise phone call from a man named Camron Carter. After introducing himself, Camron said that my dad had saved his life when he was in Vietnam. I listened intently as Camron shared his memory of my dad and Doc Russell treating him on Valentine's Ridge. Camron told me about his life in Illinois and his involvement with his church. I could tell from our conversation that Camron was making the most of every day he had been given and that the life my dad had saved was a life worth saving.

In 2016, Eric, Casey, and I met Camron in his home. It felt surreal to embrace a man who was gravely wounded on Valentine's Ridge but was alive and happy. It felt wonderful to meet him. He was authentic and kind. Camron's girlfriend, Michelle, prepared food. As the five of us sat around their dining room table, Camron shared his experience on Valentine's Ridge and sobbed. I felt so much empathy for him and wanted to show him how much I respected him. I placed my hand on his shoulder and hoped he felt comforted. His emotions were so raw. It was as if he had not shared that traumatic experience out loud with anyone before. I was glad Eric, Casey, and Michelle were also present. Camron gave me a printed copy of an article, "Purple Hearts on Valentine's

Ridge."* It was the first time I had heard about a man named John Edwards who survived the battle.

Camron also shared his deep faith with us and gave God all the glory for sparing his life on Valentine's Ridge. I rejoiced with Camron and believed that God had saved him both physically and spiritually. The next day on my father's VVMF website, I posted:

> So much has happened since I first posted a remembrance on this site. I will forever be thankful for the Marines and Corpsmen who have embraced me. I started out on a search to find information about my father but found instead much more than I was searching for. There are still missing parts to my dad's story. I have learned to be OK with not knowing, though it is my prayer that I hear from more men who served with my dad.
>
> Today I want to publicly thank a brave Marine who contacted me in 2014. PVT Camron Carter was gravely wounded on Valentine's Ridge. Corpsman Marty Russell and my father treated Camron's wounds that day. He was medevac'd out with the captain and thankfully lived. His willingness to reach outside of his own pain and contact me is something I will forever be thankful for.
>
> Oh Dad, how I wish you had been the one to embrace Camron last night. Because of the life you gave me, I will forever stand in your place and help veterans to the best of my ability.
>
> I am so thankful that your life touched Camron's that day. You did your job to the best of your ability and I am very proud of you. Camron is a kind and giving man. Your brave actions helped him live. Thank you, Dad! You would be so happy that he and I met.

My relationship with Camron has continued because he is such a kind and considerate human being.

---

* Steve Luhm, "A Vietnam War Nightmare: Purple Hearts on Valentine's Ridge, *The Salt Lake Tribune*, Feb. 13, 2008, https://archive.sltrib.com/article.php?id=8252160&itype=NGPSID.

With Camron Carter in March 2016.

\* \* \* \* \*

I've heard the expression "Wall magic" to reference the transcendent, almost spiritual experience that Gold Star families have at the Vietnam Veterans Memorial. I can attest that there is something very special about that place. In 2016, I attended a Memorial Day ceremony at the Wall. At the close of the service, I walked to my dad's panel and observed a man weeping. I waited off to the side, not wanting to disturb him. When it seemed appropriate, I approached him and asked, "Will you please tell me about the person on the panel you love so much?"

He told me he was there to honor his best friend, David Schneider. I recognized that name. David was killed in the battle on Valentine's Ridge. When I told the man that my dad had also been killed in that battle, he was astounded. His name was Larry Broy, and he was a Marine who had served in Vietnam. He shared his contact information with me and offered me a place to stay anytime I wanted to come back to the Wall. The following year, he sent me a tape of him speaking at church about my dad and his dear friend David Schneider.

The following year, Jerry and I returned to the Wall on Veteran's Day weekend to read together the names of the men on my dad's panel. Mary and Eric read names too. At the request of Gary Mayo, my dad's childhood friend from Home Corner, Eric read the name of Donald Smith, another young man on the Wall from Home Corner who was a father to a little girl.

I wanted to look up the stories of all the men whose names we were reading before we left, but I didn't have time. Without knowing that, Jerry looked up their stories and brought them with him. It felt good to have his support. As Mary, Eric, and Jerry were with me, I did not grieve what I had lost but enjoyed what I had. Larry Broy drove into the city to see us and brought me a corsage. Walking around Arlington with Jerry and Larry made me even more mindful of my dad. If he had the ability to look down, I know he would have smiled because of the way these men treated his little girl.

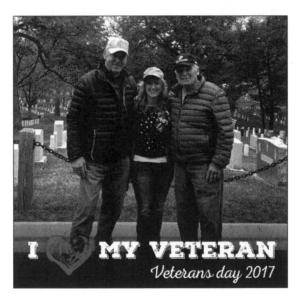

With Dr. Jerry Behrens and Larry Broy on Nov. 11, 2017.

I wrote this poem to describe the way I felt about these incredible men:

*Courageous Men*

*Many years ago, a hole was punctured in my heart*
*I was only six months old, so it*
*was a rough way to start*
*Living life without a father to nurture and to care*
*The wound was so deep that at*
*times I could not bear*
*The intensity of those emotions so I*
*focused on goals I could reach*
*Like taking care of others and getting*
*my doctorate so I could teach*
*As long as I had a mission, I did*
*not have to feel the pain*
*I moved too fast for it to catch me and*
*packed in all my life could contain*
*This worked for me for many years*
*until I met some courageous men*
*Who gave me a portion of what I lost because*
*they walked where my father had been*
*So today I say thank you for your*
*service and your love*
*To your families and to me you are a gift from above*
*There are many reasons you came*
*home, and I am really glad*
*That men of such noble character*
*served in Vietnam with my dad*
*So today I hope that you feel very*
*proud of who you are*
*A brave and gallant hero—to me a real rock star*
*For all you chose to do for me I never could repay*
*But hope you know how fondly you are*
*thought of on this Veterans Day.*

\* \* \* \* \*

Although "my dad's doctorate diploma" has my name on it, my mom and Eric deserve it too. It was important to me not only to honor my father with my life choices but also to fully thank my mom for all she did to raise me with so much love. Eighteen years earlier, I wrote the following about her and submitted it for inclusion in a book on strong women:

> I admire my mother Martha Nell Cannon for the strength and courage she portrayed throughout the Vietnam War. My mom was only 23 when she received the devastating news that my father, Hospitalman Second Class Larry Jo Goss, was missing in action. On March 6, 1968, six long weeks later, my father's body was recovered and sent back to the U.S. for burial. My mother was then left alone with me, her six-month-old daughter, to raise and teach about the wonderful man she so dearly loved.
>
> My mother was determined to keep my father's memory alive. She taught me about his character and values. She instilled in me the heart of this very noble man. She communicated so openly with me, there was never a question I couldn't ask. She kept an incredible amount of memorabilia which told the story of the man I never got to know. Cassette tapes of his voice, reel-to-reel movies of he and I, love letters sent to each other, diaries, date books, cards, newspaper articles, and various scrapbook material which I dearly treasure today.
>
> The letters are sometimes difficult to read. They tell a sad story of two people passionately in love, looking forward to a life together with their little

girl when his tour was done. Tragically their dreams never came to pass. I admire my mother because she didn't let fire, war, or even death destroy her. She knew I needed a mother and she was always there for me putting my needs first. Her love and respect for my father and for me molded me into the strong and determined woman I am today.

While my dad did not get the opportunity to write a dissertation, he wrote something far more important: a last letter to his dear grandma. She was more a mother to him than Marie ever had been. Grandma Bradford received this letter from my dad four days before he was killed:

Dear Grandma,

How are you feeling? I hope this letter finds you well and happy. How is the weather there now? The papers we get here say the temperature is up to 38–42°. Getting a little better than zero and 12 inches of snow, Ha!

How is my little wife and darling daughter? She writes and says you come down every day and visit. Thank you. Gives Marty a little chance to talk about her No. 1, Me. I sure do miss living home. This is the longest I've been gone in a long time. Since Boot Camp. The time does go by fairly fast, but a year is a long time.

Only 11 more [months] to go. Not too long huh!!

I wrote Mom last night. She has only written once, so I told her to get on the stick. I can't write her every day, but I can answer a letter about once a week. She'll probably start writing after they receive my letter. I sure hope little Jim is getting better. The flu is the wrong thing for him to catch. I hope he's walking or standing a little when I get back. I wrote and told him I was going to give him a boot with my jungle boot if he wasn't. I haven't got his reply yet. Bonnie Kay sure is writing me a lot. I've got four letters from her already. She really does a good job.

Has Mona got her letter yet from me? I wrote it on her birthday. I'm trying to write everybody a little. You and Uncle Russ & Marge, and Don & Dan can get a lot from Marty. I hope you are because I write her almost every day or two. She is doing an outstanding job. She keeps me informed about everything at home and says everything's fine. Thanks for having Marty's birthday dinner. She really was thrilled. It doesn't take too much to make my little wife happy. She's happy with me [and] that's proof. We've been very happy and haven't really had too much to live on, but we survive fairly well and got a darling little offspring don't you think. Well I guess I'll close for now take it easy and enjoy yourself. That's what life is for. I'll write more later.

Love,
Larry
P.S. Tell my Sweet Little Wife and Daughter I Love Them Very Much

Bye! Bye!!

# PART III
## *Finding Peace*

With Casey in Vietnam, July 7, 2019.

# CHAPTER SIXTEEN

# Honored at the White House

Tony Cordero, founder of Sons and Daughters in Touch, contacted me on April 24, 2018, to tell me that the White House was honoring Gold Star families for Memorial Day and that my father had been chosen as the Navy representative. The event would be held on June 4, and he wanted me to join them. I responded that I was thrilled and would be honored to attend.

I was allowed to bring two members of my dad's immediate family, but not his grandchildren. Right away, I called my mom and Aunt Marge. Although my aunt was ninety years old and Washington, D.C., was a long flight away, she agreed to join us after I told her we could visit baby Madelyn (my granddaughter).

In Washington, we met Tony at a small ceremony where he presented my mom and me with Gold Star pins, and Aunt Marge with a Vietnam Commemorative pin. Three other families were there, and it was the first time my mom had met another Gold Star widow. Aunt Marge and I were in tears.

We arrived at the White House a little early and found a park across the street where we rested. We noticed a dashing gentleman walking toward us dressed in his Navy dress whites. He introduced himself as Adm. Bill Moran. He said that he learned "one of his own" was being honored and wanted to be our escort for the night. As I watched him walk Aunt Marge and my mom to the entrance, I thought how wonderful it was that the president of the United States would be honoring my dad's life, and that the three women (Aunt Marge representing Grandma Bradford) who adored him the most were receiving this honor on his behalf. I hoped Dad was watching from heaven.

With Mom, Aunt Marge, and Admiral Moran by the White House (June 4, 2018).

The evening could not have been more perfect. I enjoyed looking out for Mom and Aunt Marge, making sure they were enjoying themselves too. We did not have a lot of information about the itinerary but were told we could walk freely through several rooms of the White House. U.S. history was all around us. I was in awe.

A few weeks prior, a White House aide had asked for information about my dad. I sent in a few pages and then she called my mom and asked for more. I assumed there would be a small write-up, so I was astounded to learn that it was actually for the president to review.

We did not realize we were going to meet with Donald Trump, the president of the United States, until a line in the corner started to form. They took us in third, just Aunt Marge, Mom, and me. He greeted each of us personally and then spoke kind words about my dad. He had read what we sent in about him and remembered. I was so impressed. The respect we were shown in that moment and the entire evening still affects me. My dad's sacrifice was not just remembered as a token, it was understood—as was our family's sacrifice.

With Mom, Pres. Donald Trump,
and Aunt Marge in the White House.

After this short meeting, we were led to a different room in the East Wing. We were seated behind Vice President Pence and his lovely wife, Karen, with no idea what was about to take place. The president and his wife joined us for a beautiful candlelight ceremony. Fifty servicemen were honored, each one represented by a lit candle. We were asked to stand as my father's name was read. The First Lady tweeted a photo of that incredible moment in time.

Tonight @POTUS & I were honored to pay tribute to our fallen heroes. Thank you to the Gold Star families that joined us in celebration & remembrance.

Melania Trump
mobile.twitter.com

I felt as though I was finally able to attend my dad's funeral. On March 24, 1968, when my family mourned my father in a little Jonesboro church, I had stayed with a sitter. I had no realization of how much I needed that experience until I stood by my mom's side in the White House on that day in June 2018.

Chief of Staff John Kelly and his wife spoke with us afterwards. Their son, Robert Michael Kelly, was killed in Afghanistan in 2010 when he was twenty-nine. As John spoke with Aunt Marge and my mom, I was struck by the ease of our connection forged by a shared sacrifice.

John Kelly, Aunt Marge, Mom, Karen Kelly, and me at the White House.

The next day, I took Mom and Aunt Marge to the Vietnam Veterans Memorial. It was the first time either had been there. I left a note for my dad and told him about his sweet wife and dear aunt visiting him that day. Although my head knew he would not receive the letter, my heart again hoped that he knew.

We also met with Rep. Susan W. Brooks, who served as our district's Congressional representative. She listened attentively as we told her about my father.

With Representative Brooks in her office in Washington, D.C.

When I returned home I received this wonderful note from her:

OFFICE OF CONGRESSWOMAN SUSAN W BROOKS
WASHINGTON, D.C. 20515

FIFTH DISTRICT
INDIANA
June 27, 2018

Dr. Lori Goss-Reaves
4292 N 325 W
Marion, IN 46952

Dear Dr. Goss-Reaves, *Lori,*

Thank you for taking the time to visit my Washington, D.C. office. I am truly touched by the story of your father and appreciate you sharing that special story with me. Being a Gold Star family is one of our country's highest honors, and you, your father, and family are so deserving of the honor. I am pleased you were able to enjoy an evening at the White House honoring your father's sacrifice to our great nation.

As your mother said, saying their names and sharing their stories is essential. I shared the impactful story of Petty Officer 2nd Class Larry Jo Goss and your family with my staff and constituents. I hope that your story can impact others like it did me. I am proud to represent amazing families like yours in Congress and value the opportunity to make a difference in the lives of the people I serve. If my office can ever be of assistance, please do not hesitate to reach out.

Sincerely,

Susan W Brooks
Member of Congress

After we left D.C., we traveled to New York City by train to visit my son Cody, his wife, Kylie, and my twenty-two-month-old granddaughter, Madelyn. At one point during the train ride, I took a break from writing and looked over at Mom and Aunt Marge. They were holding hands. At that moment I became more aware of my father's sound judgment at such a young age. He knew that if he did not make it home, my mom would be comforted by his beloved aunt. Witnessing their connection on this trip healed another piece of my heart. Later, I went to buy them a snack on the train. When I came back, my mom was reading my dad's last letter to her to Aunt Marge. It was in Mom's purse.

At the JFK airport in Queens, as we were departing from New York City and heading back to Indiana, I noticed some decorative lanterns moving slowly above our heads. I looked up and felt a sensation I'd never experienced before: my dad's presence. It was unlike anything I'd ever felt. As the lanterns swayed ever so slowly, I got the sense my dad was there. I took in the lanterns a little longer, soaking up the feeling, and then snapped a picture. I knew I'd never forget that moment—it was the beginning of something new.

Mom and Aunt Marge in Grandma Bradford's kitchen in 1966, and on the train traveling from Washington, D.C., to New York City in November 2018.

*Top:* Their first visit to the Wall (June 5, 2018).

*Bottom:* I always leave a kiss on my dad's name.

# CHAPTER SEVENTEEN

# Retracing His Steps

My dad wanted to take Mom and me to Vietnam one day to show us the beautiful country. As with all his other dreams, I was determined to make this one come true. I knew I would not get my mom there, but I would go and share the experience with her through pictures.

Since Casey was graduating from high school in 2018, I decided that would be the year Eric and I would go. I truly believed that if I could just walk up Valentine's Ridge myself, I could put together all the different accounts I'd collected and know how my father was killed. Jerry and Mary offered to go with us; they had been there several times. An Indiana Wesleyan University journalism student interviewed me about my upcoming trip. Her article in the school newspaper chronicled my feelings leading up to our departure.

Grant County local, Navy Chief Corpsman Larry Jo Goss, paid the highest price 50 years ago when he was killed in action during the Vietnam War. Today, his daughter, Lori Goss-Reaves, continues to pay the highest price, living a life without her father.

After many years of waiting, Goss-Reaves will travel to Vietnam at the end of the month to retrace her father's last steps.

"I always knew that I had to go there and find out for myself what happened. I don't know that it is a desire, I don't really want to go, to be honest," she said. "I'm not looking forward to it, there's a sadness, even to think about it, let alone experience it. But I really think that this is God's timing for me to go."

Goss-Reaves' father served in Vietnam for around six weeks before his death.

"My father went to Vietnam in Dec. of 1967, right before Christmas," she said. "He was killed on Valentine's Day on a place called Valentine's Ridge."

At the time of her father's death, Goss-Reaves was only six months old. Her mother kept her father's memory alive and present in her life by saving everything of her father's, including the letters that he wrote to her mom during his deployment.

"My mom kept everything of my dad's for me," Goss-Reaves said. "So I grew up with this knowledge, always, of who he was. My identity was formed in a very positive way because I was his daughter."

In addition to retracing her father's steps, Goss-Reaves received a research grant through the Lilly Foundation that will allow her to focus on an academic aspect of her trip. While in Vietnam, Goss-Reaves will be exploring, through the lens of resilience theory, the effects of parental death on Gold Star children in the United States and Vietnam.

"I'm going to look at how they grieved the loss of their fathers," she said. "When I get home, I hope to write an article on resilience and reconciliation and peace."

Goss-Reaves said that she is thankful for her research because it will give her a break from the emotions she anticipates she will experience in Vietnam.

Traveling to Vietnam has two primary purposes for Goss-Reaves: to find answers surrounding her father's death and to seek reconciliation.

Growing up, Goss-Reaves did not know the story of her father's death. After her father's death, Goss-Reaves's mother received a telegram stating that her husband was missing. 5 telegrams later, her mother was informed of her father's death, three weeks after her father had died.

Because of this, Goss-Reaves said that she used to imagine that her father was a prisoner of war and that he would come home to her one day.

It wasn't until 1995 that Goss-Reaves knew for sure that her father had died. In 1995, Goss-Reaves received a phone call from Dr. Jerry Behrens, the doctor who her father served under during his deployment.

"He told me that he identified my dad's body," she said. "That was when I knew for sure that he had been killed. I probably knew before then. Dr. Behrens told me that he identified my dad's body by the picture of my mom and me in his breast pocket."

Behrens was able to connect Goss-Reaves with several men who had served alongside her father. They were able to tell her the story of her father's death. Goss-Reaves still has questions and hopes to find the answers in Vietnam.

"I've got to do this so that I can come back home and help my mom know what happened, or find another part of my dad there," she said.

Along with answers, Goss-Reaves hopes to find reconciliation. For Goss-Reaves, reconciliation is putting aside differences and choosing unity.

Goss-Reaves said that she remembers experiencing resentment for the people of Vietnam when she was growing up.

"There were these negative feelings about a people group that I didn't even know. I knew that wasn't right and I knew that wasn't okay," she said. "But I had no other experience with that group of people other than, because of that war, I didn't have a dad."

Goss-Reaves expects to experience something different than she imagined when she arrives in Vietnam.

"What I expect to experience in Vietnam is that I am going to find amazing people who had a war come to their land that they didn't want, that they didn't really have a lot of say in and that I'm going to meet them and reconcile in my heart that they are great people," she said. "And that they are not responsible for my dad's death."

Her whole life, Goss-Reaves has searched for answers and reconciliation surrounding her father's death. As she prepares to find possible answers, Goss-Reaves believes that her perspective will change.

"A part of my story is very sad when it comes to Vietnam. But I think for 14 days, I'm going to experience something very different about that culture and I am going to come back home with this peace in my heart about a group of people that are just like me," she said.

A change in perspective requires Goss-Reaves to put aside her resentment and anger-a task that defies human nature. She is determined to focus on her potential gain and not her loss.[*]

Eric and I left for Vietnam on Friday, November 30. The airplane ride was long, so I spent many hours reflecting and writing in my journal.

Departed our house at 7:33 p.m.
Amazed today by my dad's courage, and thankful Eric has always wanted to come with me on this trip. Oh the anguish my dad's heart had to feel as he flew to Vietnam alone, knowing he might never again see home or all of the people he so deeply loved. Leaving my mom was the hardest and then me and his grandma. The three girls he loved the most. His letters told me so. I always wished he would have gone to Canada. Surely my mom and I could have joined him there. His character would not allow him to do so. My mom said they had discussed it. His optimism helped him survive a painful childhood. He drew on that trait as he flew, holding onto the hope that he would hold us in his arms again. Yet his intellect told him that he might not make it out of Vietnam alive. He told my mom to remarry if that happened. He wanted her to receive the love she deserved, he wanted me to have a dad. His words continue to impact my life so positively. They are with me today on a luggage tag made by my sweet "Wall sister" Shari.[†]

---

[*] Mariah Woeste, "Retracing My Father's Last Steps—A Journey to Vietnam," *The Sojourn*, Dec. 2, 2018.

[†] "Wall sister" is a term used to describe the relationship between daughters of the fathers whose names are on the Vietnam Veterans Memorial Wall.

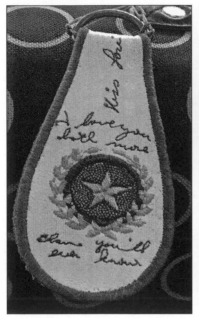 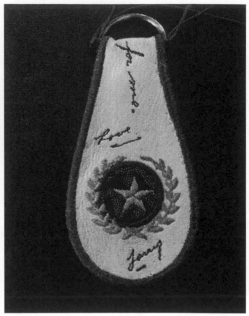

Shari used my dad's handwriting from one of his letters to make this luggage tag.

When we got off of the plane, I felt scared. Mary and Jerry were waiting for us, and their presence brought me comfort. Jerry had a cab waiting and Mary knew exactly where we were going. It felt surreal to be in the country I had harbored anger toward my whole life—the "land where my father died." The next morning, we met Mary and Jerry for breakfast. The Christmas music playing over the speaker took my thoughts back to my only Christmas with my dad. I had to push back the tears. We walked outside and the traffic was chaotic, yet no one appeared stressed. It was like New York City, except that the cars had been replaced by motor scooters carrying heavy loads. The temperature was hot and the air felt stale. I took it in the best I could but my heart only wanted to be in the area my dad served, not the city.

Mary, Jerry, Lori, and Eric in Saigon (Dec. 2, 2018).

We were in Saigon for the first part of our trip so I could conduct a research study on participants of the 2 Sides Project. The night before the meeting, I wrote in my journal:

I can't sleep so I just played out my dad's ceremony in my head—what I need to say to him. I hadn't cried yet today but I must have needed to. This is too sad, yet with life there are happy-sad moments. I'm very happy for Courtnee Jo and so proud of her.* She carries my dad's middle name, the shape of his chin, his love of school, and his work ethic. Not to mention his frugality and dislike of spending her own money, lol! I will take her college brochure and write a note to my dad about Courtnee's acceptance into dental school, on the back. We have a long car ride Wednesday through the countryside to the area where he served. I'll write the letter as we drive there. Good idea, Shari!

---

* Our daughter had just called to tell us she had been accepted to the Indiana University School of Dentistry.

The next morning, we left the Saigon hotel and headed toward the Quang Tri Province. We drove through the countryside for two days. This was the Vietnam I envisioned when I was a child. Memories flooded my mind of my fantasy of my dad being a POW awaiting the day he could escape and come home to Mom and me.

The support I received from home, through social media, helped me tremendously. My friend Kim and cousin Tina asked me for specific ways they could pray for me. My replies flowed effortlessly because I knew exactly what I needed from the trip. As soon as I finished typing we drove out of a tunnel into beautiful rain. I love rain and my dad and I both love water. The rain became a sign from God, several times on our trip, that He was with us.

Mary told me we were nearing Dong Ha. I remembered reading about that place in my dad's letters. Seeing it gave me a whole new perspective on his journey. It felt good to retrace his steps, and as we got closer to Valentine's Ridge, feelings of anticipation filled my heart.

Jerry called the hotel we stayed at the night before "a tad Spartan." The mold on the walls and dirt in the water cups were so prominent that I had slept in my clothes from head to toe. I had awakened at 4:00 a.m. the day we were set to depart and, unable to go back to sleep, wrote my dad another letter:

Dear Daddy,*

I made it!!! Didn't you know I would. :) It's because of you and Mom that I did! She loves you so much and so do I. Your darling daughter, as you always called me!

Thank you, Daddy, for asking God into your heart. Thank you for writing home about it. Now I know you are in heaven and that Mom and I will get to be with you again forever—like we were supposed

---

* I do not remember ever calling my dad "Daddy." To me he was always "my dad," but in the letter I wrote to him that morning, "Daddy" felt right.

to be with you here on earth. Thank you for being such a great corpsman. Camron Carter says thank you, too. I am bringing you this cross earring that mom bought me and this heart she wants you to have. She carried it in her purse and wanted me to bring it to you. You were with her always. She carried your letters in her purse and you and me in her heart.

I am also bringing you, for Mom, the last letter she ever wrote you. She never stopped loving you, Dad—no one ever forgot about you either. We still think about you every day and carry you with us in our hearts.

You have five grandchildren—four boys and one girl. They are incredible human beings. You would love them so much. Your oldest grandson is named after Grandma Bradford. Christopher after Ruth Christine and also after Jesus Christ. He played baseball in college and loves it as much as you did. He is a sports encyclopedia. He and you would've talked a lot about basketball and baseball games. He looks like you. He's a great daddy and husband too.

Your second grandson is named after you. Cody Lawrence. He's a lawyer. He's very smart and loves school like you. He calls Mom about once a week and loves her just like you love Grandma Bradford. Cody Lawrence has a strong work ethic and is a great daddy and husband too. He looks like you too. Mom says he acts so much like you.

Your third grandson was born with Down syndrome 23 years ago. I needed you so much then, Dad. I was 28. I cried for you and him every day for two years. He has the middle name Michael.[*] You would love him so much! Mom takes care of him every day. He's filled a void in her heart that was created when you didn't get to come home. You would have loved him like you did Jimmy. Jimmy's buried right next to you at home.

---

[*] My dad's cousin Michael Cummings was only eight when Dad was killed in Vietnam.

I finally had a little girl, Dad. I needed to watch my husband love her the way you would have loved me. My husband is an excellent father and a man you would really love too. He takes good care of me—which is hard to do because I'm strong-willed like you! He loves me so much—you would love that, and he honors you always. He even asked me to marry him at your grave on his knees in the snow. Your precious granddaughter is named after both of us. Her middle name is Jo. She loves medicine like you, and school. She just got accepted into five dental schools. Dad, she's going to be a doctor just like you. She is so brave that she went to college in California—near where you went to Field Medical School. She is strong and assertive and a fighter like you. You would love her so much!

Your youngest grandchild is a boy. God really gave me an incredible gift when he gave him to me. God knew I needed this boy who looked so much like you as a baby. It was unreal. He still looks a lot like you. He has your hair and your love of dancing and laughter and singing. He also has your caring heart. He's in college now studying to be an actor. He went to California too!

Dad, you wanted to go to college but didn't get to. I'm very sorry about that. Two of your grandsons have graduated from college. One got a degree in communications and sports management. The other is a lawyer. Can you believe that? Your granddaughter will graduate in May and then go to dental school. Wow! Your youngest will graduate in three years. I wish you could see him on a stage. He captivates every audience. He's truly that good! You and mom had great genes. Thank you!

I got my doctorate degree because of you. I'm Dr. Goss, just like you! You are who I always wanted to be like. I will honor you every day of my life, and Mom too. I love you very much. In heaven, I will get that kiss you wanted to give me and a father/daughter dance, too. I will forever be your darling daughter. Thank you for calling me that. And thank you for all the letters and for every night asking God to bless Mom and me. I feel you here, Daddy. Will you come with me?

Your darling daughter,
Lori Jo

I knew it was far-fetched to think that my dad would be able to see me on the ridge, but I hoped with all my heart that he would. Before we left the hotel, I washed my hair by bending over the shower, fully dressed. I needed to look my best for my dad. I wore a photo button of each of my children so my dad could see them—if God gave him the ability to watch us on this day. I knew my dad would recognize the wedding ring he bought my mom, the one I have worn every day since the day I said "I do" to Eric.

We left the hotel and walked to a small market. Mary wanted to buy incense and I wanted to purchase flowers. Jerry struck up a conversation with a Vietnamese man who fought in the South Vietnamese Army. He was the only person from that generation we saw during our trip.

The car ride seemed long, but we were getting close. I opened my dad's Bible to a random page—chapter one of the Book of Acts. I did not realize then what God was saying to me but I thanked Him for bringing me this far.

Minutes before arriving at the ridge, I received an email from my son Cody. He wrote a letter to his grandpa for us to read on the ridge. Tears flowed as I read his beautiful words. I hoped my dad would be able to hear them.

Eric held the GPS device that my "Wall sister" Jeanette Chervony had mailed us. He was determined to find the location of the coordinates where my dad was last seen. Eric realized we had passed the ridge, so we turned around in an area that had a restroom. When we all returned to the car, Jerry said, "Let's find it," and instructed our driver to head back. Eric suggested a place to stop on Route 9. When we stopped, I hopped out of the van with all the things I wanted to show my dad: Casey's Marion High School socks, a Cubs T-shirt showing they won the World Series, the Bible he carried with him to Vietnam, a copy of our doctorate diploma, a poem from my mom, newspaper articles about him, a picture Mom asked me to bring, and a deck of playing cards.

We looked for the Montagnard village that Ray had told us about, which was at the base of Valentine's Ridge, but we could not find it. We found a village across the street from the ridge and stopped there. Our guide and Jerry talked to the people but no one seemed to know where a path was that went to the top of the ridge.

The ridge was steep and the new Route 9 was busy with traffic. Jerry scrambled up the side of the ridge. He found notches in the dirt that enabled him to climb up approximately ten feet. He then reached down a stick to assist us.

Near our landing spot just ten feet up the ridge, we found a section of the old Route 9—the one that was there when my dad served. Eric felt like it was significant and possibly the place where my dad's body was laid when it was brought down from the ridge. I felt the chance of that was slim, but I had heard that the bodies were brought down to Route 9 and loaded into a truck before they were taken to Ca Lu, where Jerry and the chaplain were waiting.

Though I had planned to climb all the way up Valentine's Ridge, there was no way to get up there. The terrain was simply too rough. I now understand why it had taken the Marines so long to move from place to place that fateful day more than fifty years ago. Although I was disappointed and wanted to go further, I felt the Holy Spirit clearly telling me to be OK with where we were, approximately ten feet up the ridge, in the middle of foliage that did not allow me to see the whole landscape. I was not going to be able to put together all the accounts I'd collected and see with my own eyes what they were describing, but I was there, standing on the land where my father died.

We had a beautiful ceremony. I had thought many times about all the things I wanted to tell my dad. Eric displayed the ceremony through Facebook Live so my mom could be present too. It was 4:00 a.m. at home but she was patiently waiting, as were some veterans and Gold Star daughter Shari Bennett. They were able to see the whole thing. I held my composure as I read my letter, and I was talking to my dad so I felt strong. Then from my phone I played my mom and dad's favorite song, "Hold Me, Thrill Me, Kiss Me" by Harry Noble. I put my head in my lap and sobbed as these lyrics played:

*Hold me, hold me*
*And never let me go until you've told me, told me*
*What I want to know and then just hold me, hold me*
*Make me tell you I'm in love with you*
*Thrill me (thrill me), thrill me (thrill me)*
*Walk me down the lane where shadows*
*Will be (will be) will be (will be)*
*Hiding lovers just the same as we'll be, we'll be*
*When you make me tell you I love you*
*They told me "Be sensible with your new love"*
*"Don't be fooled, thinking this is the last you'll find"*
*But they never stood in the dark with you, love*
*When you take me in your arms*
*And drive me slowly out of my mind*
*Kiss me (kiss me), kiss me (kiss me)*
*And when you do, I'll know that you*
*Will miss me (miss me), miss me (miss me)*
*If we ever say "Adieu," so kiss me, kiss me*
*Make me tell you I'm in love with you.*

As I was reading my letter, I noticed several butterflies, but thought little of it. After the song finished playing, Jerry read the letter my

317

son Cody had sent me for his grandpa. The entire time Jerry read it, a white butterfly stayed on his leg.

While Mary read the poem my mom sent with me, I observed the rest of the butterflies that were still in our midst. One was blue, my mom's favorite color. I didn't think I had ever seen a blue butterfly, so I took it as another sign from God.

I left the photos Mom wanted me to bring her Larry. One was of their wedding. The second was just of her, standing in their Chicago apartment. She had sent that one to my dad at boot camp.

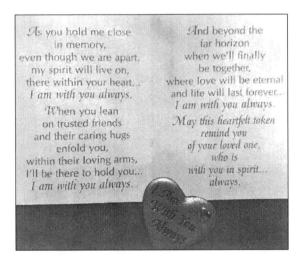

As you hold me close
in memory,
even though we are apart,
my spirit will live on,
there within your heart...
I am with you always.

When you lean
on trusted friends
and their caring hugs
enfold you,
within their loving arms,
I'll be there to hold you...
I am with you always.

And beyond the
far horizon
when we'll finally
be together,
where love will be eternal
and life will last forever...
I am with you always.

May this heartfelt token
remind you
of your loved one,
who is
with you in spirit...
always.

Mom asked me to bring this poem and heart to Dad. She had carried it in her purse along with his last letter for fifty years. We buried it for her on Valentine's Ridge.

I also brought my dad a copy of the newspaper article that pictured Jerry and me standing by the monument Eric designed. We are pointing to my dad's name. I wanted Dad to see that Jerry chose to be a part of my life because of the impression my dad had made on him. There was so much to show and tell my dad. I had waited so long.

Eric was the final speaker, and it was perfect. He spoke from his heart, thanking my dad for me. After we stopped the camera, Eric dug a hole to bury the things we had brought. As we were departing, Eric spotted bamboo, and I knew we were at the spot where we were supposed to be. During the last two weeks of my dad's life, he had made bamboo cups for mom and me. Today, they proudly sit in my family room, a constant reminder of my dad's love. On the bottom of my mom's cup he wrote "LOVE Feb 68." On the front, he wrote "Kilo 3/9" and "MARTY." On my little cup he wrote "Kilo 3/9" and "Lori," and on the bottom, "Feb 68." My dad paid so much attention to detail and was always giving to those he loved. On a C-Ration box, he wrote a note that he included with a gift to us. He thought it would be one of many, but it turned out to be his last. My dad was in a war-torn country fighting for his life, yet found a way to make these for us. I had not seen bamboo growing before. It felt like another sign.

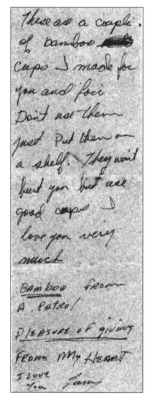

Dad's last present for mom and me (February 1968), and
the bamboo on Valentine's Ridge (Dec. 7, 2018).

The next day, we stopped to take pictures of the Little Rockpile on our way back to Valentine's Ridge. I had communicated with Ray Felle that morning, as I had to make sure we were on the correct ridge the day before. Ray had described an "east ridge" and a "west ridge" and said my dad was killed on the west one. I could not go home without knowing that we had found the right one.

Our guide, Mr. Hai, parked the van. We got out quickly and Eric pointed out two playing cards lying on the ground. We crossed the road to look at the river my dad had crossed on the February 9 patrol. Ray said the rock formations were still in the water when he returned to the ridge in 2003, so finding them assured me that we were in the correct place. I needed that confirmation.

When we got back in the van, Eric handed me the cards: a ten and a five of clubs. If I had not been present, I would not have believed it. Dad and Mom loved playing cards together, and he wrote about playing in Vietnam, too. Mary said she was sure that one was for my mom and the other for me, but we needed to figure out the significance of the numbers. I pondered for a while and decided that the five was for me—my dad's way of letting me know that he knew he had five grandchildren. As I held them, I praised God for this gift from my dad.

My parents were married in the tenth month.

Several people at home were faithfully praying and following my trip through Facebook posts. My friend Bekki told me that I had everything I needed. Her words ministered to me as I thought about everything I still wanted to do at the ridge in the little bit of time I had left. I had brought along a photo of my dad sitting on a weapon. I did not know which base he was on but noticed a distinct rock formation behind him called "the Razorback." Jerry took us to the Rockpile earlier and we saw something that looked the same. I told Mary I needed one more hour in the afternoon to go back.

Jerry wanted to take me to the Khe Sanh museum. It was important to him that I understood the history. As we walked around Khe Sanh, a peddler kept following us and would not go away, and I had the thought that maybe I was supposed to buy something from him. Did God have something for me there? Maybe the peddler had my dad's dog tag. How cool that would be! But Jerry kindly convinced him that we were not interested in his trinkets. I felt relief mixed with a little regret and hoped I was listening to the Holy Spirit closely enough.

We stopped and had a soda. My dad wrote about hoping to have one in Vietnam, so I had one for him. The peddler came back and sat next to me. He pointed out VC stuff to me, and then I saw a cross charm. I felt like my dad wanted me to have it. I could take it home as a gift from him, even though he had not served in Khe Sanh. I held it in my hand as Jerry, Mary, and me talked about my childhood for the first time on the trip. It seemed like my dad needed to know the things I shared. I felt his presence strongly there. I loved rolling the cross around in my hand. As the conversation took place around me, my thoughts remained on the gift from my dad.

The plan was to get lunch in Khe Sanh. We stopped at three places, but none had food. The fourth had a smorgasbord with already-prepared food, but several flies were also there, so we decided to pass. I knew everyone was hungry, but I wasn't ready to leave that area. We drove by Valentine's Ridge again, and the cross did not leave my hand during the long van ride.

Finally we found a place to eat, and to my delight the tables were covered in blue tablecloths, my mom's favorite color. The table we sat at had six chairs. Since there were five in our traveling party, I imagined that one was for my dad. I sat next to the empty chair and my dad and I "had a date" while Mary, Jerry, Mr. Hai, and Eric conversed. As we were leaving, I felt strongly in my spirit that my dad and I had to say goodbye. On the ridge, I had asked him to come home with me, but it seemed as though at the restaurant I knew he couldn't. As I imagined him walking me to the van, we stopped at a tree with flowers. I picked one, imagining it was from him, and felt an indescribable peace.

In the van I held the cross and continued to rub it all the way back to the ridge. I envisioned placing it on the windowsill in my office at the university and being reminded of this special trip. Our guide parked along the river, across the street from Valentine's Ridge again. I wanted to read the Bible verses God seemed to put in my heart the day before. When I got out of the van, I still had the cross in my hand but realized within a few minutes that it was gone. Without telling anyone, I looked down into the tall grass but could not find it. I don't like to inconvenience others, so I decided to let it be. Eric joined me as I read the opening lines from Acts chapter one:

In my former book, Theophilus, I wrote about all that Jesus began to do and to teach until the day he was taken up to heaven, after giving instructions through the Holy Spirit to the apostles he had chosen. After his suffering, he presented himself to them and gave many convincing proofs that he was alive. He appeared to them over a period of forty days and spoke about the kingdom of God. On one occasion, while he was eating with them, he gave them this command: "Do not leave Jerusalem, but wait for the gift my Father promised, which you have heard me speak about. For

John baptized with water, but in a few days, you will be baptized with the Holy Spirit."

Then they gathered around him and asked him, "Lord, are you at this time going to restore the kingdom to Israel?"

He said to them: "It is not for you to know the times or dates the Father has set by his own authority. But you will receive power when the Holy Spirit comes on you; and you will be my witnesses in Jerusalem, and in all Judea and Samaria, and to the ends of the earth."

After he said this, he was taken up before their very eyes, and a cloud hid him from their sight.

They were looking intently up into the sky as he was going, when suddenly two men dressed in white stood beside them. "Men of Galilee," they said, "why do you stand here looking into the sky? This same Jesus, who has been taken from you into heaven, will come back in the same way you have seen him go into heaven."*

I was not sure why God gave me these verses until I posted it on Facebook. A dear friend, Evelyn, replied that when my dad's body was left behind on the ridge, my dad was not really there. He had already gone to be with the Lord.

This truth filled me with more peace. The part of my dad's story that had bothered me since the day I found out that he and the Marines were left behind was now different. It was as if God was telling me Himself, through His word, that while the NVA had had control of my dad's physical body and animals had eaten away his flesh, my dad was OK. He had been with Jesus the whole time.

---

* Acts 1:1–11 (NIV).

We went back to the Rockpile and I saw the rock formation again—Jerry confirmed it was the Razorback. This steep rock formation resembled a man lying down. Eric took a photo of me with it behind me, just as my dad had done. I was retracing his footsteps and it felt great.

Standing near the place where my dad had stood,
with the Razorback in the background.

That night it rained throughout dinner. The restaurant was flooded so they put us in a "VIP" room upstairs. I walked over by myself to the window to feel the rain, and it seemed as though my dad joined me again just to play. I cupped the water and threw it in the air. I smiled and was reminded that even though he could not physically come home with me, his presence was still here. I started to cry.

I envisioned my dad having picked up that cross I dropped. The thought brought me comfort. It seemed like maybe the purpose of that trinket was so that my dad could have a part of me in Vietnam too. Finding the cards, a part of him, had been my favorite part of the whole trip.

Before leaving the hotel in Da Nang, Mary presented Eric and me with a gift. Once again, she knew exactly what I needed. Our Christmas present from them was a two-night stay at a resort in Nha Trang. Their generosity left me speechless. I love the ocean and needed a relaxing few days after all I had just experienced.

It was very clear to me when I was flying away from Vietnam that my dad would see me again. My job now was to take care of my mom. That's what he wanted me to do. He will come be with us when she is dying, and he will help her get to the other side. He will hold her hand and take her where they will spend eternity together. I am sure of this.

In my dad's portfolio that I brought with me to Vietnam, I found several envelopes, unused stationary, and one stamp. I used it to write a letter to my mom from my dad. I gave it to her for Christmas that year. I had received the blessing of my dad's presence in Vietnam, and I wanted my mom to have that gift too.

*Top left:* Items I took to Vietnam to "show" my dad.

*Top right:* Eric buried the things we brought to my dad on Valentine's Ridge, December 7, 2018.

*Bottom:* With Jerry, Eric, and Mary after our ceremony.

*Top:* The Little Rockpile, the river, and Valentine's Ridge.

*Bottom:* Part of Valentine's Ridge as seen from Route 9.

# CHAPTER EIGHTEEN

# My "Second Tour"

A key person in my search was a Marine named John Edwards. I had known that I needed to find him after Camron Carter shared the newspaper article with me that contained quotes from John. Sitting in the airport with Jerry, ready to leave Saigon, John Edwards responded to one of Jerry's Facebook posts. I did not know that Jerry knew him, but I looked forward to connecting with John when we returned home.

John accepted my Facebook friend request, and on February 16, 2019, I sent John this message:

> Good evening, Mr. Edwards. I am the only daughter of Doc Goss who was killed on Valentine's Ridge. I don't want to ever do anything to increase your pain regarding the war. If it would not harm you emotionally, would you please tell me what you remember about that terrible battle? I've heard different versions but only talked to one person who saw my dad's body after he was killed. I know there has to be someone living who knows more. I just got back from seeing Valentine's Ridge with my own eyes. I have heard good things about you and want to tell you how glad I am that you made it home!

John sent me a message that said, "Lori — If you can call [number] day or night we can talk about Valentine's Ridge." I called him right away. As I had done numerous times before, I grabbed a note pad and pen and wrote down every word John said:

Your dad was a part of H&S Company. He was a Petty Officer 2nd Class, which is equivalent to a sergeant in the Marines. Two companies were at Ca Lu: India and Kilo. The major was the battalion executive officer at Ca Lu. I was the communications chief. They sent me down there before the battle. My job was to make sure the radio operators did their job. I was crazy so I liked to go to the field every so often. I had direct contact with the major, who took his own life years after returning home from Vietnam.

The major said I could go on the 2-14-68 patrol but I had to get the CO's permission as he was the commanding officer of Kilo 3/9. When I spoke with the CO his reply was, "Oh good—we are going to go get that mortar." I kind of bit my tongue. I thought, what makes him think that's just a mortar up there? I knew there could be a whole group of NVA on the ridge. I had a fitful night sleeping that night knowing I was going to the field. It was to be a one-day operation; the company was supposed to be back before sundown. The company left the north perimeter going to the jungle and got to Valentine's Ridge without any problems. We started hiking up the ridge. There was some shooting up there. We ran up the hill and closed up the column. It turns out Schneider had been killed and another one had his arm blown off.[*]

I was lying down near the Command Post [my dad's group] and could hear the major on the radio say; "You have to do something! You can't be there after dark." For half an hour we didn't do anything. That was a mistake. Then the CO gave orders to move

---

[*] I remembered this part of the story from Doc Russell's account. This is the time in the battle where my dad came up to aid Doc Russell in treating Camron Carter.

forward. There was a machine gun firing from the ridge ahead. It was a machine gun on wheels. You could hear the tack, tack, tack, tack sound. Two men went down in front of me, but they were not killed. Then we got tear-gassed for a while. We were near the top of the ridge when the mortars came in. We could hear the mortar in the tube. It sounds like a Champagne bottle pop. We got down. One piece of mortar hit me but it didn't do much. The XO and the CO were both hit. I was real mad because I knew it was not supposed to be like this.

After that first round of shooting it got pretty quiet. The CO couldn't do anything so we did not have a leader. I was a radio guy looking for radios as I went back up. I saw a corpsman working on a wounded guy. I didn't know who he was because I wasn't with them [Kilo Company]. The corpsman said "He's gone," and he wept a little. The corpsman went up the ridge. I saw a guy with a pretty good ankle wound. He was laying there by himself. I started yelling for someone to come get this guy. Three young grunts came and carried him.

The injuries to the "guy" John was describing sounded similar to the injuries Doc Russell described about "Jackson from Montana." This made me wonder if John was near my dad when the mortars came in. John said he was not sure which platoon he was with until he spoke with Don Carter years later at a Kilo 3/9 reunion. John and Don both experienced the tear gas, so John knew they were close in proximity on the ridge. Don was Lieutenant Wszolek's radioman and was with Third Platoon. The Command Post was with Third Platoon near the top of the ridge.

The corpsmen from Third Platoon were Doc Russell, Doc Porter, and Doc Lindell. My dad was the only corpsman in the Command Post. I've communicated with Doc Lindell and Doc Russell. Their accounts make it clear they were not the corpsman John saw treating a wounded Marine who died. Doc Porter declined to share his memories. From this I deduced that the corpsman John saw was Doc Porter or my dad. I called my mom and asked if Dad would have wept if a Marine died whom he was trying to save. She said yes.

I was astonished to find another person who was near my dad that day. John suggested I call Don Carter, who I had spoken to at the Kilo 3/9 reunion. Don and I talked on the phone, and he said they had gathered the bodies on February 15, which was something I had read in an email Ray shared with me many years before, but had not explored further.

Determined to run down this loose thread, I called Zeke, as his platoon had brought the remains of my father and the nine Marines off the ridge. Zeke insisted that all the bodies were not gathered together. I was perplexed and knew I needed to continue searching for the truth about what happened to my dad on that disastrous day.

John reached out to a friend and then suggested that I write the National Military Personnel Records Center in St. Louis and ask for the complete packet of my dad's military records. I had done this before but had received nothing that resembled an autopsy report. I assumed one had not been done because of the condition of his body after being exposed to the elements for three weeks. John, however, thought there should be something.

The large packet that arrived this time contained documents I'd never seen before. They were stamped "Declassified." I went through the pages quickly until I found this:

A military report filled out March 13, 1968, shows the
fractured and missing parts of my dad's body.

My heart beat rapidly as I looked at each place where my dad's
body had been injured. The dark marks on his mouth indicate that

his teeth were not recovered. I assumed the NVA kept his dentures or that they fell out as his body decomposed and are now buried on Valentine's Ridge. Mom said she never saw him without them, and they were together for two years. There were also dark marks on my dad's top three vertebrae, indicating that they were not recovered either.

My dad had broken bones on his left arm. I thought back to Doc Russell's account. Without closing my eyes, I envisioned my dad shielding the wounded Marine, causing his left arm to be struck by the blast. This new information seemed to support the accuracy of Doc Russell's account.

The first line on the next page bothered me the most. It said: "The remains present for examination is that of an adult male, Caucasian, of medium body build and muscularity with light brown hair attached to the body." The visual that brought to my mind was in stark contrast to the well-groomed pictures I have of my dad. He was particular about his hair. I knew this from my mom's stories and a letter my dad sent home; he told her he was happy with a haircut a man named Leech had given him.

Page two of the report describes the condition of my dad's body.

The next line said my dad's remains were "semi-skeletal with seg-ments of decomposed tissue attached." Nobody's father should be de-scribed that way, especially someone who gave his life for his country. He gave his life for someone that day. The report said they measured my dad's clavicle to determine a match between the skeleton and my dad's age. His height matched with the measurement of his left femur. I had no doubt in my mind that these were my dad's remains. Jerry's account made that clear as well. My dad's dental characteristics were also an excellent match. I could not read any further, so I put the packet away.

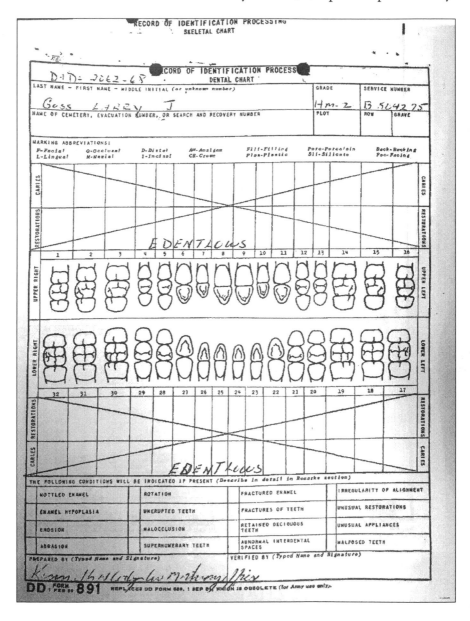

The report includes my dad's dental chart.

\* \* \* \* \*

John invited me to go with him to Vietnam in the summer of 2019. The thought of returning six months after my trip with Jerry and Mary Behrens was daunting. The emotions I felt during my 2018 trip were intense. I did not want to feel them again.

John did not pressure me to go with him but left the invitation open. My son Casey had wanted to go in 2018 but was in college during our trip; John's plan for a summer trip would allow Casey to go. The dates of John's trip aligned with what would have been my dad's seventy-third birthday. When John told me we could climb Valentine's Ridge on that day, I knew my answer was "yes."

The day after we celebrated my granddaughter Olivia's second birthday, Casey and I boarded an airplane for Vietnam. We met John, his friend, and his friend's two grandchildren. John's friend is a Marine who served with Kilo 3/9 prior to my dad's arrival in Vietnam. The itinerary for their trip was full but John's friend promised me that July 7 was carved out just for me. On this day we would climb up Valentine's Ridge.

On July 6, John told his friend he wanted to conduct some reconnaissance. He said this meant going to Valentine's Ridge to look at the terrain and make a plan for our climb. We found the Montagnard village that Jerry, Mary, Eric, and I could not find. Our guide, Mr. Thang, spoke to the villagers and gained permission for us to walk around their property. We found two paths and John made the decision to climb the steepest one the following day.

Casey and I in the Montagnard village at the base of Valentine's Ridge (July 6, 2019).

I knew John would need a place to rest and looked for a chair to take. I could not find one but John was determined to make it. He came prepared with a knife to chop the brush and C-Rations for our lunch. He also had six bottles of water in his pack that he treated with chloroquine to prevent malaria.

I was concerned about the weight of John's pack. I tried my best to get him to let Casey carry it but to no avail. That was the first indication I had that we might not reach our destination. Tears came to my eyes but I quickly changed my thoughts. I breathed in the moment, hoping my dad could see us once again, this time observing his handsome grandson, who looked so much like him.

We stopped to rest and held a short ceremony. Casey led us in singing "Happy Birthday" to his grandpa and John's friend played the song "Corpsman Up" on his phone. Our guide threw paper money in the air, a custom of the Vietnamese to send money to those who are dead. I had not told our guide about my father's childhood and found his words interesting as he spoke into the sky about the riches my father was receiving.

We held our ceremony on what would have been my
dad's seventy-third birthday (July 7, 2019).

John's friend wanted to stop. The terrain was challenging and he was concerned about John's health. John's GPS indicated that we were about five hundred meters away from the coordinates listed on the Marine chronology that indicated where the battle occurred.

John's friend encouraged me to get John to stop. I tried, but John was a Marine on a mission. He had returned to Vietnam as a tour guide several times but this was his first time back to Valentine's Ridge.

As John proceeded up the trail, his friend approached him and asked me to step away. I heard him tell John that he would bring him back the next day. I was devastated, but John's needs came first. I told myself I would come back to Vietnam a third time and would be OK.

Casey and I walked up the path a little further, but without John's memories and his GPS, we had no idea where to go.

We joined the others in the van and our guide drove us to a hill where John's friend had fought. John and I stayed in the van. He recalled out loud once again his memories of Valentine's Day 1968. His story remained consistent every time he shared it. I knew without a doubt that his account was accurate and not tainted by the stories of others or of time.

The next day I awoke with a deep feeling of sadness. I had come to Vietnam twice for one purpose: to see the part of the ridge where my dad was killed. John's stomach was upset and so he chose to stay at the hotel. In a boat with our group, my tears fell once again, but this time I could not contain them. Normally I could compartmentalize and put my thoughts and feelings away, but on this day I could not.

Mr. Thang was kind and compassionate. He asked me if I was OK. I asked him if I could pay him to return to the ridge one day and capture a video for me of the area John was leading us to. He said yes. I cried tears of happiness at the thought of at least getting to see the terrain from the top of the ridge. John told me that the "kill zone" was a flat area near the top of the ridge. I needed to see it with my own eyes, and a video was better than not seeing it at all.

Then I found the courage to ask Mr. Thang if he would take me back. We were only a two hours' drive away from the ridge. I offered to pay him all of the money I had left: five hundred U.S. dollars. He said yes. Casey and I would not have John or his GPS but I had a copy of John's map. I did not know how to read it, but it would have to do.

Casey, Mr. Thang, and I had ninety minutes to see as much of the ridge as we could. I knew better than to be on the ridge at dark. My precious Casey was incredible as we climbed as high as time allowed. Once again, my heart felt incredible peace. On the hill where my father died, I felt his love and knew that for reasons I could not comprehend, everything was somehow OK.

*Above:* With John Edwards and Casey on July 7, 2019.
*Below:* Casey on the ridge, July 9th, near the spot where his grandpa was killed.

On the ridge with thankfulness in my heart
and beautiful flowers (July 9, 2019). Getting to go
back to the ridge was the best $500 I've ever spent.

*Left:* Dad's photo of Valentine's Ridge taken from
Ca Lu Combat Base in January 1968.

*Right:* My photo of the same tree from Valentine's Ridge.

Dad's photo of water buffalo in January 1968.

My photo of the water buffalo Casey saw on July 7, 2019, my dad's birthday.

# CHAPTER NINETEEN

# Valentine's Ridge

It took me thirty-five years to complete the search I began when I was eighteen years old. Though my search took many twists and turns, it remained focused for all those years on discovering whether my dad truly was killed on Valentine's Day 1968 and on discovering who he was and who I was in relationship to him.

I thought that if I found and interviewed everyone who was near my dad on Valentine's Ridge that one accurate and cohesive story would emerge, that I would be able to recreate my dad's final hours on this earth, that I would finally know the truth about how and why my dad died.

Thanks to Jerry Behrens, I learned that my dad was killed on Valentine's Day, but accurate information about when he was actually killed during the battle was not revealed until the spring of 2020. When COVID-19 shut down our world, I finally had time to focus 100 percent of my energy on the search. Nevertheless, no matter how many hours I spent listening to story after story from veterans who were there, the cohesive story I hoped for remained unclear.

My final account is the result of a decades-long journey to discover the truth. It's no doubt somewhat muddled and confusing, but all are essential pieces of my quest for the truth.

\* \* \* \* \*

Several months after Casey and I returned from Vietnam, I opened the packet of my dad's military records once more. Sitting in my living room alone late one night, I found a paper I'd never seen before. My mouth dropped open and a sense of shock filled my heart. A missing-in-action progress report said that my dad was not killed by mortars. The rumor I had been told by others was not true—my dad was killed by a grenade.

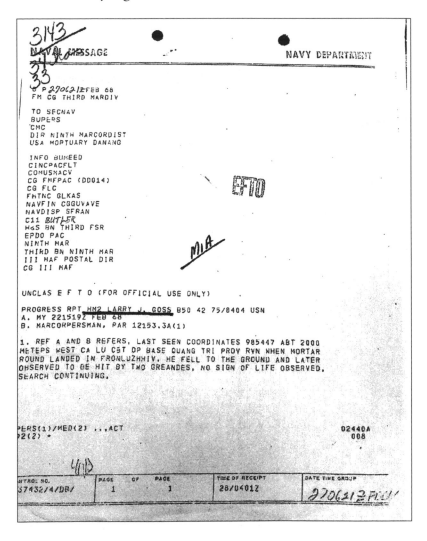

My heart always knew that my dad *had* hugged the ground when the mortars came in, just like he told us he would. He fell to the ground, but the mortars did not kill him. He was alive after the mortars landed, just like Doc Russell had said. Later, he was "observed to be hit by two grenades, no sign of life observed." The truth had been there the whole time in a classified document. I also found a copy of a letter my mom sent the government in April 1968. She had not saved a copy for herself, so it was not in the scrapbook.

The search I thought began in 1986 actually began in 1968. The information in my dad's MIA progress report would have saved my mom years of wondering and believing her beloved husband was alive.

I wanted to find the person who gave this after-action report. Was he still alive? Would he talk to me? I pored over the notes of my conversation with Rick Foster at the 2007 reunion, and the notes of my conversation with Don Carter and the other men who courageously shared their memories with me. I also reviewed many emails Ray had shared with me over the previous twenty years.

I learned from interviewing numerous Marines and corpsmen that people see the battle only from their vantage point. And in the dense jungle, that point may be only a small space around them. Still, I thought, if I could talk to all living survivors and review all command chronologies available online, I would be able to reconstruct the battle with words.

I had a large volume of information written by the Marines and corpsman from First Platoon, but only one from Second Platoon. Thanks to John Edwards, I knew the Command Post was with Third Platoon. In 2011, Ray had connected me to the lieutenant from Third Platoon, Dan Wszolek. I knew it was time to connect with him again.

From my email with Lieutenant Wszolek years before, I knew that the story passed down to me that my father was looking at a map with the CO and the XO when the mortars came in was not true. Wszolek said *he* was the person who had been looking at a map with the CO and the XO. He stayed on the ridge that night, and fought the next day, yet his voice seemed absent. After answering my many questions, he sent me his full account:

Before I present my account of the patrol on Feb. 14 & 15, 1968, a short prelude is in order. My journey to the truth which gained momentum about 10 years ago consisted of one epiphany after another. I suppressed it all for 30 plus years. This expedition was initiated when I was contacted by Lori Jo Goss-Reaves, my participation at the 3/9 reunion in Vegas in 2010, for which I commend Don Carter my radioman in Vietnam for his constant encouragement for me to attend, and several conversations with Larry Bearden.

Over the years I have had sporadic contact with several Kilo company members, but we never discussed Valentine's Ridge. I was reacquainted with several Marines at the 3/9 reunion who were with me on the ridge. No discussion prevailed. The majority of my information was gleaned from the research conducted by Lori Jo. Although much of what she was told was bogus and common-sense analysis dictated this, it did lead to a viable and constructive path to the selection of the pieces that indeed fit the puzzle. [For] this I am eternally grateful. Now I suspect I am supposed to attest to my fallibility and absolve all but I for any errors or malapropisms or spoonerisms (if they indeed exist in the written form) that are displayed in this account. I so do!

The account next written will not be influenced nor guided by information I now have. It will be written from the perspective of what I witnessed, felt, and remembered then, not what I have learned since.

We were informed, I believe that it was on Feb 13, 1968, that a company-size patrol would be heading out the following morning at daybreak to sweep through the hills just west of the Ca Lu base and north of highway 9. The base was intermittently subject to being shelled by mortars by the NVA. We knew that they were up there somewhere. Our mission was to find them and destroy them or at the least force them to leave. So much for the second part of the task. The entire conflict in Vietnam was a futile exercise of sacrificing men in order to seize a small piece of real estate only to rapidly depart and present that exorbitantly priced parcel back to its initial occupants.

At daybreak on Feb 14th, 1968, Kilo Company departed the wire at Ca Lu and headed west along Highway 9. There was no doubt in my mind that if the NVA were still in the hills, they could see us and were clearly aware of our plans as we were mortared on a previous patrol not too far from where we now were. We were a company consisting of 3 platoons of about 50 to 60 men each. With the command group and a few tagalongs, we numbered about 200.

We left the highway and headed north into the bush just a bit west of the hills we planned to search. The CO attempted to orchestrate a semi wedge formation, but this was only possible with limited success for a very short distance through the valley just southwest of our objective, which were ridges on our right (east). Soon this formation with my platoon (3rd) in the middle and in front with the other two platoons, one on each side of me, was futile and ineffective. This clearly became evident when we reached the base on the northwest section of the ridge. Insurmountable obstacles materialized, averting any resemblance of a tactical formation to be implemented. It required many hours of uneventful slogging to reach this point and as we started up the ridge our company formation morphed into an ill-advised very long line. I was still the lead platoon as I had been for the entire patrol. The two other platoons along with the command group were behind us. I was not aware of their order. My platoon was also strung out in a long line.

My point man was Ernesto Martinez. I along with my radioman were right behind him. It was well after noon, probably around 3 pm, when we got to the section of the ridge that we felt would lead us to its apex. Radio contact with the CO was intermittent but comprehensible in that I knew that he wanted to get back to Ca Lu before dark. Right about this time I came to a well-used path that was heading in the direction we wanted to proceed in. I radioed the CO with the information and was ordered to continue along the path. Moments later we discovered a fighting hole along the trail that we knew was recently occupied. This was determined by the condition of the hole and the body odor within. In addition, at about the same time there was noise up ahead which sounded like digging (metal hitting rocks) or something similar. I relayed the information to the CO. My orders were to "expeditiously" proceed. I have hated that word ever since.

Contact was established almost immediately; Martinez was killed right in front of me. The NVA had us pinned down. I along with others returned fire but had no visible targets. David Schneider was nearby, and I witnessed him getting killed. I was still in contact with the CO and relayed the information I had. A short time later, maybe 10–15 minutes, the CO & the XO joined me. It was dusk and difficult to see much. The three of us were prone and consulting a map. I do not recall that any radiomen were with us, but I am certain that they would have been nearby. I suspect that we were attempting to formulate a plan but do not remember what it was or what it could have been. The section of the ridge that we were on was very narrow at this point with steep declines on either side. We were at the crest, and the aforementioned declines is in all likelihood the reason that I am still alive.

As we were lying there, the hollow sound which was emitted from several mortar tubes being fired presented an imminent and consequential threat. For a reason still unknown, I rose to my knees and in a half squatting position hurled myself through the air in an attempt to reach the decline. Why, I will never know, as it is not something that is noted as an evasive action in a mortar attack. One of the mortars landed where I was and between the CO and the XO. I was hit with shrapnel in the back of my legs, back, and ass. In fact, there is still some metal in my body, which is constantly revealed to me whenever I have had X-rays and other diagnostic procedures.

Both the CO and the XO were hit hard, both still alive but in critical condition. I did not know who else was injured or dead. By this time, it was dark, and it was eerily quiet. The only Marines that I saw and was aware of were from my platoon. I did not give much thought to the others as the immediate task at hand was to round up all that were alive and settle into a defensive position. Someone called in an air strike of napalm, which was much too close. My eyelashes and eyebrows were singed. In addition, someone called in a mission of flares, which lasted quite a long time and was welcome as it aided our recovery of wounded Marines.

We gathered all of the live Marines and was certain that we left no one behind and moved back along the ridge to a small swale on the west side of the ridge. We were out of the direct line of small arms fire and prayed that the NVA would forgo employing their mortars in an effort to keep their positions concealed. The XO died along the way. I was in radio contact with the base at Ca Lu and apprised them of our situation along with the number of Marines that I had with me. I was being clever in divulging the number by saying the number is what Jack Benny's claimed age is, just in case that the radio communication was compromised. I had no idea where anyone else was nor was I provided with any information.

I was not given any orders or instructions. I requested a medevac chopper and gave the coordinates of our position. We set up the perimeter and settled in. Around midnight a chopper arrived and along with it was a Marine Captain (Conger) and his radioman. We made our introductions and I relayed all of the knowledge that I had. We got the severely wounded on the chopper along with the lone KIA (the XO) in our midst. As this was happening, one of my Marines who was only slightly wounded or possibly not wounded at all bolted for the chopper and quickly got aboard. I yelled and cursed at him but I suspect that I was drowned out by the noise of the chopper. I wanted to shoot him and came pretty damn close to doing so. The chopper left.

I did not know what to think about Conger arriving. His presence was not requested nor was it a requirement. I knew what was expected of me and what was expected of the Marines with me. Although Conger was not a necessity to me, his presence was comforting. I thought that maybe he knew more than I did about the situation like where in the hell was everyone else and did we have any back up or how much air or artillery support was available. Questions yes, answers no.

The night was quiet and uneventful other than the constant trepidation of what could be imminent and what we knew lay ahead. Sleep was impossible.

I was not sure that I welcomed the sunrise but there it was. The plan was simple, cautiously move to the base of the hill, call in artillery, and move up the hill and clear it. Simple in plan, yes, but much more arduous in execution. I am not sure how I felt at that moment, apprehensive, anxious, yes, but not frightened nor in a state of panic. I did think about that and although I was mildly astonished, I took comfort in that feeling.

Eventually we reached the top of the hill. This was not planned but for some reason I was the first to reach the top and when I did, I witnessed several individuals dressed in green utilities running from my right to my left about 20 or so meters in front of me. Because I sent the one M-60 machine gun and its crew to our right flank, I hesitated, thinking that these might be our Marines. I soon learned that they were not. One turned and fired his AK-47 in my direction, thankfully missing his intended target. I emptied my M-16 in their direction with the results unknown. Several more popped out of their fighting holes and took off.

We all made it to the top of the hill and the Corpsmen tended to the more severely wounded. We set up a rather loose perimeter and I encouraged the able Marines to remain vigilant as I knew that we were not yet out of danger. The only Marine not wounded on the assault of the hill was one of my squad leaders, Cpl McKenzie. The thought of the rest of our company entered my conscious state, "Where the hell were they?" I had no answer for that question. Then Cpl McKenzie said to me, "Lieutenant, I never thought that I would see a Marine company run." At the time I did not assimilate, or I was not capable of, digesting that statement.

We were all alive with some more badly wounded than others, but it appeared that none were in critical condition. That being the good news, the bad was that we were not capable of getting off the ridge on our own. I called for a medevac chopper and when it came close to us it drew heavy small arms fire from the NVA still in the area and had to abort the mission. We were in radio contact with Ca Lu and we were informed that a unit was being sent to our position and to assist in our departure from the ridge. A platoon from India company reached us late that night. I believe that it was close to midnight.

They escorted us off the ridge down to Highway 9. Some required assistance in walking, others had to be carried. Vehicles awaited us for the short trip to the base at Ca Lu. I was now on the highway waiting for the last of my platoon to reach the vehicles. Some idiot somewhere ordered an artillery fire mission, only a couple of rounds, but they hit near where Cpl Mark James was being carried down. He was killed. For me, confusion presented itself. We did not need nor require the artillery. Although I was not certain it was ours (friendly fire), the sound and suspected trajectory dictated that it was. I never heard another word about it.

Of course, I knew we had bodies still on the ridge and I guess that I thought that they would be retrieved by the unit that rescued us. No one said anything about them at that time. We were hauled into the wire at Ca Lu and patched up with some being sent somewhere else where more sophisticated treatment was available. I was not interviewed, questioned, and not even asked about the past two days. I did not see or speak with Conger ever again. I was then assigned the duties of being the company's liaison officer, coordinating activities with the Battalion headquarters at the Rockpile. This did not last long; I was soon transferred to the 3rd Marine Division Headquarters at Dong Ha.

I did not know what to think, how to act, how to behave. There were rumors about how a company ran from contact. No one asked me anything. I did not offer anything. Did they think that I was a coward and was one of the many who ran? I was not confronted about the ordeal, so I offered no information. I felt betrayed and still do.

I needed help to sort it all out so I contacted a Marine named Larry Bearden. He was a lieutenant in Vietnam attached to Kilo 3/9 from Fox 2/12, an artillery battery. He was with the major during the battle and heard all the radio communication. My hope was that he had heard something that could help me make sense of the various accounts. There were discrepancies about the orders and the retrieval of the remains of the nine Marines and my dad. One Marine told me that the heads of those left behind were removed. I had to find out the truth. Lieutenant Bearden sent me this email:

Lori,

Always here if you need me and so admired your Dad and all Corpsmen and Doctors that kept us going with medical treatment and attempted to keep us all healthy in a terrible time.

When the remaining dead were retrieved, bodies of those found were stacked on the ridge. There were 10 men left there, including your father. The recon team was ordered to remove the heads but did not and returned to Ca Lu Base Camp. The Battalion Commander issued the order to the major and later denied doing so and hence an Article 32 investigation was indicated on the major as the Battalion Commander denied issuing the order and lied to Regiment. The major was relieved of command and carried the humiliation with him till he tragically ended his life.

The men of Kilo Company later on retrieved the ones on the hill with all of their body parts. Would have been an awful task as the remains would have deteriorated due to heat and high humidity.

Lieutenant Bearden also spoke with me on the phone. I found him not only kind but also instrumental in helping me understand parts of the story that had me stuck for some time.

Lieutenant Bearden began by sharing with me that unit diaries are "somewhat factual" but "don't tell the whole story. The story is between the sentences." He said, "I would encourage you to keep going. In some ways it's going to help you close a wound you still have."

I knew he was right but I feared sounding critical or disrespectful. I was dismayed by information I received from the wife of Eddie Conklin, a Marine from Second Platoon who survived the battle on Valentine's Ridge. Eddie passed away when he was forty-eight. His son found me in 2008 and told me about a paper his dad wrote in college about that day. He said he would share the paper with me when his mom found it. On April 1, 2020, Janice Conklin finally found it and graciously sent it to me.

Valentine's Day Massacre
Eddie Conklin

It was a hot day as the patrol moved slowly through the jungle. The point men were out; all you could hear were the machetes cutting a trail through the vine-covered jungle. This is February 14th, Valentine's Day 1968, Vietnam.

My mind was just on one thought: "Will we make contact with the enemy?" Then the patrol stopped and everyone got down, each man facing in a different direction. Silence. My heart pounded and I could smell the different scents from the freshly cut brush. The point men were coming in to make their report.

At that time, I was a radio operator with the 2nd Platoon, Kilo Co. 3rd Battalion 9th Marines. We were patrolling one mile south of the D.M.Z. I listened to the radio to find out why we had stopped. The call for all platoon leaders to report to the C.P (Command [Post]) came back.

The point men had sighted the enemy and heard them setting in mortar tubes. We were on a hill, and just across to the next they had sighted the enemy. I heard the company commander say on the radio, "We'll probably get the shit kicked out of us, but move out."

We made our way down the hill across a short valley and I prayed they wouldn't open up now, [or] we would be trapped. Then we started up the hill that they reported being on. Just then, pop! pop! pop!, they were dropping in mortars. You could hear them whiz overhead and explode in the valley we had just moved through. At this point a machine gun opened up. I could see the point man laying curled up in a pool of blood, like a freshly shot deer.

There was much confusion. Men yelling, "I am hit, corpsmen!" Orders to move up. At this time I could hear the enemy moving around our right flank. We were trapped. The machine gun made it impossible to move forward and the mortars were moving up to the rear.

An air strike was called [. . .]. We popped smoke grenades on each side of our position to let our jets know where our position was. The jets made a few passes and dropped napalm, which landed behind us. I could feel the heat on the back of my legs. Then a few dropped on the top of the hill where we were taking fire from.

We slowly moved up an inch at a time. At this time, I was ordered to move to the left flank with my radio. I made my way down the line over the dead and wounded to a crater on the left side of the hill. The crater started filling up with wounded Marines.

We must have been pinned down for hours, [but] it seemed like a matter of minutes. You could smell the gun powder and blood and hear the moaning of the wounded and dying.

This was Valentine's Day. When on the other side of the world people were exchanging cards and words of love, we were exchanging bullets and death.

Now there were about twenty of us left on the hill. Most were wounded. Over the radio came the order to move forward. This was in the direction of the machine gun. We [relayed] the message that we were in bad shape with many W.I.A.s and needed more manpower to take the hill. Then we were told to make our own decision.

We decided to pull back and follow the gully out to the road that led to our base camp. Our wounded could then be taken out by helicopter to a hospital unit for treatment.

As we moved down the hill, we hoped that the Viet Cong hadn't set up an ambush in the gully for us. Suddenly we heard movement in front of us. Our fingers were on the triggers ready to open up. Then we heard the password. It was a patrol sent to meet us and cover our return to the base.

It was so difficult to read Eddie's words. A few days later, Janice found a letter he wrote to his mom the day the remains were brought down from the ridge:

6 MARCH 68

Dear Mom & Family,

Hi ma, how's my great girl doing today? And how's Dad, Bob and the rest of the family?

Well today has been pretty busy, we got up at 05 o'clock and went out to get those bodies up on Valentine Ridge, that's the name they gave that place where we were hit on the 14th. We got the bodies off O.K.

Everyone feels a 100% better that we got them off of there. Now the B52s are going to work out on the ridge; the Gooks have bunkers and troops all around Valentine's Ridge.

I saw Cavenagh today, he's in recon and was sent out to help recon the ridge. There were signs of Gooks all over the area, we could hear them moving around and talking. But the gooks will only hit you when everything is in their advantage.

They thought we were all going up to the ridge but we just sent up the recon and a few men, and sat in on a nearby hill.

The only reason we did lose so many people the 14th is because the captain and the Boot Lieutenants didn't do their jobs, but we got rid of all those assholes. The Captain died from his wounds and the other relieved.

One new Captain is really squared away. And we have a platoon commander that's been here for some time and knows what he's doing. He just a SSGT but is better than a 90 day wonder.

We accomplished our mission and everyone is happy about that. I'll have a lot to tell you when I get home. But right now, I just want to forget it.

Westmoreland says that the gooks are going for broke.

This looks like their last push. But we have a lot of strategies for them that I can't tell you because of security reasons. I have 122 days to go. I just pray to God that they'll go by fast. I have a good job now, the platoon operator will not be coming back.

He was sent back to the States. So I'll be platoon radio man till I leave in July.

We are still at Ca Lu on O.P. Texas. It's a good place to be compared to a few others; so, God is still working for me. I haven't had a chance to get to church seeing [as] how we don't have one, but take time out every now and then to pray a prayer or two.

The one I always like is the one that goes "I will fear no evil, for thou art with me."

It's a funny thing but you can see God working every day over here, some of the things that happen you could never understand. Some call it luck, but I know its God working.

You could see it at Con Thein in every time things get hairy.

Well everything is fine now, I hope we get sent some mail soon. I'm still looking for those packages, I sure could use it now.

I hope everything is fine at home. That's about all the news for now.

Take care ma, say hello to all for me,

And May God Bless,

Love Always,
Your Son & Brother
Eddie

I read this entire letter to Lieutenant Bearden and asked him about Eddie's assessment of why so many men lost their lives on February 14, 1968.

Lieutenant Bearden said, "The major would tell you the same thing if he were alive today." He went on to tell me about the mistakes he made while in Vietnam and the mistakes he observed from captains and others. He also shared with me what he heard over the radio and conversations he had with the major. I was crying as I wrote down all he said.

"From a global standpoint," he said, "here it is 4:00 in the afternoon. Why would you want to engage anybody at that time unless you have the advantage? And you have at least an hour and a half to get back."

Lieutenant Bearden again encouraged me to write what I had learned about the battle. He also said, "I know your dad was Johnny-on-the-spot all the time. I'm sorry you lost him. I'm sorry your mother lost him. I met all these young men who were great and had wonderful futures in front of them. Some of them never got married or had children. Their dreams ended that day."

Lieutenant Bearden suggested I contact a Marine named Jim Lockwood from my father's sister company, India. A friend of Bearden and Jerry Behrens's, Jim could objectively help me put this all together.

Jim was one of a small group of Marines who went up the ridge in the late afternoon of February 15 to help bring the wounded off of the ridge. Jim sent me the command chronologies from that day. They mentioned the "Dusters"[*] at Ca Lu.

In 2008, a man named Hoff contacted me by email. He told me he fired the Dusters and personally knew my dad. He shared with me stories about them playing cards together and described my dad as a "rosy-cheeked thin person who was very nice." The description fit and I had no doubt that he knew my dad because of the things he knew about him. Mr. Hoff told me that he had never heard my dad cuss or seen him drink alcohol. He also knew Dad's nickname: "Cherry Larry."

Mr. Hoff's story about how my dad was killed was secondhand and did not match up with the other things I had been told. Significant to me, though, was that Mr. Hoff told me his Dusters could have bombed the ridge, eliminating the need for the patrol. Although I did not know if that was true, the command chronologies Jim Lockwood sent me provided evidence that Mr. Hoff was at Ca Lu.

---

[*] A "Duster" is an M42 40mm self-propelled anti-aircraft gun.

It was wonderful to have Jim come alongside me in my search. Jim sent me the command chronology entries from March 1968 and gave me his honest assessment of what he read:

> When 3rd Platoon of India Company went up on the 15th to help bring the wounded down, several bodies were laid out together on the ridgeline. When Team Delmar, a recon team, went up on March 5th, they found 5 bodies together and then found 2 more, leaving 3 MIAs. That's why the Recon report on the 5th says, "Located 7 bodies." They requested a unit to come up and get them. And then on the 6th they located the other 3 missing preciously reported MIAs reporting that they had 9 bodies and one "skull." I think that the team following orders may actually have removed one head but found they couldn't proceed further. Delmar returned to Ca Lu the evening of March 6th and then flew back to Dong Ha. I think they may have had a debrief, at which time they revealed what they had been ordered to do and that's when it kicked off the big investigation.

DECLASSIFIED

| JOURNAL | | | | UNIT OR SECTION |
|---|---|---|---|---|
| NAVMC 219 GS (REV 5 63) | | | | 3d Battalion, 9th Marines |
| SUPERSEDES 2 52 AND G-3a EDITIONS WHICH WILL BE USED | | | | PLACE |
| | | | | THON SON LAM, RVN |
| (Classification) | | | | FROM (Date and hour) __050001H__ TO (Date and hour) __052400H March 1968__ |

| TIME | | SERIAL NO | DATE TIME GROUP | INCIDENTS MESSAGES ORDERS | ACTION TAKEN |
|---|---|---|---|---|---|
| IN | OUT | | | | N—Maps  I—7 reps  S—Staff  r—File |
| 0855 | | 1 | 042300H | Counter Electronic aircraft picked up on anti-aircraft (37mm radar operated) position at XD 998488. A TPQ is not possible because of friendly troops in the area. Company I checked out area with negative results. | S-3, 4th Mar. |
| 1207 | | 2 | 051117H | CA LU COB received 7 rounds incoming 82mm mortar fire at YD 012445, from enemy at XD 987446. It is believed an enemy FO is located at XD 998452. 81mm and 4.2 counter mortar fired, three (3) secondary explosions at XD 987446. A twin 40 fire mission was fired on the suspected enemy forward observed at XD 998452, with unknown results. | S-3, 4th Mar. |
| 1630 | | 3 | 051600H | DELMAR, a 20 man Recon Team, has located all of the previously known USMC KIA bodies (5). They also found 2 USMC MIA bodies, leaving 3 MIA still unaccounted for. They will continue to search for the remaining 3 MIA.  987447 | S-3, 4th Mar. |
| 2110 | | 4 | 051800H | OP ADAM spotted 4 NVA/VC digging in at XD 990564. Called arty fire mission, fired 30 rounds HE 105mm, with good coverage, observation hampered by darkness, unknown results. | S-3, 4th Mar. |
| 2155 | | 5 | 052135H | Co M reports sighting lights at YD 004588. Called arty fire mission, fired 8 rounds 105mm HE, good coverage, unknown results. | S-3, 4th Mar. |

(See reverse side for instructions)          PAGE NO          (Classification)

①

DECLASSIFIED

Command chronology entries of the 3/9 Marines from March 5–6, 1968.

I thanked him and said that these documents provided clarity. My father was one of the five MIAs. Could it be that only five of the bodies were gathered on February 15? I also wondered why a document on the Virtual Wall says that my dad's body was identified on March 20, when his remains were brought down from the ridge on March 6.

"I try to tell myself to 'let it go,' but I can't," I wrote Jim in an email. "I started the search 34 years ago and have uncovered many truths. I need to find someone who found the MIAs. Both groups of them. Thank you for helping me. I really need to complete this search for my own peace of mind."

Jim explained that since the corpsmen were Navy, they had a different "parent" organization. They were assigned to individual Marine battalions under the battalion H&S company, but not carried on the battalion roster.

Jim pointed out that some write-ups posted online indicated there were eleven KIAs, but there were actually thirteen. The two not listed were John Bellanger from Fox 2/12 and Ernesto Martinez from Kilo 3/9, 3rd Platoon. The CO and the XO were airlifted from the ridge by the medevac chopper that dropped in Captain Conger and his radioman. The XO had already passed away and the CO succumbed to his wounds two days later. Left behind on the ridge were nine Marines and my dad, the senior corpsman. Delmar recon team located the remains of ten on the ridge, and Jim felt confident that my dad was one of them.

# CHAPTER TWENTY

# Putting It All Together

As new information came in, my search expanded. For the first time, I heard about other Marines who were with the CP group that day and survived the battle. One was Gy. Sgt. George Herring. The others were a forward observer from Fox 2/12, whose name no one knew, and Lieutenant Brazier from weapons platoon.

Through a group called Buddy Finder, I found possible addresses and phone numbers for Gunnery Sergeant Herring, James Nat Lloyd, Lieutenant Brazier, and Jan Russell (Doc Russell's widow). I mailed each one a personal note. I also searched high and low for Corpsman "Jackson" (name unknown), the corpsman Doc Russell said was wounded on the ridge and possibly from Montana.

I had often wondered whose life my dad was trying to save when he was killed. Doc Russell said my dad and the Marine he looked to be shielding were both dead. Jim Lockwood and I searched for all the information we could find on the ten men left behind. This enabled us to determine that the five men who were listed as MIA until their bodies were found by Team Delmar and brought down the ridge by Kilo First Platoon were:

PFC Frederick W. Bungartz
LCpl Ernesto Martinez
Cpl Lowell Thomas Combs
LCpl John Bellanger
HM2 Larry Jo Goss

The five Marines carried as KIA, body not recovered, were:

Cpl Dennis Fleming
PFC Melvin Jones
PFC First Class Barry Rigsby
Cpl David Schneider
LCpl Jeffrey Wentzell

Thanks to the eyewitness accounts of the Marines who were in the area of the ridge where there was fighting, we were able to determine how and when three of the MIAs were killed. That left only my dad and PFC Frederick Bungartz.

My heart began to beat heavily in my chest as I looked at Frederick's DD1300 report of casualty. He was killed by a grenade, just like my dad's MIA report said. Could it be that he was the Marine my dad was trying to save?

I needed to know that my dad gave his life up for a good person. The sacrifice would seem less bitter if that were true. On May 3, 2020, I found Frederick's brother, Dave, and learned that "Fritz" was a kind young man who loved his mom and siblings dearly. He and my dad had a lot in common, although I don't believe they knew each other. My dad was the senior corpsman and would not have had a reason to interact with Fritz outside of responding to the call "corpsman up!" and attempting to save his life.

I needed to know for sure if Fritz was the Marine my dad was trying to save, and I believed there was someone alive who knew. I chased a few leads and felt discouraged by the lack of responses.

Then I received a surprise phone call on June 18, 2020, from the CO's radioman, James Nat Lloyd. He was in the Command Post with my dad and had received a letter I sent him. He wrote back: "I think about Valentine's Ridge a lot. The only reason I'm talking to you is because of the Good Lord. He got me through a lot. He's my caretaker." My own faith needed that assurance that God was helping me in this exhausting search. Corporal Lloyd was clear about what he remembered and willing to say what he did and didn't know.

Corporal Lloyd told me that he and my dad sometimes monitored the radio together and talked about their families at home. He said, "Your dad was like one of us. He couldn't wait to get back home. He didn't talk a lot. He was sociable but didn't strike up a lot of conversations. To me, he was a good guy. We all had each other's back over there. We would relieve one another on radio watch and we always talked about what we were going to do when we got home."

He talked about filling sandbags with my dad at the Ca Lu combat base. He then told me what he remembered about the battle:

It was getting late in the evening on the 14th of February. We started receiving small arms fire and spotted the NVA. We changed directions and made a sweep up the valley. We were on top of the ridge when we encountered the NVA who were close enough to throw grenades. The CP group was with 2nd and 3rd Platoon. 3rd was with us when we got hit. There was so much chaos on the radio. All three platoons were coming on the radio at the same time. We didn't have what they called Old Salts. We were learning the ropes. When I was wounded, they got me over to where there were some guys in a ravine. I don't remember seeing your dad. I was attached to the CO. He was gung ho. When we started taking small arms and moved up to where 3rd Platoon was, we were right up there with them. We were all in a U shape. We were on top of the ridge. The lieutenant from 3rd Platoon was there, the CO, me, and the XO.

Corporal Lloyd described seeing a radio operator who was dead. He said there were more still laying on the ground when others took him to the ravine; they were supposed to make a sweep on the ridge and return to the base.

I could tell Corporal Lloyd was experiencing stress from talking about his memories. He stopped talking about the battle and then said more about my dad.

"We had some conversations about finishing our tour and getting back home," he said, choking back some emotion. "He cared about his family and loved them dearly. He hadn't ever been in a situation like that before. I don't want to mislead anybody. I will only tell you what I truly know."

I told him that living without my dad was really hard but that it was a little easier to know he was such a good guy. I started to cry and thanked him for talking to me. He then said, "Larry really loved his family."

I talked to Corporal Lloyd again on July 10, 2020. I wanted to make sure he was OK after our conversation. He told me he'd had some dreams, but that was not out of the ordinary. He gave more details that he hadn't shared with me before. I wrote down every word he said.

Bits and pieces of the twenty-three accounts I had collected in my search bounced around in my head. I reread these accounts dozens of times, trying to make sense of what happened and sift out the truth. The account of Rick Foster, the man who had paced back and forth at the reunion in 2007, held particular value for me because it emphasized how tragic Valentine's Ridge was for all involved and for those like me who feel the loss every day. Rick's account also helped me weave all the accounts together. He shared with me openly on the last night of the reunion and I took extensive notes. These notes helped me "see" the formation of the Marines and corpsmen during the first part of the battle when Camron Carter was injured and my dad helped Doc Russell save his life.

Rick said:

The enemy was close, maybe 30 yards. They were throwing hand grenades at us almost vertical. They shot mortar straight and it hit where we were. Someone was saying, "Captain, Carter's really bad, we've got to get him out of here." Every few minutes or so a corpsman was yelling over to CO, "Carter's really bad." The CO said, "We're not leaving without Schneider's body." But they could not get it. Nobody ever went up there. What occurred on Valentine's Ridge was a royal screwup.

Rick reported that after the first mortar landed, the CO said, "We are getting off; I want everybody off this way." I asked him when my dad would have tried to get himself off the hill. Rick said, "Once he determined there was no one else alive, he would have gotten out of there. He was probably shielding a body while working on the body and got hit by a mortar. He was probably giving morphine."

Sitting at the table with Rick Foster back in 2007 was a Marine whose name I do not know. The Marine shared his memories with me, and mentioned the day the bodies were brought down from the ridge. He said a recon platoon located the bodies but refused to bring them down. He said they "could not do it," but gave no explanation why. He told me that Zeke volunteered his platoon to do the job. "Jed and Corporal Williams took two squads up" the ridge, he said, and reported that the major told them to bring in everything they could find. I didn't understand what that meant in 2007, but now I do.

In this Marine's words:

Bodies were there. Some fingers gnawed and mangled, etc. So hot. 21 days on Valentine's Ridge is a big big deal—Marines don't have MIAs. No other time where they laid there 21 days. Stacked like cord wood. NVA covered them. That's ugly.

When I see my dad, I see the man who held my mom and me. To think that he had been reduced to liquid lying on the ridge for twenty-one days turns my heart inside out. I know our bodies aren't supposed to matter, but when I see what happens when an animal, let alone a person, is left dead and disintegrates, I can't help but grieve. Those men deserved better.

The last thing the Marine said to me in 2007 was that "corpsmen were heroes of immense proportions." What I learned while writing this book showed me he was right.

\* \* \* \* \*

Jim Lockwood and Dan Wszolek continued communicating with me by email and I was so grateful. Jim and I read through every account multiple times, the DD 1300s of everyone killed that day, and every entry in the command chronologies that pertained to the battle and recovery of the bodies. At the end, we were both convinced that Fritz Bungartz was the Marine whose life my dad was trying to save when he was killed. Although my dad's DD 1300 suggested that he was killed by a mortar, his MIA report, dated February 27, 1968, said he fell to the ground from the mortar but was later seen killed by two grenades. The only other person whose records indicate he was killed by a grenade was PFC Bungartz. He was also one of the five men still listed as MIA the day the bodies were recovered on March 6, 1968.

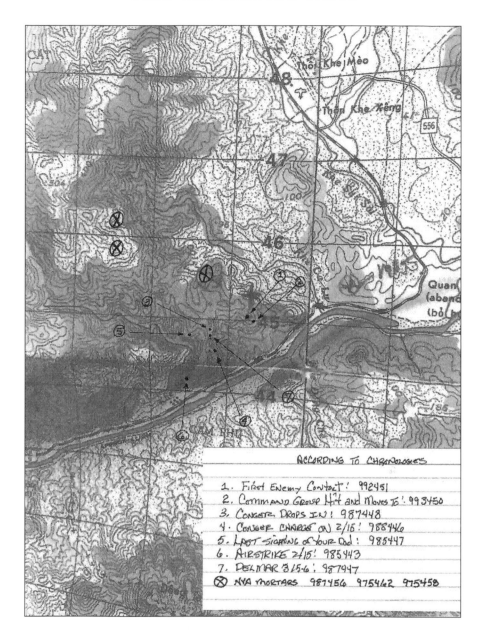

The map John Edwards carried in Vietnam in 1968. When John returned home, he drew the cross on the map at the spot where the battle began. Jim Lockwood created the notecard and dots to help me understand the battle, and added them in 2020.

On December 5, 2020, Fritz's youngest brother, Mike, contacted me after seeing my post and phone number on the Wall of Faces. He told me his mom also believed her son might have been captured because of the telegrams she received. He described her on her knees pleading with God as she watched the POWs exit the plane after their release. When her Fritz was not one of them, she wailed. He said that his father gave permission for his Uncle Bob to view Fritz's remains. Bob said the smell of formaldehyde was so strong he could only observe for a short time. The remains were skeletal and wounds were observed near his ribcage. As Mike spoke, I imagined my father's remains.

Finally feeling like I had a grasp on the events of that fateful day, I looked for the families of the other KIAs. I copied their pictures and put them in a collage side by side. Their stories mattered and their families deserved to know the truth, if they wanted that information.

And some wanted to know. One of them was the cousin of Ernesto Martinez, a young man who died on the ridge. Because of the delay in recovering Ernesto's body, his family suffered greatly. My information helped him sort through the stories he had been told. His uncle, Ernesto's brother, was still living and willing to talk with me. We talked on the phone and shared our mutual pain. I promised him I would never forget his brother and would share his name in my book so others would learn of his bravery.

\* \* \* \* \*

As I started to write this portion of the book, after hours of interviewing and reviewing government documents, I realized that I was not going to be able to write one account that included everything that happened—the stories were all from different vantage points and many accounts conflicted. But I could lay all the gathered information side by side and see what information was showing up consistently across the many accounts and interviews.

Several people around my dad on the evening of February 14, 1968, lived. The ones I know of are Lt. Dan Wszolek from Third Platoon; Cpl. James Nat Lloyd, radio operator for the CO; Don Carter, radio operator for Lieutenant Wszolek; John Edwards, Camron Carter, Gene Miller, Richard Foster, Steve Miera, Gy. Sgt. George Herring, Corpsman "Jackson," Doc Marty Russell, Doc Jerry Porter, Doc George Lindell, the Forward Observer from Fox 2/12, and Arthur Sayward.

I will forever be grateful to the nineteen Marines and four corpsmen from Kilo and India Company who chose to communicate with me about the battle. I'll never forget their willingness to relive dreadful memories in order to help a corpsman's daughter. Through their shared memories, I have written—to the best of my ability—an account that includes elements corroborated by those who were near my dad. I know that perfect accuracy is impossible—the trauma from these events and the time since they have passed have taken their toll. To the families whose loved ones did not make it home, I hope this is helpful. I am very sorry your son, brother, husband, or father did not make it home to you.

This is, from all the accounts and interviews I collected, what I believe happened around my dad during the last three hours of his life:

Ernesto Martinez was point man on the patrol for Third Platoon and the first person killed. PFC David Schneider from Third Platoon was also killed. The NVA was very close and shot PVT Camron Carter in the arm. Doc Russell moved up to treat him and my dad came up to assist. Together they stabilized Camron and he was moved down to the area where a part of Third Platoon's third squad was located.

My dad or Doc Russell told the CO that Camron Carter was hurt pretty bad and that they needed to get him out of there. The CO said, "We are not leaving without Schneider's body." This was the first engagement that the command chronologies recorded as happening at 1645 military time, or 4:45 p.m. Vietnam time.

As sunset was approaching, the CO, XO, and Corporal Lloyd moved up to Lieutenant Wszolek's position. When the CO reached

Wszolek's position, he ordered Lieutenant Wszolek to send someone to move up the ridge to find out what they were up against. According to Wszolek, he directed Cpl. Lowell Combs, who responded by saying, "This is *** crazy." As Corporal Combs crawled up the ridge, he too was killed.

While the CO, XO, and Corporal Lloyd were at Lieutenant Wszolek's position, they knew the NVA's exact location. As the three leaders looked at a map, everyone in the vicinity heard the NVA's mortar tubes pop. They only had seconds to hit the ground before the mortars landed. One mortally wounded the CO, the XO, and Lance Cpl. John Bellanger. Near these Marines were Corporal Lloyd and Corpsman "Jackson," both wounded.

Consistent in the accounts is that my dad did not move up to Lieutenant Wszolek's position when the CO, XO, and Corporal Lloyd did. Doc Russell said he saw my dad "run from one battle to the other." I believe this meant my dad was moving quickly around the battlefield during the first engagement and the second, when the mortar round came in. My dad's MIA report states that a mortar round landed in front of him and that he fell to the ground. My dad told us, in his letters, that he would hug the ground. I have no doubt in my mind that he did.

John Edwards saw a corpsman "working on a wounded guy." John approached the corpsman because he was looking for radios. The corpsman said, "He's gone" and wept a little, according to John. Two radio operators were killed on Valentine's Ridge: Lance Cpl. John Bellanger and Lance Cpl. Jeffrey Wentzell. I believe Bellanger was the radio operator Don Carter saw lying on the ground near the CO. The forward observer (whose name is unknown) from Fox 2/12 who survived the battle told Larry Bearden that Bellanger was killed by a mortar.

I also believe the radio operator John Edwards approached was Lance Corporal Wentzell, and the corpsman trying to save his life was my dad.

I reached this conclusion because both Doc Russell and a Marine from Third Platoon, Arthur Sayward, saw my dad's body "up the hill" from where Jeffrey Wentzell's body was. I had never heard anyone mention Arthur Sayward's name, but in October 2020 I saw a post he made in a 3/9 Marines Facebook group. His post made me wonder if he was in the battle on Valentine's Ridge. Arthur had not attended a reunion or talked to anyone he had served with. On October 30, 2020, he messaged me: "I've thought about it and I would like to give you as much information as I can."

Arthur said he saw my dad's body and "his hand and a part of his arm were lying on the dead Marine." Arthur continued, "I didn't know it was him at first. He was kind of lying on his side. I had to pull him a little bit to look. I checked his neck for a pulse and there wasn't. I checked them both real quick."

Arthur said my dad and the Marine were lying below the areas where the CO and the XO's bodies were, just like Doc Russell said. They also both reported seeing Jeffrey Wentzell's body a few feet below my dad's. Wentzell was carrying a radio on that patrol.

Arthur Sayward had not talked to Doc Russell or seen his written account. This left no doubt in my mind that this is true. My dad was trying to save the life of one of his Marines when he was killed.

John said the corpsman went up the hill after the radio operator died. I believe my dad moved up the hill to respond to the call "corpsman up!" because PFC Fritz Bungartz was wounded. My father attempted to shield Fritz's body with his own when the NVA threw grenades that killed both of them.

This is consistent with my dad's MIA report, which says that after he fell to the ground he was "later observed to be hit by two grenades, no sign of life observed." Jim Lockwood and I both believe with confidence that PFC Bungartz was the Marine my dad was trying to save.

Doc Russell's email to me and Ray Felle said the same thing:

On the morning of Feb. 15, 1968, I observed the body of HM2 Goss and a Marine whose name I do not know. HM2 Goss was immediately behind the Marine's body. Because of the positions of the bodies, it appeared to me that HM2 Goss had used his body as a shield for the Marine.

I was not able to find answers to all my questions, but I was able to learn that there were things I was never going to understand, no matter how long I searched. I realized it was time to stop looking for answers and do all I could to honor the Marines and corpsman who died in service to our country on February 14–15, 1968. Lieutenant Bearden's words from my conversation with him echo in my mind and heart:

I think you need to see the tragedy of all of this. People make mistakes, and when you do this in combat, it costs lives. Even when you think you don't make mistakes, it costs life. You need to have peace about your dad's devotion to his men. He is out there, running around, when we are getting shot at, trying to help us. That takes incredible courage. His death is tragic, but his life is honorable. Courageous. You will find one day that he lived serving others and it cost him his life. It's unfortunate what happened on that hill that day. We're all human and there are no guarantees. A corpsman does not run around shooting back. He's trying to help people that are hurt. You need to rest well with that for the rest of your life. A corpsman saved my ass and I am devoted to all of them.

We must always remember their sacrifice, my dad's and so many others, and never forget the value of their lives.

# CHAPTER TWENTY-ONE

# My New Wish

I always wanted to get to the end of grief as quickly as possible. People talked to me about "closure," but I didn't know what that meant. Was closure something I was supposed to find? Something that would happen automatically if I just did everything right? I knew there was no one way to properly grieve. For me, grief came in waves after my son Colton was born, and then again after he was diagnosed with autism. I had heard that new grief brings up past grief. When I was inconsolable in 1995, I was not only lamenting my current and past loss, but I was also feeling the impact of my dad's absence. Not having him in my life at the time when I needed him the most magnified the pain.

In 2010, after Harry and Willie died, my dad's little sister Bonnie gave me the letters my dad wrote to his dad from Vietnam, which I had not seen before. I was awestruck by the way my dad focused on what everyone else needed. For Bonnie it was his praise, and for Mom and me it was for others to take care of us until my dad returned home.

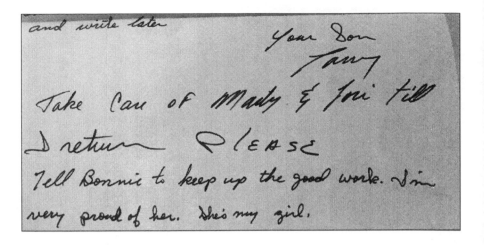

On Jan. 19, 1968, Harry received this letter from his son, my dad:

Dear Dad, Mom, Bonnie, and Family,

Received two letters today. I'm glad to hear from you. I really felt all good inside. I hope we get closer as the years go by. Bonnie, I think you are a nice little sister. You write quite often. I hope you'll keep writing me. Keep me informed on my little daughter O.K.

There isn't too much to say about the weather here. It is just the opposite of yours. Instead of cold and snow it's hot and rainy and real muddy. You sink down until you think you can't move along or get out. But we move on.

Today the "Gooks" hit us again with more than automatic AK-47 rifles. We chased them back up into the hills. The helicopters with rockets and 30 cal. machine guns are keeping him there. So, we won't have to worry about them tonight. They only hit when they know they can get away. They are really smart. He's [Charlie] hard to find when he digs in. You go looking for him and you find nothing. He really knows how to camouflage his bunkers; they are all underground.

So, I guess I'll sign off for now. I will write more when I can.

Your son,
Larry

Although my dad always focused on the positive, you could some-times see behind the words and feel the pain in his heart. His whole life he wanted to be Harry's son, and now he was hoping to have more time. On February 9, 1968, Harry received this letter:

Dear Dad, Mom, and family,

How are you this morning on February 1, 1968? I hope this letter finds you well and happy and without worry. I'm fine here. I'm on radio watch now. It is 0400 in the morning, so I'm a little sleepy, but that's the least of my worries. I received another charming letter from Bonnie Kay. She really writes a good letter. Better than myself.

We were going to move today and go north to a new position, but our orders were canceled at one o'clock this morning. So, I'll probably move later. We usually move about every 35 to 40 days. You never stay in one place too long. Pretty soon we will be going out in the bush for about a month. That's sleeping in a hole for 30 days and sweating Charlie and his mortars. Where we are now, we made a perimeter here at Ca Lu (it is an outpost we have to hold). It isn't very large, but it keeps Charlie from moving freely in this area. We have patrols, but they usually just go out during the day and back in and then ambushes at night. Every once in a while, we go out for a few days but not 30. You become an animal after that long.

Well I'm receiving mail fairly regularly here. So, the mail isn't too messed up. We receive it about every four days. You keep busy so it seems to come regularly. Well, my family is fine. Our little girl hasn't received any presents from the fairy yet. She is having a little trouble, I guess. I hope they come in soon. Everybody else seems to be OK. So, I'm not worrying a bit.

Things in the world are uptight. That's the way it should be here. Maybe they'll do a little about talking peaceful terms soon. I think they're moving troops in so they can get a little better deal.

We'll see. I know one thing he's got plenty of gooks already. I wish somebody would tell him that.

Well I will close for now and write later.

The next letter my dad wrote his father revealed more information about the forthcoming battle on Valentine's Ridge.

Dear Dad, Mom, Bonnie & Family,

How are you all doing this fine morning? It is 0215 on the 9th of Feb. I am on radio watch now. It is something a Corpsman doesn't have to do, unless he wants, but everybody here stands radio watch in the C.P., even the captain. It shortens the watch time for everybody, so they can get more sleep, and also gives you some time to write letters.

The mail here is messed up just like everything right now. We can only get supplied by helicopter and they have so much work to do to supply Khe Sanh. We see them about every 5 to 7 days and that's when we get our mail, food, etc. They really only come when we run low on food. We have been eating lately supplementary foods like beets, noodles, corn pie filling, no meat (we got some yesterday) and of course good old C rations. It's really not bad, considering when you're out in the bush it's C rations for 30 days and sometimes no mail at all.

Well, tomorrow we hit the bush again. We are going down the valley along the river. Hunting for Charlie. He's out there and we will probably see him. He's been causing some trouble in that direction lately. But we will have plenty of men and if we don't walk into an ambush we will be OK!! Charlie likes to catch small units in crossfires, but I think our captain knows what he's doing, so I don't think we'll get surprised. We hope to find him with his pants down and then blow the hell out of them. Well that's enough from me.

How is everybody there? Marty said you were down on 21 January and that she was going to come see you soon, when Dan and

Donna come to Indianapolis. I am sure glad you see each other regularly. Marty really likes you all and talks about you all the time. She told you of my phone call. I was back in Dong Ha getting my pay straightened out and they have a Mars station there where you can call stateside once a month if the things are working properly. It's really something but three minutes sure go fast.

How is Bonnie Kay? I'm sending her some small sheets of paper like the US drops to the VC. It tells them that if they come over to our side we will give them this and that. She can find out what they say at school if she wants. I pick them up when we're out on patrols, so I'll send them often.

Marty says you're looking fine and that you're your old jolly self again. I'm glad to hear that. She said you listen to my tapes. They are wonderful. I love to hear Marty and Lori. It really makes you feel good inside. I'm trying to get a real good tape recorder now. I'm using the captain's at the present time. Our man on R & R is supposed to pick me one up. It's hard to keep them clean and dry over here so it doesn't pay to buy a real good one. Tell Willie to take it easy on you now that you're back on your feet and to write a letter about herself. I'll sign off for now. Write more later.

Harry received this letter from my dad on February 15, the day after he was killed. My dad had much faith in his captain and in the goodness of his father. Gratitude filled my dad's spirit. He was raised with little and grateful for every ounce of kindness that came his way. The daddy he longed for was choosing to be a part of his life.

After my dad died, Harry lived with regret the rest of his life. He knew Larry was his son. He had chosen his other family for many years and had thought he had time to make it up to Larry Jo.

The research I did for this book revealed something else, too. Had my dad's dog tags been returned, my mom would have been spared from so much sorrow. She asked me the other day where I thought they were. I still don't know. Jerry identified my dad by his identification card. The pictures of my mom and me were right next to it in Dad's breast pocket. For twenty-one days, while his body decayed away, my mom and I were with him, in the pictures that laid right next to his heart.

\* \* \* \* \*

A part of Mom and me died that day on Valentine's Ridge. My dad's death changed her forever and it radically altered my life too. People have told me that I wouldn't be the person I am today if my dad had lived. They think those words will make me feel better, but the truth is, I know I would be a better person if he were in my life today. It was as though his death pushed me forty feet below the water and I had to spend years swimming to the surface. If only I could have just started on the surface instead!

Many people have told me how proud my father would be of me. I truly appreciate their kind comments and believe them to be true. My prayer is that all sons and daughters will experience the blessing of knowing their fathers and mothers are truly proud of them. The approval of both parents is central to a child's identity. It is like balm to a wound. It seems to make everything better and to have life-giving properties.

For children whose parents are absent due to death or other reasons, having a person in that role makes all the difference in the world. Of course, no one can replace a parent, but one good person can fill a portion of the void.

For children who have lost fathers, I pray that a man steps up to play that role. It was important to me to hear my dad was proud of me. It was more healing, however, to have a male father figure tell me he was proud of me. That assurance felt real; the other felt abstract. A kiss on the cheek and an "I love you" from a man who viewed me as a daughter was critical to my healing. It was in the present and able to be ingested in a way that filled the hunger I had for acceptance and the longing to feel my father's love.

Though my journey was long, my faith has come back around full circle and landed in an even sweeter spot than before. By accepting that I will never have a father here on Earth, I learned to trust in my Heavenly Father. Though I had tried to do this many time before, I learned that it wasn't a "how to" but rather a process. I had given all that I had to try to figure out *how* to rely on God—*how* to trust Him and *how* to not need my biological dad anymore.

The truth is that I still need my dad, but I have accepted that life includes grief and mourning because we love deeply. There are times when the sadness surfaces and now I let the tears fall. In the past, I pushed them away and told myself to be strong. I held on to my wish that someone would take my dad's place so that the grief would go away. I fought with the bitter pill of acceptance but have learned that this is OK. My dad was strong-willed too.

Grieving is a long process—a journey that requires good support along the way. The good news is that we get better at managing the sadness by allowing ourselves to sit there for as long as it takes. I hope all who are reading this book are encouraged to know that it took me a really long time.

When I was a young mother, I read the book *The Power of a Parent's Words*.* The words my father left me helped me find peace and know how much he loved me. For my mother, his words kept her flame burning and reminded her of how much she was loved.

Fourteen days before my dad was killed, he sent my mom an audio tape. Here's an excerpt of what he said:

> You keep asking me every time you write if I know where Stan is. Well I don't know where Stan is right now. I am going to try to write him a letter. He's in the Third Marine Division but there's so many separate things in the Third Marine Division. I mean they're

---

* H. Norman Wright, *The Power of a Parent's Words: How You Can Use Loving, Effective Communication to Increase Your Child's Self-Esteem and Reduce the Frustrations of Parenting* (Grand Rapids, Mich.: Baker Pub. Group, 1991).

all around this area but like I say where you're at you're there. You can't go too far because ole Charlie's out there. It's something because you're here and he's around you 360 degrees, he's watching you all the time. He knows what you're doing. He's watching you all the time just waiting for you to make a mistake so he can come in there and kill a few of you and run away.

But I'll tell you as soon as I know where Stan is. I hope to God he got a halfway decent company where you know they're not getting shot up all the time. I hope he's not in Con Thien or anyplace like that. Yet when we were out on that place, we were close to the DMZ. You just get on top of the hill and you see the DMZ down there. I mean that's too close for comfort. I don't like it. They bring those big rockets and arms in on you anytime they want. We are just lucky we didn't get hurt you know like say those recon patrols did. But anyway, I'll look for some more things to tell you have been asking questions about.

Well, I guess that's about it. I guess I've answered just about every question that you had on your tape there and what I can think I wanted to ask you or tell you. So, I'll say goodbye now. I love you very much and Lori sounds like she's really content so I'm not worried about her at all so take care of yourself. I pray for you every night when I write in my diary so take it easy and I'll see you soon. God bless you. I love you very much.

My dad's belief in God was evident in his letter, diary entries, and tapes. Why did I doubt? I think it was because no one could tell me for sure that my dad had been spiritually saved—that he had surrendered his life to God and asked for forgiveness of his sins. These tapes did not tell me that, but they sure solidified in me an assurance that my dad was mindful of God. That he prayed. That he relied on God to bless those he loved. In fact, my mom once told me that my dad's favorite hymn was "How Great Thou Art," and that she had found someone to sing it at his funeral.

I no longer wonder if I will see my dad in heaven. Oh, how amazing that day will be! I have lived fifty-four years without my dad. Many of those days have been hard, but the assurance of an eternity with him makes those years seem so small.

I continue to hope this book will help my search, but I am at peace with the search ending with the publication of this book. I have no doubt in my mind that my dad was shielding the body of a wounded Marine, as Doc Russell said, and that the Marine was Fritz Bungartz. Doc Russell said my dad talked to him after the XO and the CO were hit. My dad told us he and the ground were good friends. I am sure he "hugged" the ground when the mortars came in but could not—and would not—resist the call for "corpsman up!"

My dad wrote about reading the Bible in Vietnam. I wonder if he read this verse from John 15: "Greater love has no one than this: to lay down one's life for one's friends."[*]

John teaches us the importance of loving one another and the depths of God's love for us. In this picture that my husband drew as a potential cover to this book, he included the words "Love never dies." This gift of love brought instant tears to my eyes. My husband understood. As he patiently stood by supporting me as I searched, he grew in his understanding of the love between a father and his little girl.

---

[*] John 15:13 (NIV).

*Love never dies*

As I reflect on all I have learned since beginning the search for my father, I continually come back to the words in Romans 11:33:

Oh, how great are God's riches and wisdom and knowledge! How impossible it is for us to understand his decisions and his ways! For who can know the Lord's thoughts? Who knows enough to give him advice? And who has given him so much that he needs to pay it back? For everything comes from him and exists by his power and is intended for his glory. All glory to him forever! Amen.

God's time is so different from ours; His ways are so different from our ways. If I could have changed the events of February 14, 1968, in a way that would have resulted in my dad coming home to my mom and me, without a doubt I would. But God is in control and I am not, so I must trust that His ways are much better than anything I could hope for or imagine. The scenario I dreamed up of my dad walking in the front door of our house in Fairmount, Indiana, and my mom and I embracing him was an image that helped me cope. Some would call it denial, but I call it a gift.

That wish sustained me as a child, but as an adult I had to seek the truth about what happened to my father the day he was killed. Though the details of how my dad lost his life are not 100 percent clear, the brave men who chose to communicate with me and share their stories helped me have a clearer picture of the events surrounding my dad's death—a much clearer picture than the one my mother had in 1968.

The Bible says that there is a time to mourn and a time to die. I choose to believe that it was my father's time, just like my Mamaw always said. My mom told me that everything happens for a reason. My quest to find out why spanned many years. The result was that the "why" had much to do with choices made by men. The interplay between human choices and God's will is still a mystery. I know for sure that my dad chose to save the life of others on the ridge instead of getting off of the ridge himself. The little girl in me still feels sadness and sometimes even anger. The adult in me, however, has to look no further than my dad's own words to gain understanding. In a letter on January 17, 1968, he wrote: "I just do my job the best I can and the safest way I can to do the most for everyone involved." On the battlefield, my dad's character allowed him to do nothing except what was right and noble. My dad died the way he lived: working hard in the face of adversity and giving to others because he deeply loved.

Dad's character led him to die attempting to save the life of one of his Marines. My dad and Fritz Bungartz were not friends, yet on the battlefield they were brothers. They likely had never communicated because they were of different ranks and different platoons. On Valentine's Ridge, however, Fritz Bungartz was a Marine who needed help and my dad was a Navy corpsman whose job it was to do everything he could to save him.

As I reflect back on this journey, I can't help but smile. This search has been a lifelong journey, and a worthwhile one. I've come to know both my dad better and myself better. I started as a young girl who was mature on the outside but sad on the inside. As I have grown older, my faith and my many talks with veterans have helped me look at my dad's death from a new perspective. I am sure, as I grew older, each new loss revived the old. But I now know that my father would want nothing more than for me to embrace the now, remember the past, and look forward to the future. Heaven is so much sweeter with my dad there.

My wish today is no longer for me. My wish is for all Gold Star Children to know the love of their mom or dad who gave their life in service to our country. I wish for them to be loved and to know love in a way that makes them want to give it in return. I pray that they will hear stories to sustain them while new memories are being made; that they can know their history and focus on their strengths.

I also hope that all who are grieving have someone significant come alongside them and hold their hand while they heal, and that they will be patient in the journey, keeping their eyes on Christ. I will forever be grateful to the men who chose to do this for me in my adult years.

The unsung hero in my story is my beautiful mom, Marty. She had the daunting task of passing along my dad's love to me while longing for it herself. She shared stories and personal items that helped me know the love of my dad. To love and be loved is life's greatest gift. My father loved us well in the short time he had. As I searched to find him, I found so much more. I will never forget his last words to mom and me:

> Well I'll sign off for now.
> Kiss Lori for me
> I love you very much.
> Love Larry

## P.S. Sleep Warm

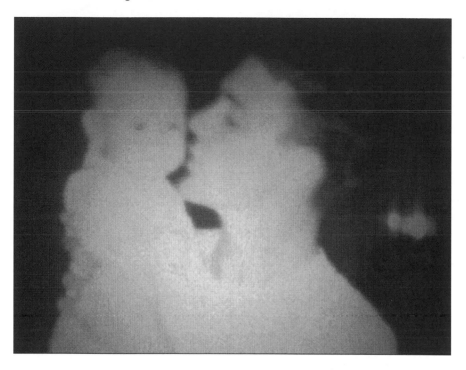

A screen shot from a video taken of my dad and me
(December 1968). *Photo credit Chris Conway.*

With Casey and Eric at the Traveling Wall in Greenfield,
Indiana (July 14, 2019). *Photo credit David Hine.*

Family portrait taken June 3, 2018. Back row: Madelyn Ann, Kylie, Cody Lawrence, Colton Michael, Mom, Courtnee Jo, Casey Jordan, Christopher Eric, Becky, and Olivia Grace. Front row: Eric, Wrigley, and me.

# Epilogue

During my second trip to Vietnam, my son Casey and I were greatly affected by the poverty we saw in the Montagnard village at the base of Valentine's Ridge. John Edwards, his friend, and I handed money to our guide and asked him to give it to the families for us. The jubilation they expressed was unlike anything I'd ever seen before. My heart and Casey's heart were struck by a precious little girl and her young mom. I knew we had to do something about the poverty we witnessed, but I did not know what.

In 2021, through the 2 Sides Project, our family was able to raise the funds to build a home for that young family. At a place where so much death and devastation occurred, something positive happened because of the generosity and kindness of people who wanted to honor my dad. Near the place where he died, there will now be a better life for a young Montagnard family. I will forever be thankful to the wonderful people who donated. My dad would have made this world a better place. Building that home was a way to let him know I received his kiss and will honor every day the legacy of love he left us.

With Casey and the Ms. Ho Thi Hieu family who captured our
hearts in the Kje Ngai village of Vietnam (July 7, 2019).

*Left:* The Ho Thi Hieu family original home in July 2019.
*Right:* Their new home in July 2021: the Larry Jo Goss Peace Home.

I began raising funds for a second peace home that will be built in the same Montagnard village. It will be dedicated to Master Gy. Sgt. John Edwards, who passed away on January 10, 2022. His clear memories of February 14, 1968, helped me learn of my dad's final hours on this Earth. John retired from the Marine Corps in 1988 and was truly one of the best! That home was fully funded by memorial donations honoring the life of Jody Carlson, widow of Captain John W. Carlson, KIA 12/7/66 in Vietnam. If you would like to contribute to our third Peace Home, built in honor of the twelve Marines and one corpsman killed on Valentine's Ridge, please contact the 2 Sides Project at www.2sidesproject.com/donate.

Master Gunnery Sergeant Edwards, our faithful friend (July 7, 2019).

Made in the USA
Monee, IL
05 January 2023

24451152R00240